FAITH AND REFLECTION

HENRY DUMÉRY

FAITH
AND REFLECTION

Edited and with an Introduction
by Louis Dupré

Translated by Stephen McNierney
and Mother M. Benedict Murphy, R.S.H.M.

HERDER AND HERDER

1968
HERDER AND HERDER NEW YORK
232 Madison Avenue, New York 10016

Library of Congress Catalog Card Number: 68–54078
© 1968 by Herder and Herder, Inc.
Manufactured in the United States

Contents

Sources and Acknowledgements

2. "The Act Law"
   from: *Philosophie de la religion*, vol. I, Paris, Presses Universitaries de France, 1957, pp. 47–54, 59–71.
3. "Revelation"
   from: *La foi n'est pas un cri*, Paris, Editions du Seuil, 1959, pp. 214–225.
4. "The Early Christian Community"
   from: *La foi n'est pas un cri*, pp. 19–33.
5. "The Easter Mystery"
   from: *La foi n'est pas un cri*, pp. 71–89.

Preface

Henry Duméry, of the University of Paris, is probably the best known philosopher of religion in France today. Born in 1920, he remained relatively obscure until 1957 when he published five books in one year. His work touched off a storm of controversy, particularly among Catholic theologians, which has never subsided. Only one of his books, *The Problem of God,* has been translated into English and, except for a few specialists, his name is virtually unknown in America. This obscurity seems to be due to the silence which separates Anglo-Saxon from Continental philosophers. Most of the time one group acts simply as if the other did not exist or was not worth talking to. Yet both pay dearly for this neglect, for the absence of any significant dialogue between the two Western traditions is one of the major reasons that philosophical discussion more and more spins around itself far from the real world. To the ordinary intellectual, philosophy seems to be the business of a group of inbred academic coteries which have removed their interests to a distance sufficient from those of ordinary mortals to be safe from any outside criticism. What ought to be the most stimulating of all disciplines has turned into an esoteric game totally irrelevant to what really matters in life. The purpose of the present systematic anthology is to introduce to the American public a first-rate Continental thinker who could substantially contribute to the present important debate on the meaning of religion in modern life.

The main significance of Duméry's philosophy of religion lies in its method. Philosophy of religion has always encountered a great deal of difficulty in making itself accepted by the believer. This is often due to the believer's distrust of any interference by reason with faith. But more often the philosopher provokes the believer's negative attitude by "explaining" the religious attitude as part of a different phenomenon. How could the religious man accept an interpretation that reduces his unique experience to a projection of a purely subjective fear, or to a mythical foundation of morality, or to a communal neurosis? The names of Hume, Kant, and Freud come first to mind. But the problem is much older. It antedates the religious crisis of the end of the 17th century. In fact, the misunderstanding between philosophy and religion started when philosophers first constructed arguments to prove God's existence and invented names to describe his essence *independently of the religious experience* within which the very thought of God originated. It was this severing of the philosophical reflection on God from its religious source which made Pascal exclaim: "The God of Abraham, of Isaac, and of Jacob—not the God of the philosophers."

Several religious thinkers in the last century have tried to lead philosophy of religion away from self-adoration and back to its religious origin. The exodus started with Schleiermacher. Unfortunately, even though the German philosopher had the vision of faith, his romantic lack of appreciation for the intrinsic necessity of symbols prevented him from ever reaching the promised land. Another religious thinker, Søren Kierkegaard, concentrated on deflating the presumptuous claims of philosophy but spent very little time considering what philosophy *could* do with religion. As a first step in that direction Newman and Blondel attempted to delineate exactly what belonged to the province of faith and what to that of reason. Yet they succeeded merely in establishing a parallelism between reason and religion. Also, at least in the case of Blondel, his discussion *about* the religious experience never seems to touch the actual experience itself. If philosophy cannot accomplish more, it remains at best irrelevant to the religious man.

Then phenomenology came and opened up entirely new avenues. The phenomenologists set out to discover the meaning of the religious act in the act itself. Rudolf Otto (who was not formally connected with the phenomenological movement but applied its method more successfully than any of its members), Max Scheler, Gerardus Van der Leeuw, Mircea Eliade, all brought reflection to religion without jeopardizing or by-passing the original experience. Some of these results had been anticipated by the American pragmatists William James, Josiah Royce, and William Ernest Hocking. All reflected upon the actual religious experience, instead of attempting to define *a priori* what the religious experience ought to be.

However, the more phenomenology progressed, the more the need for an interpretation of the *roots* of the religious experience was felt. No experience fully reveals its own foundation. The foundation itself, then, can never be phenomenologically described. The case of religion is further complicated by the fact that to the believer religion is not a mere experience. Religion even as it is actually lived does not coincide with the religious experience. To believe means always to accept more than one can understand, see, feel, or in any way experience. Experience in religion is an iceberg that hides more than it reveals. Either religion must remain closed to the light of autonomous reason, or it must be scrutinized by a philosophy that probes beyond experience, that is, beyond what appears. But can a philosophy which is not restricted to the interpretation of experience be prevented from developing into irrelevant constructivism? The question presents Kant's old predicament in a new form.

Duméry's philosophy offers an affirmative answer. Starting from a phenomenological analysis of the religious experience, it soon moves beyond this experience in order to discover its ontological foundations. By keeping constantly in touch with theological reflection *without ever accepting it at face value,*

Duméry avoids losing contact with the believer who finds in theology an authoritative, and, to the extent that he accepts this authority, *intrinsic* interpretation of his experience. This dialogue with theology is all the more justified in that the religious experience itself is not limited to pre-reflective, "lived" religion but includes also the interpretation which religion gives of itself in theology. Faith itself urges on to reflection—*fides quaerens intellectum*. This reflection *on* faith becomes part *of* faith, leading to new religious experiences which in turn will lead to further theological reflection. All too often we think of the religious experience as one thing and theology as another. But, at least in Christianity, theology is part of *every* religious experience. And it has been a serious mistake of philosophy of religion in the past to separate the first "crude" experience from the reflection which continues that experience. This mistake is probably due to the strange but common assumption that the true image of religion is to be found only in its initial, most primitive form.

At any rate, by writing a philosophical critique of religion in its full reflective development, Duméry is able to probe beyond the mere experience without ever abandoning the critical method. He thus avoids both losing philosophy's autonomy by making it an extension of theology (a danger which Blondel has not always escaped), and lapsing into philosophical constructivism by giving an interpretation of the religious experience which ignores that experience's self-interpretation. At the same time, Duméry considerably narrows down the scope of his reflection. His is not a "philosophy of religion," but rather a "philosophy of Christian faith" and primarily of Catholic faith. This is undoubtedly a limitation, but a necessary one. The time of the general philosophies of religion is past. Their success was due partly to the initial need for general introductions and partly to the ignorance of positive data on other than Western religious traditions. The field of comparative religion is relatively new. It has definitively dissipated the philosopher's dream of a common-denominator religion. There are basic differences in religion not only between the primitive and the civilized man, but also between the various traditions of civilized religion, and even between the various historical stages of one tradition.

Nevertheless, this specific character of Duméry's philosophy does not restrict its relevance to the Catholic world. In probing the Catholic's response to a transcendent call Duméry reaches the universal depth where every man's being is related to the transcendent. The fact that this relationship is expressed in the specific terms of one tradition rather than in generalities makes Duméry's work more concrete and therefore also more catholic in the original sense of the term.

L. D.

Introduction

No epoch has been more aware of man's freedom than our own, and no philosophy has given a stronger expression to this awareness than existentialism. To be free, for the existentialist, means more than to choose among given possibilities—it means to create possibilities. Authentic freedom, then, is incompatible with any fixed and predetermined order of values and ideas. For the same reason, Sartre asserts, freedom also excludes God, for if God exists man can no longer create his values—at most he can accept and ratify pre-created values. But such an acceptance is an escape from the task of authentic freedom: it leaves man none but a negative creativity of evil. "A God who would be the arsenal of eternal truths, who would have made all the good and the true, would not have left us anything to do but evil which is the opposite of being."[1]

In Sartre's philosophy freedom has no ulterior foundation. The free act reposes entirely upon itself. As soon as it accepts anything as *given,* freedom loses its authenticity. Of course, Sartre does not deny the opaque reality of the world within which freedom operates. But this reality is a resistance—to be fought rather than accepted. Nor does authentic freedom ever become trapped in its own creations. As soon as a value has been conquered, it becomes part of an objective, thing-like universe and must be rejected if freedom is to remain free. Sartre's freedom, therefore, is bound to remain entirely negative: it destroys

[1] *Foi et Interrogation* (Paris, 1953), p. 33.

but does not construct. And since this negative freedom has no further foundation, it cannot be but a useless passion.

Duméry agrees with Sartre that a preëxisting realm of truth and value would indeed restrict man's intellectual and moral autonomy and would, therefore, be destructive of authentic freedom. But he denies that the existence of God implies a pre-established order of values. In the neo-Platonic tradition which Duméry follows, God is without any determinations. All values, intellectual and moral, are created by the finite spirit. Yet the creative impulse itself can be explained only by means of a transcendent and trans-ordinal principle. "The creative freedom which for Sartre and Polin is possible only in the refusal of God, is declared to be impossible without God by Plotinus."[2]

God creates no values, but he is at the origin of man's value-creating *activity*. Dependence, then, is the source of man's autonomy, and createdness the root of his creativity. Creativity requires an energy beyond all determinations: the finite spirit creates all determinations but God creates his determining activity. No conflicts can arise because the determinate order and the trans-ordinal belong to different levels. Rather than imposing values upon me, God has made me able to create them myself.

Nevertheless, Duméry feels that theism can profit a good deal by the criticism of existentialist theism. It forces the believer to face his responsibility in this world, instead of leaving to God what is essentially man's own task. Sartre, then, may lead the way back to a more authentic affirmation of God such as was made by Plotinus for whom God is active in his creation without ever imposing any finite determination.

Important practical conclusions follow from this insight. One of them is that any form of faith which impairs freedom of conscience necessarily conflicts with the nature of true religion. Religious intolerance always results from an erroneous notion of God. It conceives him as an object, the supreme object con-

2 *La tentation de faire du bien* (Paris, 1956), p. 153.

taining all the values and ideas which the mind must obediently accept. Since truth in this attitude is to be received rather than created, there can be no truth in the non-believer except where he agrees with the believer. At most the believing community can "tolerate" his error and this only on condition that intolerance would be even more detrimental to a universal acceptance of the truth. But in a homogeneous religious society the tendency will always be to make the non-believer conform as much as possible and to force him to accept a truth which is by its very nature monolithic.

Such an attitude jeopardizes God's transcendence. God is not the *locus veritatis*—his truth is above human knowledge, just as his goodness is above human striving. As long as the believer fails to see this fact he will be intolerant of others and cheat his way out of his responsibilities. For if God is the ultimate answer to all questions, then the acceptance of his revelation guarantees the believer the full possession of all religious and moral truth. He then is dispensed from the painful search for truth and can confidently consider his view on life superior to that of the non-believer.

The intolerant believer always identifies his religious experience with an objectivistic value theory. But far from being implied in the religious experience, objectivism can only diminish its authenticity. Few ideas have proved more harmful to religion than the idea that the religious man *possesses* the truth. To be sure, there is a religious truth communicated through revelation and guaranteed by divine authority. But this truth is of a very peculiar sort: it is a *way of salvation.* It presupposes that man finds his values, and it provides him with the norms to live with these values. Even these norms have been expressed in a human way, which again accounts for human perfection and human failure.

Absolutely true is only the believer's relation to God and God's own assistance (including the one of his Word) to preserve this attachment. Such a relation by no means implies an adhesion to a number of values and ideas, preëxisting in the divine essence. "The true and the good are not pre-posited in God (which in the ultimate analysis makes no sense); they are created, posited and invented by man within his relationship to God."[3]

On the other hand, autonomy is not anarchy. In creating values, it may be that freedom does not obey any extrinsic rules, but it certainly follows a law of its own. This rules out any arbitrariness or situationism and includes the possibility of accepting a supernatural revelation. Man's relation to the Absolute must be expressed in a number of representations, and even though these representations are not the ultimate object of man's faith, they are indispensable means for the spirit's union with the Absolute.

Still, this union itself ultimately consists in the private encounter of human freedom with divine freedom. "One becomes a believer by applying a norm to an experience, a testimony to a discovery of values, a doctrine to a practice. But one does not become a believer by assimilating a theory, by reciting a story or by formulating a syllogism. Without personal, actual, free and reflective invention of a world of mystical values which one reaches through a definite intentionality, there can be a learned quasi-faith or a conformist quasi-faith, but there is no living faith, the faith which touches God personally, in the human obscurity of his representations and of his signs."[4] It is obvious that this living faith cannot be imposed upon anyone—in fact, it cannot even be directly propagated. Consequently, any confidence in the salvific effect of the letter of the revelation and, *a fortiori,* every form of religious intolerance is to be rejected.

Once the primacy of the living experience is solidly established, the question arises how reflection is related to this experience. More particularly, what is the function of philosophy with respect to living religion? Does not the emphasis on the

[3] *Ibid.,* p. 57.
[4] *Ibid.,* p. 60.

God of living religion devaluate any philosophical reflection? If it does, we are back at Pascal's choice between the living God and the God of the philosophers. Undoubtedly, as soon as the philosopher starts constructing ideas about God rather than reflecting upon the spontaneous religious experience, the speculation can only be detrimental to religion. The philosopher's task is not to invent the experience, but to submit it to the critique of reason. He encounters the idea of God—he is not its author. In that sense, the religious man can never learn anything new from the philosopher. Yet, in another sense, the philosopher makes an important contribution to the *understanding* of the religious experience. A religious experience which excludes philosophical self-understanding would be just as inauthentic as a reflection which is not based upon a previous experience. For religion is not a blind experience; its own impulse urges it on to reflection, and faith necessarily strives for insight. This impulse gives rise to theology, as an attempt to understand the intrinsic coherence of revealed data in the light of the revelation. But the same religious impulse also urges the mind to understand religion, even revealed religion, in the totality of human experience. This is the task of philosophy. Without philosophy, the religious experience does not fully understand itself. We may conclude, then, that although there is no God of the philosophers, the God of religion is not inaccessible to philosophy.

To the extent that faith belongs to the cognitive order, it must be expressed in intellectual categories over which philosophy has jurisdiction. But in a sense, the entire religious experience is within the jurisdiction of philosophy, since all experience is an object of philosophical reflection. Of course, reflection must not become a substitute for the original experience, but it never will as long as the philosopher keeps in mind the primacy of experience.

This approach is obviously quite different from philosophy's handling of the problem of God in the past. All too often philosophy has simply ignored the reality of faith and, as a result, has said either too little or too much about God. It says too much when it usurps the primacy of the religious experience and substitutes pure reflection in its place. It says too little if, overly fearful of violating the integrity of the religious act, the philosopher restricts himself to developing mere proofs for the existence of God. A contradiction lurks in this exclusive quest for a demonstration of the divine existence, for it implies that God's existence can be known but not his essence, while simultaneously the philosopher endeavors to show that God's essence is identical with his existence.

Duméry proposes that the philosopher devote his energy to a more fruitful enterprise. He should make a critical study of the religious affirmation of God. Faith affirms God on various levels of consciousness: in the intellect, the will, the imagination, the sensibility. The critic's task is to distinguish these levels and to determine the conditions required for the religious affirmation in accordance with each level. He must study the religious act in and through the variety of its expressions. Such a philosophical critique by no means jeopardizes reason's support of faith, nor does it make the proofs for the existence of God superfluous. But it reunites the religious object with the religious affirmation, and refuses to consider the arguments independently of the living affirmation of faith within which they originated. Rather than restricting the role of reason with respect to religion, Duméry's approach gives it a total jurisdiction over the entire field of religious experience. Whatever is experienced falls within the competence of reason. Even the experience of the transcendent is part of the immanent, human reality which reflection has a right to scrutinize and to clarify.

The objection of rationalism which some have raised against this position is ill founded, for as long as reflection stays within the boundaries of the immanent experience, it cannot intrude upon what the religious man considers to be the transcendent origin of this experience. On the contrary, if philosophy does not uphold and exercise its right to reflect critically upon the religious affirmation itself rather than upon some problems which have been carefully excised from this affirmation, one can hardly maintain that it fulfills its task, namely, to clarify the human experience in its totality.

In claiming this right, philosophy merely returns to its origin. Ancient philosophy was well aware of its religious roots and made no attempt to hide or ignore them, as philosophy did later. It is a well-known fact that Western philosophy originated in a reflection upon the religious cosmologies of the Near East. Less known, perhaps, is that the umbilical cord with the living religious experience was maintained for many centuries after the origin of philosophy. For Socrates and Plato, whom we generally regard as the initiators of purely autonomous thinking, philosophy remained religious in form (the myth) and in content. In fact, the mystical trend of Plato's philosophy became the very heart of Plotinus's thought.

In the Middle Ages the relation between philosophy and religion was drastically altered. Revelation became the proper object of the science of theology as such. As a result, excepting a few isolated attempts,[5] revealed religion ceased to be an object of philosophical inquiry. The study of revealed religion was not to be taken up again until after Kant. And not until the contemporary phenomenological movement was it *generally* accepted that philosophy might have something positive to say about the entire realm of revealed religion. Even so, phenomenology has remained primarily descriptive. Duméry, however, wants to restore philosophy to its full critical right. The task of philosophy is not merely to describe and to analyze but also to evaluate critically on all levels of consciousness, the formation and structure of religious symbols, including the ones which the religious man considers to be strictly revealed.

As we saw earlier, this strictly rational approach is not rationalistic, provided the philosopher does not mistake his critical

[5] The most brilliant of which was Spinoza's.

xxi

work for actual religion and keeps his reflection subordinate to the living experience. Yet the question may be raised whether it is still adequately distinguished from theology. Duméry answers that the difference between the two disciplines is not one of content but of method. Theology reflects upon the content of faith and so does the philosophy of religion. But whereas the former reflects upon this content from an attitude of faith, the latter may never make its reflection intrinsically dependent upon the acceptance of the content of *faith*. The philosopher accepts the religious affirmation only as a *content of consciousness* without committing himself to the transcendent reality which it affirms. His method is entirely autonomous, not in the sense that it is independent of all experience, but in the sense that it does not share the basic commitment of the experience. The theologian, on the contrary, is fully committed: he accepts the authority of sacred writings and of the religious community whose beliefs the Scriptures systematize. For the philosopher, this authority is part of a total experience, but it is not singled out as a determining motive moving him to unconditional adherence. It is precisely the acceptance of a transcendent authority *within the reflection itself* that makes theological conclusions essentially different from philosophical ones.

The philosophical *epoché* does not imply, however, that philosophy and theology have only the material content of their object in common. Theology constantly borrows from philosophy, both in content and in method, to reach its own conclusions. Similarly, philosophy reflects upon the *total* religious experience, which includes theology. For all its autonomy, philosophy of religion would have little to reflect upon were it not for the existence of theology. Rather than avoiding the theologian, the philosopher of religion must try to situate what the theologian is doing within the *total* experience of life. In that function he provides, perhaps unwittingly, a link between philosophy and theology. "The language of the theologian is disconcerting for the philosophers only insofar as they are unable to discover what the theologian wants to say in what he actually says. As for himself, the theologian knows it very well where his practice and that of the believer is concerned. But he does not always know it critically, and he need not know it that way. The philosopher of religion understands his enterprise. Without substituting anything for the religious sense held by the theologian, he still can elucidate it in a methodical and critical way."[6]

In defining the method of philosophy of religion Duméry was strongly influenced by Maurice Blondel. Ever since his dissertation on *L'action* Duméry has retained contact with the French philosopher's thought. Today he is probably his most perceptive interpreter. Of particular influence on his own thought was Blondel's view on the relation between philosophy and living experience. The reality of living experience is accessible only to action. Philosophy does not deal with it. Its task is solely to discover logical coherence, and particularly the inner system of determinations of action. No logical structure can ever replace the primary experience of the real. But at the same time this limitation allows philosophy to reflect upon all of reality without ever chancing an illegitimate intrusion into the proper domain of action. Thus the philosopher can with all due respect for the transcendent reality of revealed religion study it as a self-contained system of thought. For he never discusses this reality as such but only the logical structure in which it is presented.

Any philosophy which does not by its very nature exclude the possibility or the cognition of man's relation to the transcendent must consider the study of the religious phenomenon a logical necessity. Blondel explains this necessity as the need to overcome the discrepancy between the infinite impulse of action and its limited achievements. "All attempts to bring human action to completion fail, and yet human action cannot but strive to complete itself and to suffice to itself. It must but it cannot. The feeling of impotence as well as that of the need

[6] *Ibid.*, p. 118.

for an infinite consummation remain incurable."[7] This discrepancy makes the question of a transcendent completion logically inevitable. Now, the believer claims that such a completion is achieved in revealed religion. In his search for coherence in the system of determination of action the philosopher cannot simply dismiss this claim. According to Blondel, he must consider it at least as a logically necessary hypothesis.

Yet, according to Duméry, philosophy can and must do much more. It must also consider the mind's positive surge toward an ultimate principle that is beyond all determination. This surge appears in all forms of human activity. Cognition, desire, feeling, all manifest a constant striving towards absolute unity. This search for an ultimate principle is precisely what, according to Duméry, Plotinus's philosophy of the One attempts to express. The One is identical with the mind as the principle which enables the mind to posit itself. Yet, the mind cannot be said to *be* the One since it labors under a subject-object opposition. The One is present in the mind's striving, not in its realization. Only a total adherence to this absolute unity will allow the mind to terminate its striving.

Plotinus's impact on Duméry's thought is so strong that one might call him a neo-Platonist, were it not for the even more considerable influence of Husserl on his philosophy. From him Duméry borrows the technical equipment for his *itinerarium mentis ad Deum:* Plotinus's stages of the mind's conversion to the One are presented as the reductions of Husserl's phenomenology.

In the first, so-called *eidetic* reduction, the mind eliminates all factual, contingent elements from the phenomena of consciousness in order to grasp their universal essences. A second reduction, called *transcendental* or *phenomenological,* "brackets" all reference to existential reality in order to concentrate exclusively on the phenomena in their relatedness to the transcendental sub-

[7] *L'Action* (Paris, 1893), p. 321.

ject. "The phenomenological reduction is the awareness of the subordination of the essences to the act which mediates itself through them, which expresses itself in them and reconquers itself upon them."[8] A third, *egological* reduction views the phenomena of consciousness as not merely related to, but also *produced* by the transcendental subject. The study of the constitution of mental phenomena thus becomes a study of the transcendental ego.

Duméry considers these three reductions indispensable in any philosophical analysis. But since, at Husserl's own admission, no ultimate absolute can be reached through them, Duméry feels the need for a fourth, *henological* reduction, grounding the transcendental ego itself in the absolute One. Without this final reduction the mind's striving for unity is not sufficiently founded. But before discussing this innovation, it may be appropriate to bring out some of the implications of the phenomenological method as Duméry understands it.

For Duméry as for Husserl, consciousness and the conscious object constitute one ideal unit of meaning. Neither an independent world of objects nor an independent consciousness confronting the world of objects makes sense to Duméry. Things first acquire meaning and become objects under the intentional gaze of consciousness. "There are only intentional objects, because there is no consciousness but objectivating consciousness."[9] Thus, it is Husserl's theory of the transcendental reduction that provides the epistemological foundation for Duméry's theory of the creative self.

Consciousness alone constitutes meaning and value. Yet, this does not imply that consciousness can create meaning at random, independent of rule and law. The meaning-giving *ego* is not the empirical self but the transcendental *ego,* which constitutes both the self and the world. Duméry calls this more profound, creative ego *act-law.* It is an *act* because it creates, produces, and regu-

[8] *Critique et religion* (Paris, 1957), p. 147.
[9] *Philosophie de la religion* (Paris, 1957), I, p. 21.

lates. The ego acts autonomously but not independently: it receives its active impulse from the One which is above all determinations. This One is the object of the fourth, *henological*
reduction. It reveals the ultimate, unconditioned condition of
the ego. In its constituting activity the self determines the indeterminate energy of the One. The self, then, is not an original
creative principle as the One is: it is an act which is *pre-ordained*
to determine being according to its immanent necessity, and
which therefore rightly may be called *law*. The determination
of all being is a necessary condition (Hegel would say a *mediation*) for the self's conversion to the One.

Still, the question remains: How can the self be a law to itself
without being arbitrary? Duméry's answer is clear. In the creation of meaning and value *the self expresses its essential relation
to the One*. Man's creative activity reveals his thrust towards
the One. This henological direction of the self's creativity
excludes all arbitrariness. Undoubtedly, man may jeopardize
the mediating function of his activity by overemphasizing some
values to the detriment of all others. Yet, this error does not
result from the creative act itself, but from man's failure to
recognize its relativity, that is, its relatedness to the One, which
alone is absolute.

It is important to keep in mind that the ego's creativity does
not follow from the awareness of the self, but that it precedes
it as its necessary condition. Man constitutes meanings and values
before he experiences himself as a constituting ego. Even this
awareness does not reveal the act-law directly, but only its
expressions. The task of philosophy consists in discovering the
ego's original, intentional impulse underneath these conscious
expressions and in understanding constituted ideas and values
as objectivations of more fundamental attitudes. Philosophy
thus brings into reflective focus the most basic activity of the
mind from which the empirical self originates.

The distinction between act-law and empirical consciousness
is essential. It allows Duméry to eliminate several false prob-

lems. One such problem is the opposition between freedom and determinism. As long as consciousness remains restricted to what is empirically accessible, freedom is simply an unexplainable exception in a deterministic world. As the positive sciences (one of which is psychology) draw ever narrower circles around its little enclave, the suspicion grows that some day scientific predictability will cover a field which a lack of knowledge alone still withholds from complete determinism. In Duméry's view, however, scientific determination itself originates in the creative spontaneity of the ego. Instead of suppressing freedom, determinism presupposes it. For rather than merely ratifying a preëxisting objective necessity, freedom, for Duméry, is the subjective but necessary source of all objective determinism.

Of course, the freedom which produces necessity is by no means arbitrary; it cannot even be identified with the traditional "freedom of indifference." It surpasses the psychological experience of deliberation as well as the unclassifiable phenomena that remain after the scientist has finished his work. If the pre-scientific concept of unlimited freedom is too simplistic, the positivist notion of an all comprehensive preëxisting determinism is even more so. "Psychological consciousness knows only those causalities which could originate from its own choices, or fragments of causality of which it does not know the ins and outs, or, finally, the not-further-justifiable shock of factitiousness. Never except by abusive majoration or generalisation is it aware of a necessity at once intelligible and impelling. Similarly, the scientist discovers phenomenal connections, experimental concatenations. He supposes determinism wherever nature does not respond *no* to his question, wherever the precision of his calculation allows him to tie together phenomena which must be integrated into an operative whole. But never does he find himself confronted by a fully constituted causalism. Order supposes an organizer. The experimental structures are those of the laboratory, that is, of man and his instruments, not of nature."[10]

[10] *Ibid.*, I, p. 60.

If determinism cannot exist without freedom, neither can freedom exist without determination. Freedom and arbitrariness exclude each other. The act-law is essentially *order,* and order means determination, but the determination is the self's determination, the order is the self's order, not one imposed from without. Even to place God under the denominator of *being* would make man dependent upon God in the order of determination, and would be incompatible with the autonomy of the *act-law.* Duméry therefore rejects the traditional notion of participation. Being and the source of being cannot share in the same being. As to the principle of determination, Plotinus's *intelligible,* it *proceeds* from the One, but does not participate in the One. Henology and participation exclude each other. "One must choose between these two possibilities. The advantage of the henology is that it simultaneously guarantees the radical productivity of the One and the creativity of the intelligible, the One as 'source-principle' and the intelligible as self-position."[11]

This radical status of the self's creative autonomy raises several questions. The first one is: If God is above all categories, how can we know about him? Any form of "natural theology" seems to be excluded. Even to prove God's "existence" is not possible —much less to discover his attributes. Duméry is not deterred by this negative conclusion, for it forces him to lay all the more stress upon the notion of *revelation.* Man cannot but make the movement towards God, yet he cannot *know* God unless God reveals himself. "Because he cannot himself speak our language, all speculative revelation becomes impossible. That is why the Bible declares fruitless all human wisdom which claims to teach us *in toto* or in part what God is."[12]

One may wonder, however, whether Duméry's radically negative theology has not eliminated even the possibility of a revelation. Some critics think that he has removed God so far from

[11] Henk Van Luyk, S.J., *La philosophie du fait chrétien* (Paris, 1965), p. 78.
[12] *La foi n'est pas un cri* (Paris, 1959), p. 216.

man as to make any subsequent contact impossible. Duméry answers this objection in the second edition of *La foi n'est pas un cri.* He admits that God is silent insofar as he transcends all determinations of language. But God can reveal himself insofar as he is the source of our speaking. If the henological reduction can be made, a dialogue with God is possible. Duméry may "reduce" a substantial part of what the ordinary believer considers to be essential to the notion of revelation. But he stresses just as strongly the possibility of and the need for a revelation. "God is beyond our grasp, our categories, but he appears through them. He is the high point of our aims, he is their soul. Nevertheless, we must increasingly purify our ideas and our plans. For instance, he cannot be called *personal*—personal as we are; but he is more. It is possible, it is normal to address ourselves to him as to a person, provided we preserve the mystery."[13] Definitely eliminated in Duméry's thought is a revelation of God through nature. Nature may help man find his way to God, but it can never teach him anything *about* God. Nature has no voice of its own—all revelation is essentially human, for man alone can give meaning and expression. So, if God is to speak at all, he must do it through man. Man alone is the image of God.

But this brings us to a second question. If man alone has the power of speech and if God is above all human categories, how can any revelation be said to be *God's* Word? Revelation seems to be an expression of man, in both its content and its form. In constituting the sacred, the human subject creates mediating schemas and categories in order to attain the Absolute. As expressions of a human experience, these schemas and categories are obviously human. So, then, what entitles the religious man to read God's Word in them? If they are merely intermediate stages in the mind's ascent to the One, they are at best relative expressions. How, then, can the believer ascribe a permanent, absolute meaning to the words of revelation? If the One is above

[13] *Ibid.,* p. 225.

all intelligible determination, why should the New Testament be anything more than the relation to the Absolute of one particular cultural group expressed in accordance with their specific needs and aspirations? Duméry would admit the relativity of all religious language, including that of the New Testament. Every language bears the imprint of the civilization which it expresses, and that civilization is, by its very nature, relative. But he would deny that this relativity eliminates the absolute element. The transcendent nature of God does not exclude an objective revelation—nor does the subjective acceptance and expression of this revelation, the so-called projection, eliminate its objective character. "Consciousness does not project anything *upon* the object, it does not cover it with something that does not belong to it. I use the term projective consciousness as opposed to reflective consciousness. I mean that consciousness itself is spontaneously projective: it projects, not something of itself upon something other than itself, but the meanings which it intends on a diversity of expressive levels. Its act is intentional: it is directed toward the object and attains it; but it cannot intend it without expressing it at the same time in a spectrum of various representations."[14] Subjective structures do not change the object: they are the indispensable means by which the subject attains objective essences on various levels of consciousness. They are the prism in which the object itself is refracted. That the New Testament projects the religious consciousness of a particular community, by no means implies that it has deformed the objective character of the *fact* Jesus. Indeed, without such a projection there would be no religious history. For what transforms these particular facts into *religious* facts if not their mode of acceptance? For meaning, history must depend on meaning-giving subjects. This is particularly true in the case of sacred history. The events of Jesus' life can have a religious meaning only to a religious subject. To *understand* the religious meaning of

[14] *Ibid.,* pp. 244–45.

Christ, it is not sufficient to register the historical facts of his existence. "The religious reality objectively contains the meaning which the believer recognizes in it; yet, this meaning is perceived only when the believer discerns this reality as religious. In technical terms: the religious object exists, but we still must 'constitute' it as religious."[15] The most essential characteristic of the religious object is that it must be received in a religious way, that is, that it must be *given* a religious meaning.

Far from being a deviation from the original message, the interpretation of faith is a necessary factor for the correct transmission of this message. For the message itself refers to faith and this cannot be transmitted by a merely factual report. It requires a personal commitment on the part of the reporter. If the evangelists had not told their story in a spirit of faith, their writings would have been no more "sacred" than the brief reports on Christ in Tacitus and Pliny. Historical reliability requires that the events be rendered as truthfully as possible—*not* that the narrator abstain from all religious interpretation, for this interpretation is an essential part of the events *insofar as they are religious.*

The religious interpretation also justifies the selection which the sacred narrators apply to their historical material, and which must appear quite arbitrary to the non-believer. Even many believers who imagine that it suffices to "get the facts" in order to have faith are shocked by this selection and prefer to ignore it. But every history requires *some* selection, and since a "religious fact" can be recognized only in a religious vision, a selection of facts on the basis of their religious acceptance becomes imperative. Duméry's position supports the conclusion of contemporary biblical scholarship, that the sacred writers found their inspiration within a religious tradition and must be read in that tradition. The tradition is the faith of the witnessing community which is able to bestow the religious meaning upon historical events.

[15] *Ibid.,* p. 258.

Yet the necessity of a subjective acceptance in faith, of a tradition, does not reduce religion to a merely subjective experience.[16] Christianity has always strongly emphasized the historical character of its foundation. The object of Christian faith can be seen only through the eyes of faith, yet faith itself requires that its object be *historical*. The religious vision of faith is empty without the historical facts which it illuminates. An attack upon the historicity of the basic events of Christianity, Jesus' death and resurrection, is, therefore, an attack upon Christianity itself. No doubt, faith in the resurrection goes far beyond the historical apparitions and the discovery of the empty tomb: it demands that death and resurrection be accepted as essential stages of the revelation of the son of God and of the redemption of man. Yet the act of faith itself needs the foundation of historical facts. Only a dialectic of seeing and believing could ever lead to the pentecostal experience. "The apparitions of Christ are proofs because they do not merely present the risen Christ to seers, but to seers who are also believers and whose belief brings them to the proper perspective, to an order of truth in which it would be contradictory to claim that Jesus is the Christ, the blessed of God, without having broken the bonds of death."[17] The apostles believed because they saw and they saw because they believed.

Another point that must be emphasized against any subjectivist interpretation of man's theophanic activity in Christianity is that the original and most basic meaning of Jesus' acts was given by Jesus himself. This meaning was reconstituted and developed by the primitive Christian community. The result was transmitted to later generations who, in turn, reconstituted these objective data into religious experiences. Since the meaning-giving activity is obviously conditioned by the personal characteristics and the cultural level of the interpreters, the religious interpretation of "the Jesus event" varies from age to age. Yet, all these variations do not basically deviate from the original

---

[16] *Loc. cit.*
[17] *Ibid.*, p. 83.

meaning given by Jesus himself. Against the position of *form-criticism* Duméry maintains that the collective consciousness may enrich an idea, but that the idea itself can originate only in a personal consciousness. What the Christian community sees in Christ was, at least implicitly, immanent in Jesus' experience. To recognize Jesus as the Lord is an act of faith that no historical "facts" can "substantiate." Still, the Christian's belief cannot be without objective support. For why is it that the believer's faith centers exclusively upon Christ, while he rejects all other "theophanies"? Whatever the basis of such a religious discrimination may be, it cannot be purely subjective. As Duméry remarks: "The religious consciousness deifies only those beings that display for its eyes a presence indicating divine authority. Every theophany is a value judgment, the value of which is proportionate to the spiritual requirements of him who formulates it. How could we deny that in the case of Christ and his disciples the theophanic judgment passed on Jesus was inspired by his own attitude through which it attained a particularly pure conception of the nature of God."[18]

Some objective religious meaning must obviously be transmitted. Since such a meaning is not immanent in the historical events as such, it must be placed in them by a religious interpretation of the events. In Christianity, this interpretation started with Jesus and his first disciples.

[18] *Ibid.*, p. 74.

FAITH AND REFLECTION

I.

Autonomous Freedom
and Religious Dependence

1. THE ERA OF CREATIVE FREEDOM

Around 1900 Gaston Milhaud claimed that the world had arrived at the fourth age of thought. The philosophy of activity was replacing the old philosophies of the idea. Now, fifty years later, should we match eloquence with eloquence by suggesting that we are entering with amazement and delight upon a fifth age of thought? The cynical will smile: "The atomic age, no doubt?" No, we are speaking of a far more subtle form of disintegration.

No doubt, existentialism is a first sign of our transition to a new age. Judging by some of its offshoots, certain critics will say that in fact we are regressing. This, to be sure, is quite possible and even probable if existentialism is nothing but some sort of measles. Only this last point has not been proven.

In fact, existentialism strikes a new note not because it is a philosophy of tragic existence (which is nothing new, even in philosophy) but because it is the philosophy of human freedom carried to the absolute. It is a near relative to that philosophy of values of which Raymond Polin has given us the clearest expression. It is not the existentialist way of looking at things as such that tells us most about our intellectual age. Rather, it is the thesis that man is invested with a radical and creative freedom.

3

So widely used is the word "freedom" that it seems a common-place thing at first sight. But here it has its strongest meaning: man is free because he creates the true and the good out of whole cloth. The true is not an eternal truth nor the good an eternal value, situated in God and destined to be ratified or chosen later by man. Henceforth it is man, each one of us, who freely creates ideas and values. In other words, the human mind no longer has to adhere to an *ideal order* of which it is not the source. It posits this order; it forges this ideal. It is free because it is creator.

To this Sartre and Polin add that God is now superfluous and an additional burden. As the source of eternal truths, God disappears when they do. A man who creates himself by his own efforts has no need of a Creator who, in creating him, prevents him from creating himself. Human freedom is the death of God. Atheism is humanism's last word.

Now this atheist conclusion will not easily be accepted as progress. After having proclaimed a fifth age, we find ourselves thrown back to very ancient times. Suppose, however, that atheism were only an impulsive gesture, an illogical conclusion, a blunder that could be recognized and corrected. Suppose man could create ideas and values without rejecting the Absolute. This would change everything.

Indeed, we would suggest that this supposition contains the great question of our times. If any problem is contemporary, urgent, and new, this is it. If a positive solution can be found for it, our fifth age will not be far off. It will be up to Catholic philosophers and theologians to attempt such a solution, but the way in which the problem is posed will be something of a shock to them—a proof that it is new, unexpected, almost insolent. Let us wager that they will easily win God's cause, which is fortunate: God does not die! At the same time, however, they cannot with impunity lose man's case. For this new man, this untrammeled soul who goes so far as to recognize within himself the power not only to opt for the values that are imposed on him but to create values by his own choice, will not easily lay down his arms. Compared with this creator of the good, the technical Prometheus, with whom Marxism is so enchanted, is a powerless dwarf. The humanism of progress is but a poor reflection of the truly radical humanism of self-creation.

It is not our place here to reveal the pitfalls of a creative freedom conceived on a human plane. It is sufficient to have pointed out that creative freedom is the salient point of contemporary thought, the sign of our times. By way of suggesting a remedy to fit the disease, however, allow me to call attention to an irony of history. The first time that so bold a thesis appeared was in the third century of the Christian era, thanks to an Alexandrian philosopher called Plotinus. (Perhaps our fifth age is going to slip away into the past.) Plotinus taught that the mind created the intelligible in an essentially active contact with the One, its origin. The Absolute, according to Plotinus, is beyond subjects or objects, which appear only through the minds that give rise to them. Thus Plotinus maintains that this creative freedom which Sartre and Polin believe possible only by rejecting God is really impossible without him. It seems to follow, then, that the creation of the self by the self does not exclude but rather requires the Creator. The most recent philosophy joins the concerns of ancient philosophy at the very point on which it seems to make the most innovations. What is left, then, for our contemporary philosophers? This, which is of prime importance: to sustain the full impact of the idea of total freedom in the human order, to support it and preserve it better than did Plotinus whose discovery suffered an eclipse for fifteen centuries. In any case, atheism will be the worst enemy of the bold thesis which it has brought to light. Perhaps this means that the fifth age which we have been talking about can only be realized or restored by Christians. What our modern philosophers learned from Nietzsche, what they would have done better to learn from Plotinus, let us learn from this unrecognized Christian tradition which teaches that God occupies himself less

5

with producing reflections of his glory than with creating creators.

2. FREEDOM AND ETERNAL TRUTHS

"One can never wrestle enough with God if one does so out of pure regard for the truth. Christ likes us to prefer truth to him because, before being Christ, he is truth. If one turns aside from him to go towards the truth, one will not go far before falling into his arms."[1] In these words, Simone Weil uttered a sound paradox. Her terms may momentarily surprise one who has been born in the faith and never had to struggle to obtain it. But on reflection, he will soon agree that the search for God is likely to pass through these phases of purifying negation. Atheism itself, provided it is intelligent and sincere, is a tribute in its own way to the true God. Men reject the Absolute only for the sake of a better absolute. Often a refusal to accept a particular representation of God involves the implicit affirmation that God is above all representation. Finding God will never be anything but a searching beyond what one has found. Thus, the dialogue between the atheist and the theist is unending: it involves the very figure of an open question. One man adores God while idolizing himself. Another refuses to adore, while striving tirelessly to surpass himself in order to reach him. We might say that each of us is always an unbeliever for someone else. We might add that it would be a pity if God's witness were to testify chiefly to his own indolent or futile tendency to place God anywhere but in God.

My intention, however, is not to renew the debate between theism and atheism. It is to preach uneasiness to the believer. I have no wish to make him scrupulous—this was done to him a long time ago—but I would like to help him to see that the

[1] Simone Weil, *Waiting for God*, translated by Emma Craufurd (New York, 1951), p. 69.

6

faith is less an answer than a question. For believing consists first of all in resisting the temptation to sleep. It challenges a man to give up all support, the rigid foundations, the cold proofs. In a word, believing is a rude awakening to a kind of activity heretofore ignored, the acceptance of a grace whose real name is liberating freedom. How will the believer react to all this? Will he be surprised, happy, or disappointed? "Newfangled apologetics," he may say. Not so. Our age has done away with apologetics, that overly opinionated scholastic method which deduced conclusions without end, but always according to its own line of thought, without ever questioning either its premises or its methods. Or better, let us speak of an apologetics of spiritual autonomy, the only kind which is worthwhile. The older apologetics, based on *esprit de corps* and confessional loyalty, is mere self-justification—petty, defensive, and, above all, ineffectual.

It is not my intention, moreover, to reëxpound the Christian faith or to bring it up to date. Adaptations such as these are mere publicity tactics and there are many who have a flair for this sort of thing. It is more profitable, I believe, to consider lived attitudes and to criticize them objectively. What the lesson lacks in amplitude, it will perhaps make up for in effectiveness. I shall proceed in detail from theory to practice. I will deal in paradoxes only when it is necessary to keep an open mind. I shall begin with a somewhat negative speculative side, but promise a less severe positive side.

Does the believer believe both in truth and in freedom? This question is rarely asked, because the solution precedes and conceals it. Once it is raised calmly, we can see why we avoid it. It is annoying because it is disturbing, and it is disturbing because it challenges indolence. We can, indeed, believe in truth or in freedom, whether we hold our convictions loosely or with rigor. But it is far from immediately clear that the believer does not cultivate the first of these to the detriment of the second.

His excuse, his alibi, is that the truth he accepts precedes him and forestalls any action on his part. A God becomes incarnate for him, a church prescribes the creed. The believer accepts it, approves it, comes on the scene after his own truth. At first he could no doubt have questioned it, discussed it, resisted it. But once he has accepted a creed, he has a ready-made truth. He has caught up with it and now follows it. But he did not create it; it does not "hold" because of him. The believer loses himself in the truth; he alienates himself in it.

I am summarizing here a current objection, one which I should not like to reject too quickly. As an objection, it is quite fair. As matter for an examination of conscience, it is terrifying. Can the truth of my faith be prior to and outside of my personal commitment? Does believing dispense me from acting and thinking for myself? If it does, to believe is to abdicate and salvation lies in revolt.

I can imagine what the apologist would answer in my place— but I am not in his place. I shall take the blow and endeavor to be as exacting on my part as my opponent demands. It seems to me, therefore, that faith is what we make it, and that we do not receive it as we would a thing. Unfortunately, I have to contend with a common prejudice. Everywhere I hear believers speaking of establishing truths, of truth *per se,* of truth unrelated to a subject. They may say this simply *pro forma,* in which case it is understandable. But it is disturbing that the basic attitudes of some among them should be penetrated with this ingenuous conviction, this objectivism which stifles the life of the mind. At any rate, if faith were to require this idolatry of a truth-thing, if, in order to possess it genuinely and in itself it were necessary to subscribe to this manner of thinking, I do not see how God's transcendence could ever escape anthropomorphism. The purpose of religion is to bind us to God, not to strengthen our illusions.

Although the faithful are not initiated into anything but the dogma and the morality of ordinary living, the simple and the learned lay claim to the same truth. This is a paradox, for *how can people who have not the same idea of salvation aspire to the same salvation?* Can anyone believe that a religion of fear or of power (or even of bargaining and chicanery) can lead as far as a religion of love? And yet, without judging anyone's intention (for appearances can be deceiving), it is clear that Christianity itself is lived, according to the individual's way of thinking, in terms of fear, servility, petty moralism, or true charity. Is it really then the same faith? Has not each one the faith that he deserves? The coward saves his body, the hero his heart, the thinker his head. Is there no one then willing to save everything, but in the right order? And above all who, while striving to save his soul, will also hope to preserve his intellectual integrity?

Presented in this fashion, the problem runs the risk of ending in a very serious division, with the learned on one side and the ignorant on the other—a division as dangerous as it is futile. For there are two kinds of intellectuals, the true and the false. The true intellectuals are those who, in the various realms of science, art, or criticism have preserved or achieved a certain simplicity that they share with all upright souls, even the less educated. Secular learning never determines the authenticity of religious attitudes. Yet we cannot fail to judge these attitudes—from selfish fear to the very gift of self through love—according to the levels of truth and reality that they have spontaneously attained.

Viewed from this angle, the faith of any man can be evaluated, whether he be learned or ignorant. The man who commits himself to God and to the Church because it is too difficult to fight alone, too oppressive to bear his problem alone and so much more convenient to leave to others the care of solving them, may indeed possess many virtues, but he is lacking in courage. The man who submits his judgment in order to circumvent a difficulty, to set aside his responsibilities *en bloc*, thenceforth to think as suggested or commanded, is not docile; he is cowardly.

This dual example, moreover, is not at all fictitious. There is a way of appealing to God that closes the question and at the same time deadens the mind. There is a way of having recourse to the Church that closes the mind and cuts it off from all progress. The warnings of the unbeliever, therefore, are salutary. If God were an arsenal of eternal truth, who had achieved all the good to be accomplished and revealed all the truth to be known, he would have left us nothing to do. Nothing, that is, except evil, which is precisely the opposite of being. If a church would not be satisfied with teaching the fundamentals of the faith but claimed to deliver the definitive word on all things, it would leave us nothing to discover. Nothing, that is, except error, which is precisely the betrayal of truth. These hypotheses are foolish but not unheard of. Some believers think that they are on the right track when they conceive of an infinite into which they can plunge and be sated, and a religious authority which each morning secretes new dogmas and certitudes. They must realize, however, that such a hunger for satiety, such a gross spirituality, has nothing to do with genuine faith. To believe the truth does not mean to deposit it somewhere, lifeless and cold, even if this were to be in the Absolute or in the parchments of its representatives. Nor is it to conceive of truth as though it preëxisted the toil of men, completely constituted before being sought, desired, or won bit by bit. Neither, finally, is it to imagine truth as incapable of being lost once obtained, guaranteed for tomorrow if today has grasped a part of it. No, to believe the truth is to *establish* it, to bring it to the light through risk, uncertainty, and groping. Mankind has never discovered anything it has not laboriously looked for. It has never found anything without running the risk of losing it. The effort of discovery and the effort of conservation together sum up the meaning and the value of truth for men. Without these arduous tasks, there is only the love of rest, of comfort, and of security, which underlie a religion of individual conformism, social etiquette, and heavenly assurance.

But how are we to *establish* the truth of our faith since it precedes us as a given? If we are to attempt a brief, condensed, and necessarily incomplete reply, we shall have to pass over many fine points. Sometimes, however, a summary is helpful. We note, then, that only one means is open to us here: we must believe, not because of Scripture, which is the letter, not because of tradition, which is the social body, not because of history, which is reconstruction, and still less by reasoning and feeling, which are simple projections of the spiritual person. We must believe through God alone, the unique and definitive Revealer, through whom Scripture is life, tradition is spirit, and history, witness. But is even this sufficient to respect the autonomy of the subject? Is not the visible Christ imposed as a fact, the Church as an institution? Yes indeed, but if we give the matter serious thought we see that it takes at least as much audacity here and now to call Jesus God and to declare the religious society divine as it did in the first decades of the Christian era. Jesus is a fact; the Church is a fact; both are empirical realities. But to go from these facts to a doctrinal interpretation and to base our existence on this interpretation—this will require in each of us a new Pentecost. The assumption of a fact into a doctrine, of a situation into a faith, is always a personal initiative, a free and radical act. Nothing—not even the Gospel—is ever given coercively and collectively as completely objective evidence. *When they are open, the eyes of faith cause a world to come into being.*

Thus the believer deceives himself if he imagines that the truth precedes him, engulfs him, and carries him away without any effort on his part. He is looking upon this very intimate action by which the grace of God is made manifest to him as existing before his birth, beyond his psychology, and even outside his consciousness. But he ought not to canonize these representations, comprised as they are of weak and at times deceptive schemas as equal to the absolute Presence. Still less ought he to forget that if God has given him the power to make himself by acting, it is indeed he himself—finite spirit, creator of finite good—who causes ideas and values to appear in the universe. And if, by God's condescension, he is raised to the heights of

11

faith, it is still he himself who must take in this new view, without God or anyone else being able to dispense him from focusing his attention or from opening his eyes.

Is this by any chance a new and consequently suspect Christian anthropology? The suspicion, should it arise, would be strange. We might as well discredit every attempt to make faith, truth, and freedom march together on the road of spiritual progress. No doubt, we fear that the awakening of autonomy may somewhat impair sincerity and obedience. But is clinging to what is not God the way to be sincere? And is obedience bowing our head instead of scanning the face of authority for the true identity of the one commanding? On the contrary, loyalty and docility exist only at the cost of a rectitude that unceasingly examines itself and submits everything to judgment. No one can deny that adoring God involves a refusal to bend our knee before idols. Viewed from this standpoint, faith is the highest contest, the one that makes Caesar capitulate and breaks the chains asunder. When we wish to keep the world and society, tyrants and glamour, the passions themselves at bay, we need extraordinary strength. For these are overpowering weights, and not even the Absolute is too much to help us lift them.

Nevertheless, a certain distrust might persist concerning such a rugged faith. For, without admitting it, does such a faith not claim for itself a kind of aristocracy of the mind? It only seems so. It does not nurture any gnosis; it assumes more risks than privileges. There is, moreover, a final and decisive criterion: charity. But even in this area a surprise is in store for us. Charity is the most inspiring idea in Christianity—not that people have not tried hard to narrow its scope. It transcends ethics just as loyalty based on love surpasses submission to law. And yet there are those who have sought to reduce the state of grace, which is the life of charity, to an accounting of virtuous and sinful acts. Charity is infinitely more noble than any effective impulse or any emotional response, although there are those who have tried to reduce it to the dimensions of sentimental pietism. But it is far from that. A religion based on love has nothing in common with a purely psychological piety, with its cultivation of the ego through countless techniques for developing in the soul a sense of gravity and importance.

Charity is, in fact, the opposite of such complacency. It is not preoccupied with self; it is forgetful of self. The universal is its hallmark, although this is a notation which, regardless of what anyone may say, is not terribly familiar. The fact that people habitually think of charity in terms of affectivity indicates how difficult it is to hold fast to the level of spiritual universality. It is nevertheless necessary to do so. For the love of God is incompatible with partiality. Charity, in the strictest sense of the word, goes beyond any limitations or boundaries, whatever they may be, whether our own or those of others. It goes straight past appearances and brings out in each being all that is infinitely precious, all that lies hidden under the cloak of passions or beneath psychological or social confusion.

But are we aware of the renunciation of egoistic categories involved in such a penetration and breadth of vision? There is nothing selfish here, nothing mercenary, no guarantee of the hereafter, no pact made with God. Charity does not pay. It obliges us to give without counting the cost; it looks for no return. More than this, it makes precarious every virtue and every value, for it is not satisfied with what has been done and brushes achievement aside as an obstacle. It admits of no definitive foundation, since it will not rest at any determination. It hangs everything on a freedom which commits itself and offers itself, a freedom which does not depend upon any object, since it challenges them all. Charity joins forces only with its source, the pure liberty of God, the *Aseity* which, through grace, permits it to transcend all nature. Finally, through the presence of each in all and of all in each one, it is the bond among all spirits and, as it were, their common avenue to the Principle of all reciprocity.

This description may seem to be playing with words. We know, however, the concrete needs to which it answers. It is the man who aims at complete disinterest who is the bearer of charity. He it is who overcomes the ambiguity of the emotional, of the psychological, of the social. He is not stayed by a religion of fear or interest or security; he is not satisfied with conversing with God, of arguing with his Church. He loves men, sacrifices himself for them, endeavors by every means within his power to free them—economically, civilly, politically, and religiously. Such a dedicated, self-sacrificing, and efficient man is the true witness of God to his brothers. He does not resort to excuses, to false show, to alibis. He shifts to no one—neither to God nor to the Church—the responsibility of discovering day by day the true and the good that can renew the human condition. And he does this out of love, a pure love closely modeled on the unique Love. Can such a religion be compared with an edifying self-worship? Let us abandon individualist conceptions of salvation, desires for a heaven which would resemble an accounting office. Those who seek such things will find that even that which they do not possess will be taken away from them—namely, the sense of the Absolute. For, according to Brunschvicg's terrible pronouncement, God will not reveal himself to cowards.

3. Freedom and Religious Escapism

Sartre's philosophy is atheistic in principle. It is a deliberate effort to achieve coherence by eliminating God. In view of this admission, some critics are quick to declare in triumph: Sartre has revealed his method of attack; his starting point is a gross begging of the question. But this is naïve. Sartre does not deny that he begins by rejecting God. He says so openly. And in saying so, he means to prove that his conclusion confirms his starting point. He has thus a very specific intention in mind: to draw the greatest possible logic from an atheistic position. This design is so explicit, and also so lucid, that he will use no method other than the dialectic to prove his point. Sartre is by no means

14

anti-religious in a hostile way. Religion simply does not exist. Atheism has matured. It is no longer negation and struggle; it has become a matter of organization and method.

If this is so, if Sartre has openly broadcast his intention, critics have no right to become indignant over his initial premise. After all, everyone is free (and responsible) to establish his own hypotheses. Challenge, wager, exaggeration make little difference here. What is important is the inference that follows. Is it or is it not at all one piece, coherent, bona fide? It is the author's duty to be unsparingly exact. It is the critics's role to try to find him at fault. Well aware that the task would be a hard one, Sartre nevertheless did not hesitate to undertake it. For that very reason we would like to show that after having chosen an untenable starting point, he resolved to maintain its untenability. Having excluded God, how can one, how should one propose this, that, or the other idea so as to remain consistent with oneself? This is the motive force of the investigation. The progressive development of the system is but an attempt to chart a straight course from beginning to end without ever appealing to theism. Doubtless, this calls for both courage and ingenuity. We should not be surprised that the denial of God requires at least as much trouble as his affirmation. The important thing is to attempt it and strain for success. How does Sartre go about it? How does he think he will achieve it? Such an approach will be more enlightening than any mere denial of his starting point. Let us begin by describing his principal themes. We shall then judge their solidity.

Once we have disposed of God in principle, nothing further stands in the way of man's apotheosis. God was an intruder. Once he is out of the way, man recovers his absolute freedom. How can we conceive this? By adjusting a few Cartesian notions. Descartes attributes to God a freedom creative of essences. We need only transfer this freedom to man. Descartes was wrong in projecting onto a transcendent absolute what properly belongs to the human existent. Man is entitled to complete autonomy.

Otherwise he would retain only the negative freedom to commit evil outside God—while the accomplishment of good would be restricted to ratifying preëxisting values. For freedom, if it is not to be sterile, not to be merely a word, must be *productive.* It must create its own good and its own truth without adhering to preëstablished values. In short, man should be called free not because he can commit sin and error, but because he is able to create the good and the true bit by bit.

This power to create essences is precisely the desired liberation. Henceforth a free act is bound by no law. Every determining principle, every metaphysical norm would be only a necessitating *antecedent state.* If there is law, principle, order, determinism, even alienation, these could not exist before, but only after the outbreak of freedom: not upstream but downstream. Freedom, therefore, is total, original, and constitutive. All truth and all value depend on man's free decree, and man himself depends on nothing. Man's freedom has no other foundation but himself. Sartre could repeat the words of Lachelier: let us not fear to suspend our thought in the void; it can rest only on itself.

This void that encompasses thought is by no means frightening. It is not an unforeseen threat but a necessary condition. Nothingness is only the other side of the Absolute. For the Absolute, entirely contained within itself, leans on nothing. It does not draw its truth from any universal order that has been imposed on it but only from its own act. It reveals itself as a supreme uncertainty and has no security other than the continuity of its own outpouring. If the mind ceases to fly forward, to create the unknown, and to burst forth in unforeseeable discoveries, it destroys itself as pure freedom. It drops down like waste, its own residue, a thing. But this anguish, inherent in freedom, is also its sharpest spur. Autonomy can realize itself only under the banner of risk. It leans on no previous truth, exterior or superior to itself.

In the light of these remarks, we can weigh the hazards conjured up by the denial of God. Is not theism equivalent to an

16

ontological systematization, to a normative determination that invites and prescribes man's adhesion but at the same time denies him any productivity? In banishing God, man has eliminated the whole metaphysical apparatus attached to the idea of God, which is only a net thrown over human freedom. God was the foundation of order, the locus of eternal truths, the archetype, the efficacy and the end of all that is or acts. Henceforth the coast is clear.

Or rather not. One *given* remains, an irreducible given that is the essence of things. Our idealism was premature and we must change our minds. Riveted as it is in nature, freedom will, even in the absence of God, be recaptured by some objectively established norm that will open everything up to question again, though under a different form. The danger is serious, and it will require all the resources of the dialectic to avoid it. Yet the solution is near. Since God is out of the picture, we cannot see in things an intelligible reference that could serve as a consistent standard, necessary for judgment and will. There is no longer a given in the strict sense of the word, because there is no longer any Giver. The reality of things is imposed as a *fact,* but only as a fact. It is brutal, opaque, and gratuitous. When it strikes us, it will cause us to turn nowhere but back on ourselves. The metaphysical heaven is closed. There is nothing to justify the world of things. We have only to understand that from it we can obtain by way of reaction an illumination within ourselves. We shall remain the only source of significance in a universe in which being means nothing, because pure fact is sufficient for it, fills it, and packs it tight.

Moreover, the knowledge is very well accounted for by the simple contact with things. Even our subjectivity will be all the better guaranteed since this exteriority will better preserve us from becoming involved in objective reality. By intentionality I aim at being; I keep it at a distance.[1] I have nothing to draw

---

[1] Unfortunately, Sartre saw in the subject only a prop for intentions without interiority. Thus consciousness becomes, as Lachièze-Rey and Varet have

from it but the shock that sends me back upon myself, according to varying degrees of resistance. Not the least idea sleeps at the heart of things. Meanings are always our own. Thus realism is rejected, along with idealism, for we need blunt and tough things to unlock our meaning-giving activity and also to qualify it in its productions. Thus no subject dispenses with "being," while being, in order to be, does very well without a subject. At the same time, however, all knowledge remains a subjective phenomenon. For if the thing is a pure fact, the idea can only be *non-fact* or value. That is why thought knows being only in negating it. Far from being ontological, it is essentially—to borrow a neologism from Wahl and Mounier—mé-ontological.

This paradox is the decisive turning point of the dialectic. If knowledge succeeds in freeing itself, not despite its involvement in the world but because of it, freedom will no longer be bound by the limits it encounters. It will rebound with the same resiliency. And that is exactly what human freedom requires if it is to remain absolute amid every restriction. In God it was child's play to conceive of a radical freedom that was uniformly triumphant. In man, however, a serious obstacle remains to be circumvented: finitude. How is this possible? How can we deify man, who is finite and limited by time and space? Yet this is what we must do, and here is how.

Finitude alone is negativity, and negativity is productivity. In fact, since knowledge and negation are synonyms, a pure freedom with nothing to negate would be a *full being,* a huge thing-in-itself. It would become contradictory. On the other hand, once it is bound within narrow limits, it is contained only in order to gush forth from them. Its situation, by providing it the necessary support of negation, allows it this "mé-ontological proof" of itself, which is its very breath. Instead of seeing any incompatibil-

---

pointed out, a "polyp of intentionalities," just as others have made of it a polyp of images. Devoid of interiority, the life of the subject loses all unity and continuity.

ity between the absolute of freedom and its radical finitude, we must see them as rigorously connected.

The loop is therefore closed, it seems. For man has organized the totality of his relations with the world, and done so while dispensing with God. He is free, not in spite of his situation, but because of it. He is the exclusive bearer of meanings, not in spite of the fact that he is overwhelmed by being, but because of it. Situation and freedom, ontology and phenomenology correspond to one another. Our finitude is indeed a dependence upon a being which escapes us. But it escapes us only to allow us to recover ourselves from its dominion. And no doubt it lays many a snare for the forgetful consciousness. But precisely he who allows himself to be caught alienates himself of his own accord. For here being is not determining, unlike the being of theist ontology, which impels and commands while pretending to extend a helping hand.

Finally, knowledge and freedom are winners everywhere. The truly real, or transcendence of the brute fact, is founded on the *unrealizing,* the denier of all facticity, that is, on the imagination. We need search no farther. Man is at last fully master of his creations. He has accomplished the feat of entering into himself without withdrawing from the world. His freedom has assumed charge of all its conditions. It has returned to consciousness that spiritual virginity which makes ideas fecund in themselves. Authenticity, total autonomy, is finally won. It is sufficient for man to possess himself by radically reconquering himself at each moment. For freedom is at the very heart of action, that is to say, of the most effective action.

The description completed, it is time to resume the rights of the critic. Now if we appeal first of all to a criterion of success, we must admit that Sartre's philosophy is superior to many systems. *Empiricism?* It is in a state of rout. In Sartre, there is no passivism of the knowing subject. The states of consciousness are anything but a certified true copy. *Absurdism?* This is merely

19

the abdication of freedom, by which it makes itself a thing among things. And even in this it is deluded without owning defeat. Camus may have given the world a bad jolt, but it is he himself who "absurdifies," which amounts to establishing some order. *Historical materialism?* This also prostitutes the dialectic to the promiscuity of things even though it has meaning only within consciousness. *Sociologism?* But social pressure cannot arise from below as a generating cause. It is only a conditioning, one more facticity. Initiative is always a question of freedom, which everything presupposes and to which everything returns. *Rationalism?* This is a disguised determinism, which saturates the mind with universal laws. *Moral stoicism?* This is merely heroic indolence clinging to necessity. *Hedonism* perhaps? This is out of the question for a freedom that constantly transcends itself, for an asceticism for the sake of authenticity. Woe to him who self-indulgently looks back. Like Lot's wife, he will be turned into stone on the spot, caught and hardened in his determinations. Thus, Sartrean logic and ethics can claim superiority over a number of incoherent or incomplete doctrines.

But destruction, however usefully and skillfully done, is not enough. The construction erected on the ruins must itself possess a foolproof solidity. Does Sartre's philosophy possess this solidity? Does Sartre hold the untenability of a position which he deliberately chose as perilous? This is what we must see.

The first point to be discussed is of course the denial of God. Sartre's philosophy cannot admit of a God who establishes a normative static order. There is no productive freedom other than that which negates. All adhesion of judgment is sterile. By saying yes without at the same time saying no, man surrenders himself into the hands of another. He compromises his creation of himself by himself. Further, the idea of God, considered in itself, is contradictory. It claims to join in the Absolute the being of ontology and the non-being of reflection. For both these reasons, theism seems to be inconsistent.

Let us concede that a normative metaphysics is too often

tantamount to a necessitating static order, which demands passive ratification and not creative initiative. Sartre would say that this is the result of those who confuse being and perception, and whose ontology makes sensible objectivity the criterion of all reality, even the spiritual. Does this inadequacy prove the impossibility of establishing any norm other than a static or constraining one? The problem is perhaps more complex than Sartre perceives it. Even in the case of realism, it is not certain that the ontological norm is a given in the sense of being a thing. There is in fact a kind of necessary reductionism which tends to harden every valuative viewpoint so as to express it more conveniently. But it remains entirely possible to escape the disadvantages of a psychological language and to avoid confusing a rough translation with the meaning that it conveys. Let us, however, refrain from insisting on the deficiency of every verbal wrapping and take into consideration only the main objection. There is a way —one which Sartre has not foreseen—of avoiding a static order without proscribing all norms. This way consists in the creation of the intelligible by the mind in its union with the Absolute. The Plotinian tradition, for example, by no means places ideas in God so as later to impose them on minds as ready-made laws.[2] While reserving to the One the privilege of a radical spontaneity and an ignorance richer than all representation, it makes the advent of systems of ideas coincide with the creation of minds. All static order and all priority of norms are therefore void. God is no longer a threat to productivity, he is its source. He is still less an obstacle to negativity, since genesis of consciousness and finitude are the same thing. Nevertheless, a norm subsists, an interiorized norm. The conversion of the mind remains to be achieved. The ego is ambiguous. It can fall into the sensible

[2] While offering Plotinus as an antidote for Sartre on a specific point, I am simply trying to meet Sartre's requirements and to turn them back upon their author without betraying them. I am not trying to make any other point in the debate. To do this would require a discussion of Plotinus himself.

or climb back to its source. Only the latter attitude offers salvation. It is unification. The other is dispersion.

With this difficulty taken care of, there remains the complaint against the very idea of God. The argument that claims to establish the impossibility of reconciling in the Absolute both being and reflection carries weight only against a God that is monolithic (inert Nature), or axiomatic (abstract Notion), or dualistic (reflected-reflecting). It does not hold against a triune God in whom plurality and unity, subjectivity and objectivity are interwoven. It is an unexpected benefit of Sartrean atheism that it obliges us to pose the problem of God at such a high level. Sartre's philosophy can confound only non-Christian theisms, just as above he was refuting only pseudo-ontological thingness.[3]

After the problem of God and of norms, a second point calls for discussion. This concerns the relationships between consciousness and the world, or again (a related question) between freedom and situation. It is easy to view intentionality as a means of rejoining being without taking it over. Such a view denounces either an irreducible dualism or else an artifice to disguise an effective regulation of nature. In fact both are present. Sartre attempts to get around dualism thus: being is self-sufficient in its compact massiveness; meaning is proper to the mind. Dualism is involved only when there is a radical dissociation from the intelligible. But does not even the most objectivized being really possess some intelligibility, despite its self-sufficiency? How else could perceptions be qualified? Can a pure shock be at the origin of the least differentiation? In holding that the object in some way provisions us, we are merely attributing a certain natural content to the cognitive act. To see in the sensible object a simple reflective limit is only concealing the difficulty. For it means recognizing that this limit has a dialectical function and is integrated in some way or other into a true dialogue between subject and object. By turns we resort to dualism in order to

[3] See Duméry, *La méthode complexe de Jean-Paul Sartre.*

maintain being in a stability apart—God is no longer there to support it and to relate us to it—and to integration in order to permit the coming and going of consciousness, which should always be consciousness of something, negativity and transcendence.

We find the same sophism in regard to freedom in a situation when shock alternates with evaluation. The incoherence becomes even worse. Indeed, objectivity is not merely an external fact, it becomes an internal fact and proliferates indefinitely in a facticity consequent upon the free act. Freedom then resembles a wild flight towards the future. It must continually detach itself from what it is doing in order to continue to act. It must repudiate what it has built as well as that which has been imposed on it from outside. Thus a refractory weight of discarded structures builds constantly upon its back. Consciousness using these structures as a springboard to push forward again and again—this is what constitutes heroism. But the past as past is indeed dead. The future compensates for it, since it allows us to recover the center of freedom insofar as it "presentifies" itself. Cold comfort. Man aspires less to escape from what he does so as to continue to make himself by doing, than to make what he has done live on in what he is still doing and ultimately in what he will have done. But in this case there is only one solution to the problem of temporal consciousness. The past must be linked to a permanent source of actualization that makes it always actual, and even, as Nédoncelle realized, transmutes it into an ever now. Time unravels stitch by stitch with no living recapitulation, no mechanical return, but rather a constant refashioning in a central point called eternity.[4]

With Sartre, however, we may prefer the ardor of creation

---

[4] Sartre speaks of an intentional recovery of the past by the present. This proves that freedom gathers with it past determinisms and uses them again for a new leap according to a renewed project. But the past, even preserved and recaptured in this way, has no other value nor other actuality than that of an impenetrable, though curable resistance. It therefore remains a dead weight, a ball-and-chain that freedom drags along with it.

to its products, for they have no value without it. We can of course lament the degradation of values and look upon moral standards which are accepted in their derived and fixed state as inferior and relative. After all, values are values even when separated from the intention that sustains them. And as Sartre remarked with calculated cynicism, the quietism of the solitary drunkard is as enviable as the futile activism of the leader of people. As regards freedom in act, each individual actualization should be considered as nought, since everything remains to be done. Nevertheless, this does not at all mean to say that freedom ought to act for action's sake and make it a point of honor to remain indifferent to the values it brings to light. And yet this is what Sartrean freedom amounts to. Its power of choice is in proportion to its power of rejection. At the same moment, it chooses and rejects, it flatters and scorns. The values it promoted interest it no longer. Thus its past, although present, remains unknown to it. We are justified in concluding that the past truly remains the obsession of Sartrean consciousness. Whether we admit it or not, the past is a distortion of freedom, like a being vowed to obstruction which blocks the reconciliation of man and the world.

A third and final point should be mentioned, the old problem of communication between consciousnesses. Sartrean freedom, which is cut off from everything (no *before*), without finality (no *after*), which is self-determining (each one establishes his existential project), cannot help but be insular. But here arises another difficulty. If creative freedom designs its own patterns in total independence, how will it happen that all human subjects weave more or less the same design in the intellectual and practical order? The introduction of a universal would take care of everything. But Sartre cannot admit an objective, static structure which would soon prove constraining. The problem therefore is as follows: how, without resorting to any supra-individual principle, obtain a society of minds that is not a cluster of hermits?

24

The example of Leibniz can help us understand how Sartre solves this difficulty. He revives the Leibnizian system of monads while excluding the preëstablished harmony. For Leibniz, each consciousness plays its little tune full force with its ears plugged. If this disjointed ensemble nevertheless produces a fine concert, it is not simply because of the conductor. Sartre rightly denounces the trickery of such mechanical direction. The symphonic success depends on something more fundamental. It derives from the fact that the scores, which each musician interprets with greater or less skill, bear the same musical notation. The consciousnesses free themselves according to their interpretive ability, which necessarily varies from one to the other. But they inevitably meet on that which is written down, fixed, and determined. The same with Sartre. Consciousnesses, as pure freedom, fly at full speed towards an unmarked future. If they could keep themselves aloft, they would fly in parallel paths without coming together. But reality is there, or even the simple past, which brings them down again. Thus the descent is inevitable. There is no use arguing that after the slightest contact with the earth they can take off again and again. No matter what we do, the real remains ambiguous. It permits both flights and captivity. Consequently, because of this common relationship with the world or with the determined in general, Sartrean consciousnesses meet below, through that which is not themselves, like the Leibnizian monads which are forced to line up by the common resistance offered by matter.

This explains why the rejection of the universal does not lead to solipsism (complete isolation). A jerky and uneven contact is maintained among existing things whose shadowy faces confront each other with weapons of hatred or eyes of desire. But such a meeting, which cannot take place in the light, is not a communication. It is a contest. For Sartre, men can conspire for evil; they cannot form a partnership for good. In the first case, they need only cling to ready-made matter. In the second, they can only fly far away from everyone and every-

25

thing, into the light but also into the void. Perhaps this is an ideal of transcendence. Can it also serve as an ideal of reciprocity capable of assuring mutual advancement? In *Les Jeux sont faits,* Pierre and Eve come together among the dead, because there everything is done, nothing is left but to be. Among the living, on the contrary, they embraced in vain and could not be truly united. For each of them to make himself each had first to break away, to become separated from the other. This amounts to saying that, for Sartre, salvation cannot be found in dialogue. We speak to each other, we brush up against each other, we rub elbows. But deep within the self, in the inalienable virginity of our hearts, we have already renounced those whom we love. Consciousnesses meet again, but in the past. The future, which is the true tense of freedom, is conjugated only in the singular.

On terminating this study, it is useless to carp at the deficiencies of Sartre's philosophy. It will suffice to stress the most paradoxical point. Sartre calls himself an atheist. But he shows no ill will towards the idea of the Absolute. He introduces it into time and into finitude. With deep insight, he maintains that consciousness chooses its own limits and goes beyond them. He rightly shows that finitude is a fall; it makes intuition bend back on sensation. But this original sin is no sooner recognized than already he adds to it the efficacious grace of negativity and summons redemption. All in all, Sartre's atheism is only an attempt at deification without theological grace. He eliminates God only to deify man. But this is not all that new. The only thing original about the venture would be that he attempted a creationism of essences at the human level. But even this is nothing extraordinary after Plotinus, and it is not necessarily atheistic. Will Sartre be left with a simple option which the system itself might or might not justify?[5]

[5] I wonder if the contribution of Sartre's philosophy might not be to induce spiritual personalism to reconsider several of its positions, so as to deepen them. He challenges personalists: (1) to elaborate a theory of creation of the intelligible and of value according to which self-creation becomes something more than a word; (2) perhaps to restore, but with discretion,

Obviously, it is somewhat provocative to say that Sartre's requirements cannot be satisfied at their own level, but can give rise to useful investigations on the part of a theistic personalism. But this is not unheard of. Not long ago, Brunschvicg's philosophy formulated a very similar appeal. Indeed, it seems to us that from Brunschvicg to Sartre or to Polin, the opposition to Christian spiritualism has hardly changed its arguments, except that the creation of values has been accented more clearly by the young masters. Despite appearances and what anyone may say, a parallel between Brunschvicg and Sartre is certainly possible. They hold many positions in common: (1) the method of comprehension and of efficient action; (2) the play between exteriority and interiority, the Brunschvicgian "mixed" becoming the Sartrean ambiguity; (3) the dualism which is unconcerned about the origin of things and attributes to the subject alone the advent of meaning; (4) the search for interiority and authenticity, but in the rejection of divine transcendence and according to an indefinite progress; (5) the primacy of freedom, which Sartre (like Polin) later dramatized by means of Hegelian negativity; (6) the notion of an absolute, adapted to time in order to establish a network of necessary relations, in the very midst

---

the Plotinian and Dionysian tradition of divine ignorance, by excluding every determination in God, which would put transcendence in its proper perspective and purify the last lingering anthropomorphisms; (3) to make it clear that temporalization cannot be reduced to empirical evolution, but proceeds from a movement of intelligible personalization, which freely and without predetermination prescribes its temporal projections. "There is no such thing as an occasion," says Sartre. Contingency, insofar as it is the expression of the existing subject, has no meaning, for it is the nature of the subject to assume responsibility for all its conditions. The subject therefore ought to be conceived as both an act of radical spontaneity and as a system of laws which it posits while positing itself. Literally, it is an *act-law,* beyond every preëstablished norm without, however, running the risk of a capricious or arbitrary discontinuity; (4) to show that the orthodox supernatural, which gives access to the pure liberty of God, is the only possible way of crossing all limits, the redemption of all finitude (on the condition, of course, that we do not confuse divine transcendence and exteriority). Since the supernatural is the obligation of each freedom to go beyond its "nature," and even beyond all nature, it is truly a principle of autonomy, not of alienation.

of the chaos of sensations and over and above the absurdity of facts.

Sartre, however, transforms Brunschvicg's position through the use of the phenomenological method. He replaces construction with a more direct grasp. He pushes psychological analyses into greater detail. He is more insistent about the function of the body and the dialectical relationship between freedom and its situation. He substitutes existential anguish for intellectual serenity. He attributes every possible evil to rationalist idealism, which he considers too proud of its efficient legalism and also too inclined to take an overview. But he fails to recognize the religion of interiority which exists in Brunschvicg. He loses the taste for true recollection. He becomes tetanized in moralism without issue. And this is perhaps the ransom demanded of every deliberately atheistic humanism: the denial of God condemns each of them to a fanatical exertion (we should also remember Camus). Christianity, on the contrary, accomplishes and transcends morality with charity. Only Christian freedom is neither strained nor shriveled. For through grace it shares in *aseity*.

The last word to Sartre, then, should be that morality can be surpassed only if God exists and summons us to share his autonomy. Sartre is right in forbidding freedom to rest on any support beneath itself. This requires a certain stamina, for man has a passion for security. But Christian freedom finds in communion with God the only way to establish itself without pinning itself down. It therefore considers Sartre's moralism rather tedious. And Christian freedom is amused to see it having so much difficulty in reconciling effort with joy.

4. FREEDOM AND RELIGIOUS INTOLERANCE

The idea of tolerance has a bad press among Catholics, since if it was not invented against them, it was at least used against them. The same holds for freedom of conscience. In themselves, these ideas are not polemical, but in fact they are weapons. It is strange, nonetheless, that the praise of interior freedom and exterior tolerance should come from the pen of a free-thinker, and rarely from the lips of a churchman. The free-thinker had to go into hiding to write, while the churchman held the foremost position to speak. Where was courage? Where truth? Where charity? I leave it to historians to fill in the particulars of this unusual case. The fact certainly betrayed the right, since the very nature of the Christian faith is to open spirits to the mysteries of God, not to establish a temporal kingdom. If the unbeliever laid claim to tolerance, his attitude was considered intolerable. And yet if he were sincere in his unbelief, if he remained faithful to his conscience in rejecting the creed, to oblige him to think or to act differently would be tantamount to doing him violence. At the same time, this propagation of the faith by force (which consents to a right established by might) was the destruction of faith, whose very worth is founded on loyalty and freedom. In a word, by silencing the unbeliever, by calling upon him to believe what he did not believe, faith took up arms against itself. By thrusting itself on others, faith repudiated itself.

This contradiction is so glaring that the mind finds it difficult to admit it. We begin to think that the theologians of the past were either very naïve or very sadistic. To suspect them of wanting to create faith through slavery is to accuse them of more than a lack of awareness. Was it not as elementary for them as for today's theologians to know that a religious act obtained by ruse or by violence is defective? It is hard to believe them cynical enough to contradict one of the best established points of their own doctrine. To tell the truth, there is another more plausible hypothesis that does not paint them so black or so thoughtless. There was a time, it seems, when all Christianity *simply could not understand* how any person could oppose the faith for any reason other than a derangement of mind and a disorderly life. If he refused to ratify the articles of the creed, if

29

he rejected the teachings of Scripture and the councils, if he broke away from the discipline of the Church, it could be attributed neither to scruples of conscience, nor to intellectual integrity. It could be due only to the development of individualism, to pride, to a culpable preference for personal opinions over the common truth. He was therefore no simple skeptic but a renegade; not an independent thinker but a revolutionary. He was holding back the collective thought; he was shaking the foundations of the social order; he was threatening the very basis of civilization. The concept of heretic took on more and more this negative, antagonistic, and criminal aspect. The fomenter of heresy no longer appeared merely as one who was isolated, but as a rebel. His revolt was worse than that of the schismatic, for the latter did not deny any point of dogma, he denied a point of discipline. The schismatic kept apart, but he continued to believe the truth. However, we can imagine that his independence cost him dearly. Schisms were successful only within the shelter of well-protected frontiers. The isolated heretic, whose only refuge was his own conscience amid a uniformly hostile group, carried his defiance to its highest pitch. He directly braved the powers while continuing to keep in touch with the community that received from these powers its charter, its instruments of thought and action. He withdrew (or was cut off) from the communion of the faithful, but he continued to relate himself to it by his very disagreement. He was dangerous because he was subversive. His error stood as an act of defiance towards everything that constituted the justification of a type of society in which the political and economic structures were accepted as the only possible projection of the Christian faith. It was necessary, therefore, to sacrifice him for the common good and even for his own good, for his refusal was merely a blind rejection of universal values which can be denied in words but not in substance. Basically, the heretic clings despite himself to what he rejects, and this indestructible belief can judge, condemn, and execute him. At any rate, he has no reason to expect anything but the retribution of a justice contained within the order he has violated.

Today this attitude of mind would be classified as totalitarian. But to appreciate it and even to grasp it as it appeared to itself, we are badly situated. The conditions of existence have greatly changed. The heretic, as we have said, is one who disputes this or that dogma. In modern times, however, unbelief has become so radical that it opposes the very idea of dogma. The Middle Ages never experienced such temerity, and would have accused it of extravagance. According to the medieval, the pagan had his belief, the heathen (Moslem) his also. Not to have any would have been tantamount to being without reason: *dixit insipiens in corde suo, non est Deus.* In our day, the commentary on this versicle would be done under a different light. We would wish at least to investigate the motives of the fool, to find out the reasons for irrationality. In times past, on the other hand, one was not supposed to look for reasons where there were none. Thus we can describe the old mentality as a condemnation *en bloc* of things which today we would not condemn until we had examined them in detail. But we must not interpret this as the tyranny of the arbitrary; it did not sacrifice recalcitrants to the whim of the prince. Despite its monolithic appearance, it was more circumspect and more expert. Paradoxical as this may seem, it relied entirely on its need to be consistent with itself. The heretic was the one who did not understand himself, whose affirmations fell short of or went beyond his own deep sincerity. No one suspected that, if he could once be brought face to face with himself, he would testify to anything other than what authority taught. If he once understood the latter's demands clearly, its teachings, its precepts, he would necessarily agree. His denials could only be so many refusals to see, a perverse determination to block the light. His stubbornness derived from a subjective illusion, a lack of logic, or moral weakness. Objectively, if he did not wish to be thwarted in his aspirations and desires, he was obliged to recognize what the others professed. In fine, he

31

continued to give evidence against himself in his very denials. He was divided within himself, he condemned himself by the contradiction of his life. He could not be in good faith because he rejected the indubitable, and because his conduct denied what he continued to need in the very depth of his own being.

Indeed, to this day we defend the proposition that it is impossible to lose the faith without some prior moral lapse. Giving up the faith always involves being in bad faith previously. However, the meaning and import of these affirmations must be clearly understood. On the one hand, it is natural to think that the person who cuts himself off from God has only himself to blame; grace is never wanting. On the other hand, it is hard to say with certainty at any one point that a conscience is insincere to the point of despising its relationship to God. Though we maintain that the loss of faith arises from a culpable refusal of grace, no one can say whether this refusal exists in any particular case—whether an implicit faith does not remain untouched.

But these distinctions remain too fine for some people. They can be grasped only after long experience, which begins with less subtle reasoning. It is much easier to connect all loss of faith directly with a mind fascinated by error, with a will overpowered by passions. The heretic thus becomes a man who misunderstands himself and cuts himself off, a man who affirms his position and recants at the same time. He continues to want what he rejects, to seek what he has repelled.

Consequently, when we undertake to check him, we try not to destroy his sincerity but to give it back to him. We try not to violate his conscience but to safeguard it. We have no intention of distorting his judgment, we aim to remedy it and set it right. Neither do we have the impression of dictating a choice that will repress his freedom. We offer him a faith which he needs and which he invokes in secret, although it embarrasses him to do so. Thus we offer him the means of recovering his moral integrity, of reëstablishing the most correct relationship

32

with himself, with society, and with God. Far from becoming a slave, he becomes a friend again, if not happy at least capable of becoming so—a peaceful and pacified man. If, out of obstinacy born of blindness, he should offer resistance, one recourse remains: when the occasion presents itself to open the way for him to abandon a life in which he has not succeeded in knowing his own will. We kill him literally in order to teach him how to live; not by wreaking mean vengeance on him, but simply by showing him that he who continues incapable of understanding the meaning of life has forfeited the right to benefit by it. He takes his own life the moment he lets go of the conducting wire of life in common.

This description perhaps seems exaggerated, unlikely from beginning to end. In fact, it follows a classical pattern. This pattern is invariably reproduced whenever a kindred mind engenders similar deeds. There is nothing more revealing in this respect than the procedures of some civil laws. When an individual has deviated from a prescribed line of conduct, he is considered unworthy to survive. He has become as alien to himself as to the community from which he received life and the reasons for living. If he renounces these reasons, he no longer has any right to life. By separating himself from the community, he condemns himself to death. What is more, the logic of Christianity did not go beyond execution for an unrepented crime. It tried to convince the heretic of his error, but if this failed, it handed the case over to the invisible Judge. Nowadays, the logic of the integrated collective prescribes repentance as almost obligatory so that the execution may be justified. In this case, the result is twofold: on one side, the regret for the condemned's lack of consistency is assuaged when he publicly admits his errors, thereby safeguarding the meaning of his own expiation; on the other hand, by recording its verdict the community is reassured of its guiding principles. It is not good for the community that one single conscience, even that of a renegade, go to the tomb with the conviction that it blocked the general system. That is why the love of the common good is so partial to conversions *in extremis*. It remains unforgiving but not unkind. It wishes to put to death only those who ratify the acts of the government. The present political situation has given us several examples of this: they were edifying, logical, and relentlessly expiatory. The new Inquisition is every bit as much in earnest as the old one— and it does not offer heaven as a reward.

However, let us forget these comparisons with current events. It is not that they are not useful but, were we to pursue them, they would lead us too far afield. We keep only the impression that establishments are unbeatable in point of applied logic. From variable premises, they always succeed in drawing those simple, smooth, and pressing conclusions which are "for reasons of state." It is obviously to be regretted that a society inspired by transcendent principles should at times have attempted to govern the interior life with the same kind of severity. This was the result of a confusion between the spiritual and the temporal, the private and the social, the personal and the communal. Only those things could be allowed to each which were conducive to the prosperity of all. All the rest was subjective illusion and objective treason. The least difference of opinion tore the social contract to shreds. Each disagreement had to be cemented over under pain of bringing about the collapse of the entire social order. When one is responsible for a universe, how admit its weakness? This would be to destroy with one blow both the ideal of the group and the values by which live each of its members. It would mean tearing the members from the very purpose of their existence and, with a word, abandoning them to the absurd—a piece of folly equivalent to a death sentence. The first duty of life in common is health; its first standard, order.

If our analysis is correct, we can see why the notion of tolerance could not enter the heads of believers in certain periods of history. To tolerate error would have been to tolerate at once social disorder and individual dishonesty. Their extreme severity was not caused by a lack of liberality, *it was a lack of imagi-*

nation. It was impossible for them to imagine an unbeliever at peace with himself. Hence their effort to suppress in the unbeliever his distressing dream of attaining his own personal internal consistency. Indeed, once one is persuaded that truth is a thing and that this thing belongs to a privileged group, and that no one is ever justified in destroying such a sacred possession, one is naturally led to think that any fault against this possession is a crime against the social being and the private being. This conviction then degenerates into imperialism, not in the name of a will for power that admits of no contradiction, but rather in the name of an inability to understand that the Absolute of faith does not impose itself automatically on all consciences. It is simply not seen that there are some among them who, because of their complicated situations, can work out their salvation in the most unexpected ways. An individual of this sort may reject God, not through ill will, but simply because the representations he has been given of God seem to him to be insufficient or distorting. Another individual may reject God because he has deified his own powers and passions, but no observer can be judge of this. God alone sounds the reins and the hearts. It would be regrettable in either case to pre-judge the position of the other and to condemn him without appeal. That, however, is what the impulsive censor does. He acts on the *a priori* assumption that the rebel is wrong—a disconcerting oversimplification that is tantamount to thinking that a moral and religious choice is a uniform and instantaneous gesture. What leads to this hasty judgment is not so much the desire to rule (this is only a result), as an inflexibility of mind, a total lack of pliancy and of irony, an ingrained inability to imagine the life of the spirit as anything but an elementary mechanism. Dealing with a world that they believed immutable, with an order of things that they considered definitive, with ways of living, feeling, and evaluating that seemed to them founded on nature itself, the direct objectification of an essential order immanent to the creative thought, the theologians could react only as they did: unbelief is unthinkable,

35

and those who profess it are fallacious reasoners, warped and corrupted spirits. Such men disregard an order that is objectively indubitable. They disobey a law of nature that is imposed on them in spite of themselves since it is imposed on everyone. Thus, unbelief could not even receive a coherent structure on the level of thought. Much less could there be any question of securing it a legal status in society. It was stigmatized and it was banished because, in the full sense of the word, it was inconceivable.

In the last analysis, the history of the Inquisition is explained less by the harshness of its procedures than by the narrowness of its judgment, by the hasty consecration of certain categories of thought which a more mature reflection would have discredited. Or rather, once certain rigid principles had been decided upon, their application could only reinforce them, so that practice and theory ended by justifying each other by turns. Nevertheless, logical priority belongs to the idea and not to the fact. Formulations appear later than patterns of conduct, but these patterns express the state of mind. Because the mind remained a prisoner of partial representations, customs remained sectarian. Intolerance in thought led to intolerance in life. To check it demanded not first and foremost the reorganization of social systems, but the reform of the intellect. The objectivism of religious consciousness had to give way under the blows of a philosophy of initiative and personal responsibility. This eventually came to pass, by which we are reminded that the first task in such matters is on the intellectual level. With the liberation of the *Cogito,* we discover, a new world comes into being.

Is this universe of freedom less favorable to faith? It seemed so in the early days. Overlong guardianships never teach the use of independence, and thus the man who has been freed has a tendency to misuse freedom when it has finally been won. Moreover, no authority willingly agrees to give up old privileges. Last but not least, the renovation of mental structures is never accomplished in a day. The old ideas linger, become encrusted, seek to delay progress. All this explains how religious tolerance could have been little tolerated by the Church and overextolled by its champions. It took centuries to regain a new balance: time for the Church to make liberalism less aggressive; time for unbelievers to make their opposition more liberal. This is a two-fold coming to awareness which in the end ought simultaneously to liberate faith and reason. But society perhaps has not yet reached that point.

The term "tolerance" and the expression "freedom of conscience" belong in fact to a vocabulary of transition. They indicate that the evolution of attitudes is far from being accomplished. To tolerate has a negative ring. It means to endure rather than to permit, to put up with reluctantly, to deplore what one must accept but cannot justify. Tolerance is a makeshift, even an inconsistency. We close our eyes to what we disapprove. Thus, we "tolerate" the separation of Church and State, the secular school, the practice of other religions, the activities of the free-thinker. But in our heart of hearts, we continue to think that an established Church would be a good thing, that secular education is suspect, that religious differences should return underground, that the works of those who teach error should either go unpublished or be thrown into the fire. Thus we "tolerate" because we cannot do otherwise. If we could, we should no longer be tolerant. The odd thing is that independent minds have begun by demanding tolerance in place of intransigence, instead of freedom pure and simple. It is true that it is better tactics to destroy the vice gradually rather than to attack it head on. But to seek to be tolerated or to tolerate is always a negative attack, merely a chipping away of authority. It stops short of rethinking the function of authority, of defining the limits of its exercise, of determining the legitimate areas of its application. We stop short at something negative which, in practice, places everyone in a false position: the emancipated mind, the dubious and questioning individual whom we grudgingly leave alone, as well as the authorities, who maintain the "thesis" while at the same time adjusting themselves to the "hypothesis." In short, the one who is tolerated does not have enough elbow room, while the tolerant authority has a bad conscience about its lenient policies, having compromised its doctrine. For both, the ideal of tolerance can serve only as a temporary expedient, half a loaf.

The theory of freedom of conscience is no less precarious. Elaborated by those who do not share the faith of others or who profess no faith, this doctrine is more concerned with defending a subjectivism of opinion than with preserving the bases of personal convictions. In fact, it was a political weapon, destined to make the Church yield its control over public institutions. But its efforts to provide itself with any intellectual justification were only half-hearted. Or rather, when it did do so, it took on a rationalist laicism which suppressed everything supernatural. Thus it opposed rank prejudice with rank prejudice. It was unwilling to work out for itself the problem of relating spiritual authority to individual freedom. On their side, Catholics were more inclined to condemn this agnosticism or atheism-in-disguise than to examine it for its good points. Nevertheless, they were not loath to claim for themselves this very same freedom of conscience whenever their situation required it. Thus freedom of conscience had a double meaning, which each side made use of in turn once it was attacked. But the notion remained shallow and ambiguous, generating more heat than light.

In fact, a freedom of conscience which simply excuses us from having any convictions at all is not justifiable. Rather, we must defend a freedom of *the* conscience, which makes conscience duty-bound to discover and to verify the convictions of which it is capable. Without any doubt, if anything can be found in favor of a cordial understanding between believers and unbelievers, it is on this side we must look. But mutual tolerance is still not charity; freedom of conscience is still not the search for truth. A theory of the freedom of *the* conscience, on the other hand, could satisfy both parties, inasmuch as conscience cannot escape its responsibilities nor refuse to make a choice.

At the present time, it seems that many unbelievers are ready to acknowledge that freedom of religious choice should not consist in struggling against the faith in a somewhat roundabout way. Respectful of the convictions of others, they know that theirs also should be subjected to careful criticism, if they are not to remain simple prejudices. Atheism that does not call itself into question, agnosticism that doubts everything without doubting itself, and especially anti-clericalism that does not recognize its own emotionalism—these are as inconsistent as sheeplike faith, lazy metaphysics, and euphoric and sanctimonious clericalism. The duty to question, to debate calmly and clearly, and to criticize constructively imposes itself on every man once he has reached a certain degree of culture. Believers and unbelievers meet again on an equal basis, faced with the same demand. Whether they will or not, they can never become fixed in their position, but must continually be strengthening them or doing them over. Many believers put security above initiative, and unbelievers have a great time laughing at these risk-all-on-the-Absolute who act only under instructions and subscribe to heavenly assurances. But there are also unbelievers whose courage is based on the current list of best-sellers. These are the virtuous thinkers of vicious thoughts. They shatter moral restraint, they lead school boys astray, they declare war against all established order. But look at them, these breakers of the tables of the law, these masters of irony who mix philosophical jargon with street-corner slang. They take a position only for their public, they assume an air of importance, they pontificate. The day we realize that a rebel can be taken in by his negation every bit as much as a dogmatist by his affirmation, we will come to understand that the way one denies or affirms is more important than the results of his efforts. We need neither skeptics who have too high an opinion of themselves, nor reactionaries who torture themselves. On the contrary, we need—and as soon as possible—unbelievers who do not believe in themselves, and believers who are ready to take real risks. The nineteenth century wanted to achieve a victory for the critical spirit over the dismal immobility of ecclesiastical sciences. It was partly successful, since ecclesiastical sciences themselves began to thaw out. But that is not enough. The task remains of redoing its own achievements —which were canonized too soon—by beginning with systems of pure reason, and with systems which enlarge reason. The unbeliever is no more free because he does not believe. The believer is no more creative because he believes. Neither the one nor the other can remain free or become creative unless he can draw from his consciousness the wherewithal to guard his sincerity and revive his courage.

Unfortunately, the mere suggestion of giving the unbeliever his chance (by accepting him in good will) will be considered unseemly by some believers, which proves that absolutism is not entirely uprooted. The honor of the Catholic Church is to teach that Christ, by his voluntary oblation, has reconciled all mankind with itself; that Redemption is universal, and that it offers a means of salvation to all creatures. Even those who do not call on the name of Christ, even those who fight him, if they are generous, simple, and upright, will be saved in virtue of what they do not know or do not recognize. This thesis, which is a dogma, is the most glorious promise made to the real faith which may hide behind an apparent lack of faith. The Church does not demand that every man acknowledge his Lord by his lips. It requires that every man, explicitly if he can, implicitly if he can do no more, hold to the presence of God in the world and in the spirit. The Church sets more value on the explicit, for the means of salvation established by Jesus give a firmer structure to the religious experience. But the implicit suffices, if it is the only thing possible. It is this implicit faith that eventually expresses itself in the form of non-Christian religions, of non-Catholic denominations, or even in the pseudo-religions of sci-

40

ence, art, philosophy, politics, or philanthropy. As we can see, the limits are as wide as the varieties of human situations. And only the absolute of union with God in devotion and uprightness confirms from within the multiplicity of commitments and codes of behavior.

All theologians must support this essential position. Why is it, then, that good will remains in the realm of theory? Why is it that even today we hesitate in practice? No doubt because the dogma of universality has not always been blessed with the theory of religious knowledge to which it has a right. School psychology has to distinguish between knowing the Absolute and knowing a sensible object. Textbook metaphysics has had some difficulty in perceiving the shade of difference between demonstrating according to a formal dialectic and discerning according to sense of values. Professional apologetics have only half understood the issue at stake in the distinction between basing faith on objective evidence and having it spring up from a meeting between the soul and the God of Jesus. Generally speaking, too many specialists in the sacred sciences have overestimated their personal interpretations, their set of problems, their methods of approach. Consequently, some theologians believe as firmly in their philosophy as they do in the faith and defend it just as violently. The two things, however, do not belong to the same order. And as far as I am concerned, I cannot conceive of a philosophy that is not continually engaged in a perpetual research, reform, and reorganization of its categories and methods. By absolutizing modes of thought which are entirely human, we spare ourselves the trouble of criticizing them. But at the same time, we run the risk of basing faith on a system of fragile representations. In the long run, we do more harm than good. By linking religious knowledge to an objectivism that does not distinguish between spiritual activity and the workings of nature, the false philosophy that was taught in the seminaries of the nineteenth century (and which distorted the tradition that it claimed to reflect) could not help but destroy the sense of the

41

faith. It created a kind of religious rationalism, the worst rationalism of all until, as a reaction, it gave rise to an equally unreasonable irrationalism. This was the modernism of which Blondel remarked that it rested on the same presumption of a limited intelligibility. We have criticized Marxism for basing itself on a materialistic psychology, inspired by phrenological ideas more than a century out of date. It is equally undesirable that a certain Catholic mentality should remain on the philosophical level of a 150-year-old empiricism, a level more faithful to Thomas Reid than to Thomas Aquinas. We must have the courage to insist that faith requires a maximum intellectual effort, and will not allow itself simply to be grafted on to an effete system, as for so long we tied liturgy to a dead language. The prudence necessary in teaching young students is one thing; the obligation of critical reflection in free research is quite another. In the thirteenth century, theologians *made* the science of their times. In our day, science will turn against them, if they themselves do not turn to it. We will agree that this would not mean progress for the Church.

The attempt at renewal is particularly urgent for the problems which preoccupy us today. A Christian philosophy centered on freedom of *the* conscience is still to be established. Until now it has been hampered in too many minds by a philosophy of truth as a thing. We imagine that ideas and values are pre-existent in God and that it is a matter of man's ratifying them. Sertillanges has clearly shown that this was not St. Thomas's position. We do him wrong by placing this notion under his patronage. We conceive of God as a supreme Object, the resting place of ideas and norms. Thus we maintain that intelligences and freedoms need only conform to the immutable essences. If they consent, they automatically establish themselves in the good and the true. If they refuse, they can only err and be lost. It is simple, neat, and unanswerable. As a matter of fact, it is too simple, too neat to be rigorous. For neither God nor spirit are ideas to be reconciled in the abstract like complementary qualities. A system like this deeply offends the divine transcendence and the dignity of the spirit. But it is a convenient way to appropriate truth or value for one's own benefit. Once faith becomes the gateway to a possession of ready-made divine ideas, we who possess God's revelation are able to persuade ourselves that we have the unexpected good fortune of being able to think what God thinks, and soon of governing all things according to his designs. But I would maintain that this self-sufficiency, this usurpation of God's point of view is nothing but the apotheosis of anthropomorphism. It is not faith and it is not religion. It is the confusion of the experience of the sacred with a simple philosophical theory which reifies ideas in order to subdue consciences and to restrain free acts. This is realism for the sake of security, which offers the creature a road map, and blocks his way with guard-rails. It is also a realism of authority and constraint, designed to transform the representatives of the Absolute into unyielding bureaucrats from a divine planning committee. Certainly, spiritual authority is infallible in matters of ethics and religion (which involves a host of values, even many which are non-sacral). This infallibility means that the Christian norm cannot lose its effectiveness for salvation. Presuming that it is authentic, such a norm is infallible in the full sense of the word, since religious truth remains homogeneous with itself. But this does not mean that the Church is more than the depositary of an incorruptible good, with the help of the Holy Spirit, which merits for it righteousness, dynamism, and fruitfulness in the order of salvation. We can draw no proof from this that would justify the opinion of those who believe in a revelation established outside those who have done the revealing in history, or who think that the Christian religion espouses a ready-made pattern instead of proceeding from the initiative of the people of God, of Jesus and his witnesses. These are two ways of picturing to one's self the world, man, and his destiny. We cannot place them on the same level nor endow them with equal value. For the first is fraught with ambiguities, is open to many abuses,

43

and could bring about the most unfortunate results. It sanctions in advance the alienation of the sacred, and does this for reasons which are hardly admissible. It is not surprising that minds molded by a system of representations such as this should one day become oppressive. When one has God's plan in his pocket and the right of command over his brothers, he will hesitate no further to bend them to his will for the love of truth. He will render his brothers the invaluable service of forcing them to get into line with God, thus solving all their problems in a single stroke. Thus society comes under control and the world enjoys a foretaste of heavenly peace. This is a consoling picture, whose features I am emphasizing for the reader's edification, but which is only a caricature. Every fanatic for order dreams of it when seeking power and, once established, puts it into practice. Thus does the innocent theory of ideas projected into the Absolute become a pretext for tyranny.

Nevertheless, many believers continue to fear that if they let this dream go, everything will go. That is because they are confused on several points. They hold, and rightly so, that the mind should attach itself to the Absolute. But they think that this means that the human subject must attach itself to the objects contained in the divine essence. Here is the trap. The imagination will be less prone to error on this problem if we recall that an essence is a *meaning*, a *norm*, not a thing nor an object in itself. Besides, if God is pure simplicity, he cannot be a constellation of ideas and values. In fact, there are objects only for a subject, and finite objects only for a finite subject. In other words, to one who admits an infinite, transcendent Absolute, it is not logical that God be the subject of determinations or essences. That is why we attribute these, not to God, but to the created mind. Yet the mind is hardly cut off from God, since it needs him in order to exist. We can sum up this thesis in one formula: God creates the mind, which creates ideas and values. There is no break between the Absolute and the conscience. But this does not mean that the good and the true are pre-posited in God (which after all makes no sense); they are created, posited, and invented by man in his relationship to God. Thus relativism is exorcized, while freedom, because it is creative, becomes active and productive—a twofold conclusion that ought to please the believer.

Actually, there is no reason here to fear any danger of anarchy. The human subject is fundamentally free, but he is also responsible. He creates his own values, but they are sound only if they help him to create himself in keeping with an ambition that will not stop at anything determined. He therefore does not create indiscriminately in any way whatever or for any purpose whatever. He remains the product as well as the agent of his own creations. The more he becomes master of his own activities, the more his responsibility increases. It is not the absence of rules and of guideposts that protects freedom, it is self-control. In order to stop being a Torquemada, it is not necessary to become a Caligula. Neither the one nor the other represents the meaning of freedom. Caprice and tyranny are the same thing. Freedom must be simultaneously *creation* and *law,* or it will cease to be freedom. Lagneau clearly understood this fact. Sartre and Polin recognized it themselves when they assigned to freedom the duty of loyalty to self. Merleau-Ponty also accepts this fact when he condemns man to *meaning* and to *freedom,* that is, to choice and to coherence. Husserl's philosophy admits various interpretations, but I think his original contribution would be this: The supreme intentionality is free and creative, but the essences it posits are objective, universal, and necessary. The self-rule of freedom is thus achieved through obligatory mediations: there is no longer either subjectivism or pure situation morality (without the permanent imperative of equating self to self). Husserl was right in thinking that, in the noetic order, freedom creates the necessary, not the contingent nor the fortuitous. In one stroke this insight destroys the ethics of passivity as well as the ethics of impulsiveness. This explains why we do not hesitate to conceive of a human creativity. This thesis cannot be the privilege of the atheist. The theist can make it his own, and with better reason.

The practical attitude that follows from all this will be very different from that of spiritual imperialism. To become a Christian means to choose to go to God by the ways of Christ and the Church. This is a meritorious choice because it is complex and not mechanical, costly and not easy. Have the apologists with their compelling proofs considered this? To elicit an act of faith means to take a triple initiative: (1) to recognize that man is linked to the Absolute and that this bond can be expressed in history. (2) To agree that those who have best uncovered this relationship with the Absolute are the founders of Christianity, Jesus and his witnesses. (3) To believe that, thanks to their witness, every man is capable of binding himself to God correctly within the modalities of the new cult, that is, to conclude that a personal religious experience cannot receive a more coherent structure than that of the Church.

If we examine these three closely related initiatives, we find that they require a free and intelligent reading of texts, events, facts, and teachings. They do not, however, imply any direct intuition of God (faith is not the beatific vision), nor any deduction based on formal evidence. Much less do they demand an arbitrary decision to believe anything whatever because it is necessary to believe something. Furthermore, these initiatives do not involve a simple comprehension of the articles of faith, for the purpose of the rigor of the formal enunciation of these articles is to direct the view, not to stop it. Rather, they testify to a global attitude of mind which aims at an aggregate of specific values (religious values, the sacred, the supernatural) through a series of representations that serve as a ladder, not as the goal itself. Faith unites with God and not with dogmas. Dogmas are only the intellectual mediation of an act of communion, which operates in secret between human freedom and the freedom of God (grace). We become believers on the day we adapt a norm to our experience, a witness to our discovery of values, a doctrine to our practice. We do not become believers by assimilating a theory, or by reciting a history, or by perfecting a syllogism. Without a personal, actual, free, and reflective discovery of a world of spiritual values which it is possible to attain through a definite intentionality, we can have a learned pseudo-faith, a conformist pseudo-faith, but not the living faith which touches God in person, in the human obscurity of his representations and his signs. This is the true price of faith. It means that there is no faith without an active searching, a definite commitment, a freedom tendered and constantly ready for action. It does not recopy a formulary, nor subscribe to it with its eyes closed. It opens itself to a presence; it welcomes a new life, joined to a new sense of existence and history. If this is not a value judgment, and at the same time a reconquest of self and all else, it will be difficult to know at what other moments a man could prove his freedom and his discernment. On the contrary, it is possible that religious conversion, when it is accomplished with lucidity and fervor, is the model of every genuine spiritual act.

But if it is correct to say that faith involves so much the vital forces of the mind, we must realize that it can neither become the object of propaganda, nor a matter of inheritance, nor a question of propriety. Faith does not appear on command nor by imitation and, despite appearances, will not persist through habit. More importantly, it will become fully explicit only among those who can and will effect the union between Christian teaching and the experience of the divine. Only those who have seen the connection to be attempted, the meaning and values to be regained, and who lack the courage to do so, can be guilty. But all the others—all those who do not grasp this meaning nor sense these values—are obliged to pursue their salvation through equivalents or at least through substitutes. It is up to these others to discover other paths, to create other meanings and other values, to tie together their thought and their life in integrity and endeavor. It is useless to want to

47

arouse them, despite themselves, to meanings and experiences which, in their eyes, remain enigmas. They are not justified in denying them on the pretext that they cannot themselves verify them—the blind have no right to deny color nor the unlettered the fine arts. But neither can they be forced to accept that which means nothing to them. They are masters of their intellect and will, responsible architects of their destiny. It is up to them to create themselves differently. To admit this is neither to discredit revelation nor to abandon each one to his whim. Whatever the individual situation may be, the demands of light and of generosity remain equally stringent. But we must understand that only those things are true or good which can be assumed by personal reflection and freedom. The true and the good do not preëxist to the acts of clarity and sincerity; they are established in them. They are absolute, not because they are inflexible objects, but because they are signposts towards the unique Absolute. We can therefore imagine an unbeliever arriving at truth and goodness by the most varied paths, provided that, despoiled of all selfishness and all pride, he directs himself towards the infinite. There is no question here of any laxity, of any demagoguery condoning the misguided. God remains the necessary goal of human aspirations. But to advance towards him, each must find the route he can, in keeping with his light and his ardor.

We are obviously far removed from objective codes, social restraints, trials for heresy and irreligion. But we are no doubt nearer a disinterested, loving, and prayerful faith. Once such a faith takes shape, it bears witness to itself and offers to serve as a sign for all those who are capable of understanding its message. Thus there is no question of suppressing its radiance, its contagion. Exhortation, instruction, and dialogue remain legitimate; they are normal means of communication between freedom and freedom. But to importune, to harass, and to compel are indiscreet and inadequate—inadequate precisely because they are indiscreet. They encroach on the judgment of another; they paralyze his reflection, they mistrust his generosity. Still worse, they put up a screen between grace and conscience, and run the risk of overwhelming the latter and obstructing the former. The temptation to do good—this is not merely an unusual and striking slogan without significance. It means self-exaltation, self-enhancement, self-aggrandizement. We are called not to do good, but to serve the good without publicizing it, and to help others to do it, not by dictating the recipe, but by showing why and how we do it ourselves. To win over by example is worth more than any conscription. It is more meritorious and in the long run more effective. But to achieve such disinterestedness, we must first change our attitude, change our theory of religious knowledge. The objectivism of the idea leads sooner or later to a fanaticism for order and to repression. Only the conviction that freedom of conscience is inalienable leads to true faith, with the attendant paradox of sincere unbelief, of the apparent incredulity which is faith in non-faith. Without this good will in principle and in act which admits that the City of God recruits from the Church of the baptized and also from the Church of the threshold, near or far, the universal of charity will be nothing but a false advertisement. If it is to become a reality, the boundaries of the temple must include the whole spiritual universe, from which no one is excluded unless he chooses to remain outside. Each must ask himself whether he is inside these boundaries or outside. But no one can use his assurance of being within as a basis for insisting that others are without. The surprise will be that some charter members will not find themselves there, while some strangers will find themselves very much at home. The converts are not always the people we think they are. All this should be a precious warning to us, a counsel to a modesty which is preferable to the boasting of the pure and the untroubled. May the self-satisfied neither reign, nor triumph. The last word is not to those who talk of truth and goodness, but to those who do it.

No doubt, our discussion to this point has been enough to

suggest that there can be faith in incredulity, uprightness and even piety in atheism. Yet the atheist must not be content with denying merely for the sake of denying. One sometimes meets iconoclasts who are fairly naïve. They go to infinite trouble to exclude certain representations of God on the ground that they are not God. They overlook the fact that God is precisely over and beyond these representations, and that they need not reject him to reach beyond the symbols. An atheist who never places his critique at the lofty height of the Absolute but remains always on the level of his conceptual expressions or his imaginative projections, is less godless than an iconoclast of false absolutes. Furthermore, it is necessary to pause over these terms. Atheist or theist, the terms are always understood in relation to certain coordinates: One is always the theologian of some positivist farther to the left, and the atheist of some dogmatist farther to the right.

Up to this time, we have not been concentrating on the situation of the atheist himself. We have been considering the attitudes and states of mind of many believers, in an effort to show why some among them succumb so quickly to the pleasure of hurling anathemas. We have even suggested how the mentality of contemporary Christianity might be ventilated. This is a matter of particular interest to the laity. Yet freedom of mind is everyman's concern, and to defend it on one score is to safeguard it on all others, so the unbelieving reader will perhaps agree that our discussion also concerns him. At any rate, we will do our utmost to steer clear of all sectarianism and to define, in the interests of everyone, where conviction stops and fanaticism begins.

The difficulty which most vitally concerns us is precisely this: Can a believer, a Christian and a Catholic, assent to a system and judge it at the same time? Is he not a prisoner of the rule of faith and of the discipline of the Church? To put the matter in a general way, is the believer not bound to an irrevocable dogma which no longer allows him a radical reconsideration of his position, which necessarily denies him complete freedom of thought and of action? At most he can elaborate on the fine points of official doctrine, or quibble about secondary issues. But, as Alain has said, the believer can indulge in these mental gymnastics only on the condition that they ultimately accord with common belief. In short, daring as he may appear and free as his movements may be within certain limits, the believer cannot finally commit himself on his own conviction. Always he must return at last to the conclusions of a collective thought, the thought of his group and his leaders. He seems to preserve himself at a certain distance from his own most serious affirmations, ever ready in advance to submit himself to the decisions of a higher authority. In a word, he is dependent, obedient, and loyal. He follows a party line. He does not plough his own furrow day by day, taking his own risks and facing his own dangers.

This objection has, no doubt, lost its force after our remarks concerning the initiative which the act of faith supposes from beginning to end. Neither the existence of God (even if we admit that a rigorous proof is possible), nor the religious experience of Christ and the Church, nor the decision to make the Christian norm one's own—none of these can be imposed or prescribed in any way other than as an appeal to the initiative of judgment. The reason for this is, as we have already said, that none of these truths becomes a compelling evidence until conscience has grasped its meaning and its value. Now conscience grasps neither the one nor the other simply from hearing a doctrinal statement. A special attention is required, one which fortifies simple formal understanding by an understanding in depth, which grasps what can be had, over and above the material signification of the words, of religious values and of their specific content. And no man comes to this type of understanding without placing himself in a highly complex intellectual and moral frame of mind. The act of faith does not consist merely in accepting the exact terms of the articles of faith.

Rather, it consists in using doctrinal statements so as to seek through them an order of reality that compares with no other, the domain of the sacred. So long as an individual is not prepared interiorly to perceive the original and irreducible quality of this new world, he will only remain blind and deaf in the face of the clearest accounts of it. Sacred history, the fact of the Church, works of apologetics—all remain closed to him so long as he remains ignorant of what it is he should be looking for in them and through them. If his mind is to open to the faith, his conscience must awaken to the mystery of a presence in which his freedom discerns a still higher freedom. In a word, if he is to understand the supernatural, he must accept it and recognize it as such. Otherwise, he will remain incapable of evaluating history as sacred, Jesus as God-among-us, Scripture and the Church as sources of revelation. All the trouble one may take to show that faith is born of sound reasoning is time wasted, for God and human freedom are not abstractions to be added together as if they were homogeneous quantities. In reality, a professed faith should spring from a living faith, and this begins the moment the conscience recognizes both that it needs to experience the sacred and that the Christian message is the adequate means of living and formulating this experience. This recognition is ordinarily effected through a witness which gives an account of these same values. But this witness would remain a dead letter if the subject himself were not capable of grasping its intent, of adopting it and of veryifying it. In any case, one must turn oneself towards the divine if one wishes to reach it by means of the signs which are given of it. Otherwise, he hears the words and observes the facts but draws from them no lesson. The mind remains closed because freedom itself has not broadened its sphere of values to the point of integrating the experience of the sacred. Many people are interested in Christianity but see in it only a curiosity. To see therein the presence of God in our history, one must first of all agree that man is linked to the Absolute and that he can discover this bond by beginning with his own situation. This requires that the soul does not enjoy the exclusive possession of its own values. Without making an effort to break out of its egocentrism or narcissism, the soul will never succeed in transcending itself.

Despite these observations, we have scarcely made clear the implications of a freedom sustained within a continued adherence to an Absolute. It is undeniable that the adoption of a rule of faith binds the believer, even though he remains the author of a free commitment, to unite his own autonomy to the regulation of the community at the institutional and social level. Now everyone knows that institutions have two faces: on the one hand they protect individual freedoms by bringing them into concert, and on the other they limit one man's freedom by another's. Besides, for their own organization and development, institutions spontaneously create the machinery of management and control, which become increasingly complex and burdensome. Whereas at the outset they appear to be the projection, on a social level, of a reciprocity of concurrent wills eager for mutual support and expansion, they soon make their members feel the weight of projects already begun and of regulations previously established. In the end, the role of established ways of doing things becomes so important that the individual member is lost sight of. The duty to preserve prevails, or risks prevailing, over the obligation to continue to create. The institution, established for and by the spirit, threatens to turn against it. It is understandable that the faithful of a Church should be even more concerned about the possibility of such a development than a member of a civil society or a private association. For if the Church were to become an archeological museum, it would no longer be a contemporary witness of a contemporary salvation. Historian and guardian of the past, it would be yesterday's magnificence in today's mediocrity, but it would not be the remedy of today and of tomorrow for the uneasiness of the men of today.

53

In fact, if an impartial observer of Christian history is struck by the permanence and the stability of one same perspective of the faith, he is even more impressed by the changing cultures and means of expression of this faith. The Church has passed through many successive modes of thought; it has not become definitely fixed in and fastened to any. Born of Jewish messianism, established by Jesus and realized in him, it began in less than a hundred years to speak the language of the theology of the Logos. Later it fit itself into the categories of Platonism, then into those of Aristotelianism. During its course of development it has renounced neither biblical categories, nor patristic structures, nor medieval concepts. Its dogma bears the mark of different eras; its definitions have a date and place of origin. The faith thus appears as an original intention which perpetuates itself through constantly changing cultural forms. Fixed in its orientation, it imprints itself constantly in the strata of expression which are constantly in the process of fusion and transformation. The only limit it sets on the mobility of the human expression is inaccuracy of transcription, contradiction or false meanings which would obliterate the original intuition. But in theory, every language and every civilization can be permitted to interpret its practical and dogmatic intentions. Its refusal, nevertheless, to allow the expressions of the past to fall into disuse arises from the conviction that a vocabulary that has succeeded in embodying its message represents a definitive structural success and a cultural acquisition. Indeed, the precise association with its meaning constitutes for a word a way to integrate itself into the life of the spirit without return. In sanctioning Jewish and Hellenic cultures, the Catholic Church does not claim to attribute to them an exclusive priority over other cultures. It merely shows that the Western mind was able to distinguish certain values, to define certain attitudes, so that if in the future faith expresses itself through the patterns of a different civilization, the Church will not have to give way to them in their turn by rejecting its old categories. Rather, it will have to blend in one single harmony the variety of old and new structures. The Church is coextensive with all attitudes of mind, without repudiating those it has met in the past, without opposing those it will meet in the future.

These precisions are not on the periphery of our development. They are at the center of it. If it is true that faith transcends the cultures in which it is embodied, no one should presume that the Christian is a docile pupil who recites word for word and willy-nilly fragments of Jewish mysticism, bits of Greek metaphysics, chapters of Roman Law which have been revised and corrected. No, even after becoming incorporated into a particular cultural cycle, the Christian is only the believer in a presence of God in history—I mean not only the kind of presence which occurred in the portion of history during which Jesus gave testimony, or during which the Church preserved his witness, but in all history, in the fullness of human history. Freeing himself from the start and surmounting the materiality of the signs he had used to discover this unlimited presence, the Christian unites himself with God, with the One alone, beyond all time and all expression. The complex system of beliefs, precepts, and rules of every kind that were imposed on him, or rather that he took on himself, is to be used only for the sake of transcendence, under the sign of adoration. If he lacks the courage or the intelligence to do so, if he fails to surmount what he cannot do without, he weakens the formulas, he goes through the movements, but he remains at the level of superstition and does not rise to the level of religion. If he adopts the creed through laziness or routine, without making it his own through a maximum of lucidity and energy, he is no longer seeking his salvation but is fleeing from it.

That is why I think that even a strict and sincere adherence to dogmatic and liturgical expressions cannot survive without an interior "detachment" from their finite and intermediate character. One has to be simultaneously attached to them, since "formulas and rites are the means to an objective, and to be detached from them, in the sense that the mediations are made to permit one to reach his end, not to conceal it. It becomes possible, even necessary, to make the system of religious norms one's own, and nevertheless to consider it relative to that which it structures, to reduce the norms to the values which they seek to express and to see clearly the dependence of the norms on the values. In short, it is no longer improper or rash to claim that a believer remains the judge of that which judges him, the free servant of a free cause. He enters into a system, he adopts it, he takes it on. But once he is praying, once he is communicating with God, the system no longer dominates him. It is at his service. He vivifies it by opening himself to grace. The danger of literalism, of externalism is here completely surpassed. There remains only a spiritual experience, intimate and incommunicable even though dependent on community norms, which at its limit borders on ecstasy. The whole machinery of rules was a means to an end, albeit indispensable. But once the end is reached, the soul is free. It rests in God; in him it has life, movement, and being.

Spiritual men and mystics have often noted this flight of the soul, but positive, authoritarian, and timid minds remain somewhat frightened by it. They do not appreciate flights outside the network of laws; they consider surpassing intermediaries an undermining of structures. But the contrary is true. We respect a means to the extent that a man can make use of it, not to the extent that he idolizes it. Misunderstanding and fear always give a somewhat unfortunate reputation to any fairly resolute step towards transcendence. It is the height of paradox that men of God should retard, restrain, and suspect eagerness for God. We can guess how they become so fearful: they are more attached to the system itself than to what the system signifies and seeks to promote. Good faith will save them, but we might hope that they would come at last to love their Lord more than that which speaks of him. They allow themselves to become attached to that which they should hold loosely, while they slacken their hold where they should tighten it. They rejoice in the abstract when it should be a question of touching a concrete valve. They become involved in the theological when they should be involved in the divine. In a word, they stop midway on the road, and never arrive at their destination.

The annoying thing is that they do not keep this learned and legalistic literalism to themselves. They spread it; they seek to impose it. This gives rise to fairly questionable intellectual habits. I shall not attempt to describe them, so painful is it to see certain men serve the Church, preëminently an "open society," with procedures dear to closed societies. Intrigues, informing, resentment, quotations out of context, tendentious interpretations are ordinary procedures. In itself, this restlessness of mischievous minds merits but little attention; it is always a conspiracy of folly weighted with envy. In alluding to it in order to combat it, I do not, of course, intend to make any apology for error. But I deplore finding errors where none exists. Certain campaigns against eminent and very sound teachers may one day be proved to be as futile as those undertaken in the thirteenth century against St. Thomas. However far I am from thinking what a certain theologian may think, the idea would never occur to me to dispatch God's sheriff after him or to stir up the five continents against him.

But this idea has occurred to some: they put themselves in the place of responsible authority, they convey their grievances outside hierarchical channels, they arrogate to themselves a competency and powers which no one, either among scholars or responsible leaders, attributes to them. This is a strange manifestation of the spirit of charity. A number of *zelanti* think that they are doing good at the very moment they are respecting neither the freedom of consciences nor the most elementary rules of fair play. Why this illusion about themselves, this ill-will in regard to others, this morbid haste to bring wrath down upon anyone who continues to be a seeker in the faith, a wayfarer in the pursuit of truth? This would be inexplicable if we did not know that certain forms of virtue pretend to go beyond mere intelligence. Indignation sometimes masks itself as a higher insight, a more demanding charity than that which insists that to understand and to love cannot be separated. To become incensed, to scold, to condemn—these are the favorite pastimes of those who, having nothing to create or to think themselves, fly into a rage because others still dare to reflect and to deal with ideas. They practice blackmail against humility, obedience, and faith that is simple and open. And they do all this in the name of insolent prejudices that they have established as the center of everything, and as judges of everything. They are too satisfied with themselves to remain disquieted and to suffer others to be so. Thus they turn to their own uses every means of suspicion and of coercion; they crusade for a holy war; they manufacture heretics and then destroy them. Lovers of immobility, iron defenders of the letter, enemies of progress—they advance from victory to victory across every intellectual Spain.

Valéry observed of these mediocrities that they went to too much trouble to make us believe that God is so stupid. And Mauriac flung at them the remark that only simpletons would say that God preferred simpletons. However, we would hardly solve the problem by submitting everyone to an intelligence test. It is not a matter of playing at who is the best in Latin or Hebrew. At the heart of the conservative complex, there is something more than psychological repression. There is an inability to understand that the faith surpasses all the human systems which it is obliged to take on in formulating itself. There is also an inability to understand that the orthodoxy guaranteed by one's agreement with the believing community has the value of a mediation for salvation, but the logical processes and philosophical concepts it makes use of are not thereby canonized. Lastly, there is an inability to understand that the Church owes it to itself to have an especially sound program of studies for its schools, and even an official philosophy, but that outside its formal classrooms it ought by no means to reject independent research, provided it in no way endangers the affirmations of the faith. In fact, very few Christian intellectuals are satisfied with a Holy Office theology or a Biblical Commission exegesis. But the conservative is astounded and scandalized at this; he does not distinguish between the necessities of social regulation and the duty to reinforce prudence with the initiative of reflection. And yet both are indispensable: if it is necessary that the main body of the troop be carefully sheltered, it is also necessary that there be pathfinders and scouts. I have no sympathy for those who set out on their own merely for their own amusement. But I admit without any difficulty that the Holy Office and the various commissions, in performing their tasks, do not dispense any seeker from performing his. The conservative, on his part, will never admit this. He confuses all the machinery of this immense organism which is the Church. He likewise confuses all the levels: those of teaching, pastoral ministry, administration, discipline, science, criticism, and so on. In a word, he adheres to a massive system that absolutizes the human and the divine, his personal sense and the religious sense, his unacknowledged biases and his desire for the good and the true. He is not merely a man of faith, but a member of a sect. He is no longer a believer; he has become a partisan. Today we see the sectarian spirit spreading into heterodox groups. Perhaps it is a phenomenon of the times. We must beware lest it affect the faithful. By multiplying clans in the bosom of the Church, we can only harm its unity. The conservative is divisive, and so is the modernist. We must prevent all unilateral appropriation. We must be on our guard lest any tendency attempt to absorb all other tendencies, since all aim at serving and giving expression to the same faith. This is something that the conservative forgets, as soon as the situation appears favorable to him. And it is difficult to remind him of it without being accused of laxity. However, I do not wish to crush him in the name of my own contrary position. I would simply like to help him to understand that among believers there cannot be two categories: those who have the true doctrine and those who do not. Once we recite the creed, once we obey the Church, we have the faith, the one and indivisible faith, which gives neither awards nor honorable mention except in the order of holiness.

However, the conservative is not freed from his confusion merely by opposing him with reasons. His sickness is that he cannot hear them. And yet, it is necessary to find a means of making deviations of this sort impossible in the future. If, as an eminent historian of Thomism has suggested, the Church does not wish to lose the intellectuals in the twentieth century the way it lost the working class in the nineteenth, it is necessary to prevent the faith from harboring those who, despite the Fathers and the Doctors, the great masters of theology and of the spiritual life, have an overwhelming fear of the daring of the spirit. Are their convictions so shaky that they fear to see them collapse at the least shock? Is the Word of God so enfeebled that it must be supported by miserable crutches? Must believers be treated as if they were perpetual minors, obliged to seek the truth through the authority of another? And must we force the hand of authority, abuse its good faith, oblige it to take measures that it is loath to, measures which it often allows only to end conflicts whose appearance and continuation it regrets? No, these doubts, these fears, these pressures on the hierarchy are themselves an insult to liberating faith, to the testimony of love and of light that Jesus brought into the heart of the Synagogue. If we persist in believing that to preserve means to prevent from growing, that to direct is to bridle, or—as Kant bitterly remarked—that it is necessary to condemn for the salvation of souls without concern for the salvation of the sciences, we no longer proclaim the truth that liberates, but the truth that enchains. In this case, we shall not be surprised if the contemporary world is scarcely swept away with enthusiasm. Our world is always ready to listen to St. Paul. It refuses to hear Torquemada.

Of course, we know very well that spiritual authority is on the side of the apostle and not on that of the inquisitor. Authority is

Paul condemning factions; before that it is Peter feeding his flock. But we are complaining of those who place themselves between us and the Church to make us believe that its countenance is that of a Medusa, not that of a mother. We shall never be able to exaggerate the responsibility of those who hide from outsiders' eyes its goodness, justice, and longanimity. Our quarrel is not with authority, for it has our respect, our gratitude, and our affection. But precisely because we have such a lofty idea of what it represents, because it appears to us as the guide of hearts and minds, because across the ages it is the witness of him who said he was the way to the Father, we shall not suffer people who lack both any mandate and any competence to presume to speak in its place. All that we have said here not only does not attack authority, but defends and preserves it. We are not evading the precept of obedience. We oppose any person, no matter his reason, who replaces lawful leaders, misinforms them, or exceeds their instructions. Indiscipline is a serious matter, but he who falsifies the role of authority is as guilty as he who does not submit to it. There are docile people who are abusive and rebels who are naïve. To multiply the truly obedient, let us have few vassals with their own private interests to serve. If the freedom of the children of God is not an empty phrase, it is up to the community of believers to prove it. The brotherly union of the early Christians conquered the empire of arms and laws. Let it appear again, and the new empires will lay down their rods of authority.

We might be inclined to think that periods of distrust or narrowness are simply an accident in religious society. Let us indeed hope so, for there is nothing so unhealthy as a climate in which one cannot assert himself, in which each plays a role and develops an attitude of mind which is either that of a courtier or of a refugee. The danger is that the most loyal teachers think themselves obliged to write in half-truths, even when their position is above reproach. If a perfectly creditable author considers it prudent to resort to expedients, to subterfuges (putting forward the ideas of an agnostic straw man, creating imaginary conversations with a deceased monk on various questions of present religious interest), in order to display a strictly traditional doctrine, it is difficult to see how the reputation of the faith will gain anything by it. No one should have two contrary opinions, one that he publishes and one that he keeps to himself. It is a matter of integrity for Catholic intellectuals to say exactly what they believe to be true and what they consider compatible with their beliefs. It is scarcely flattering to oblige them to resort to understatement or to elliptical statements while extolling those among them who indulge in cheap pieties in order to be reassuring. Their obligation is to be frank and docile: frank to their own conscience and the conscience of others, docile to spiritual leaders—but not to schemers or fanatics who inform by deforming the truth. Indeed, a police-state atmosphere gives rise to results which are either deplorable or absurd. If we condemn Catholics who are studying Catholicism, naturally they will turn, for the sake of peace, to the study of what is not Catholic. One theologian will owe the clan of petty critics his new vocation as an Indian scholar. Another will turn his attention to geological sedimentations, or to the biology of hormones (it has happened). But maybe it would be better to recruit as many scholars for the religious sciences as for the profane. The formation of a single dogmatic theologian, of a single moralist, of a single Christian philosopher is more precious to the Church than all the spy networks, the whole cavalcade of apologetics tournaments, the arrogance of doctrinaire courses, the pretensions of the ambitious servants of the prevailing ideology, and all the Zhdanovs of the faith.

But to be frank, the obsession to remain on the beaten path or to force others to keep to it is never an accident in the lives of individuals or of groups. Given certain premises, it is a logical, pressing, ineluctable consequence. Whoever fails to evaluate the system he avails himself of submits to it and wishes to submit others to it. This is obvious in politics, in literature, in philosophy, and also in religion—particularly in religion, which develops the sense of the Absolute. That is why, in order to believe in God, a believer frequently tries to project the force of his belief over everything, even over things that do not belong to the same sphere of values. To avoid such a mistake, it is necessary to unite a sense of the relative with the sense of the Absolute. If it is not permitted to lower God below God, neither is it permitted to raise the human above the human. God is not served by deifying points of view whose onesidedness make it sufficiently clear that they are by no means absolute. And it is a betrayal of man to impose on him in the name of God ways of thinking and deciding that he ought first to sift through his judgment, if he does not wish to be taken in by them. Is this setting too great a store on freedom of conscience? Is it paying excessive homage to it? Not at all, if it is true that without discernment and loyalty the quest for the good and the true would be impossible. We must choose between responsibility and servility (the latter being only a caricature of obedience). Only the first is worthy of the spirit.

If responsibility can be maintained and servility avoided, the way can be opened to a reconciliation of the critical mind and faith. For there is no real antinomy between a free opinion and a free faith; both meet in the same sentiment of rejection in regard to all that is biased, incomplete, and unstable. To affirm God's existence and to adore him constitute the highest form of liberation; they oblige the believer to refuse all that is not God, all that does not lead to him. The idea of God is the great lever of human emancipation. It makes it possible to hold in check every determination, every particular object, the whole order of the finite. Man should not use God to get the better of his fellows and to defy the powers that be, but when he has recognized God's presence at the heart of his personal freedom he is no longer dependent on any selfish, arbitrary need. Thus a man becomes impervious to hate, falsehood, and envy. In communion with God, he is invulnerable, and the charity he receives from this union is accompanied by the courage to love even his enemies, to dedicate himself and to die even for those who destroy his body or his thought. What is the difference between a faith lived at this level and a militant holiness?

Thus it seems that a believer motivated by this kind of fervor need no longer fear the snares of action or of science. A love of God which transcends all partiality urges him to a detachment from his ideas and their success. It teaches him to renounce what he creates as well as what he thinks. This is the irony of true charity, as Eugenio d'Ors used to say. It eliminates that irritating gravity, that self-importance which makes it clear that one believes more in oneself than in what is to be believed in the order of religious practice and truth. We should be misunderstood were we to speak of an unbelief inherent in true faith, symmetrical with the faith that still lurks in unbelief, provided it be sincere. But we must admit that faith is sufficiently aware of its own limitations to recognize itself inadequate to the Infinite, in need of a God who fills the soul only to make it ever more eager. The belief that leaves one fully satisfied is not good; it is only the illusion that one has arrived at perfection. True belief, the only authentic kind, is that which adheres to God not to delight in him nor simply to rest in him, but to renew one's forces in him and to learn the secret of a boundless love.

Thus we believe that a man can be a Christian, a devoted son of the Church living shoulder to shoulder with all the other faithful, without ceasing to think and to act freely, without ceasing to be at ease in the midst of those who are striving and seeking, even in the light of different principles. We believe that one can have and keep the faith even while being aware of the difficulties of exegesis, the problems of history and of criticism, the pangs of poverty, and the tempers aroused by political confusion. For faith is not something to be called into question by knowledge or technical skill. It is faith which calls into question all knowledge and every technique, which prevents our absolutizing them and expecting daily miracles or unchangeable certitudes from them. By forbidding us to rely heedlessly, indiscriminately, and thoughtlessly on our knowledge and skill, faith is the safe-guard of a courage that is always new and an intelligence that is always awake. Without faith, inquiry would soon cease, for in the long run, man is more prone to approve than to doubt, more inclined to be satisfied with evidence than to prolong his dissatisfaction. The nescience of faith is the salvation of science. Faith calls science from what we know to what surpasses all knowledge. Thus it enables knowledge to advance without ever encountering any barriers. Faith is the intellect's saving grace, because it preserves affirmation from all premature limitation, from a fixation at an intermediate plane. Fundamentally, faith does man the service of returning all of his concerns to the plane of relative truths and relative goods.

In this way, faith discredits no values, not even the profane. It restores each to its proper proportions. If the Christian must strive for justice, for peace, and for universal love, it is not because he has at his disposal an infallible recipe for resolving problems of the city, of the economy, or of politics. In fact, he has only one essential certitude to guide him: God is every-where present to those who know how to recognize him. For the rest, like any other man, he has to rely on his own counsel. Thus, in the secular order, the Christian must proceed like all his fellow men and work out desirable solutions day by day. Just at this point, however, too many Christians go off at a tan-gent: for example, they appeal to charity, not to end the struggle between the classes by disarming the rich, but so as to discourage those who have been exploited from successfully pressing their demands. This is sheer obfuscation. The loyal Christian should shun as he would a sacrilege this way of sub-ordinating his faith to material interests, his brotherly love to the desire for money. There should be no hesitation concerning the path his conduct should follow. As detached from everything and in search of imperishable treasures, he is that much the freer to prevent millions of men from being at the mercy of hunger, privation, and oppression. He should be in the first rank of this struggle for justice since, better than others, he knows that souls caught in the vise of misery and trouble cannot glimpse or even suspect true values. At the same time, however, he is not unaware that the battle is full of hazards. He will bring every effort to bear on it without thinking for a moment that his intervention will be more decisive or more infallible than that of his companions. This modesty will do him no harm, indeed it will unite him more closely to those who suffer and who seek. Contrary to what one may be inclined to believe, the sense of the possible, of the relative, of the approximate will not lead him to disregard either action or research. The fact that he knows the Absolute to be unrealizable in this world will prevent him from ever interpreting as definitive the results he may attain. When one thinks the Absolute to be where it does not exist, one is inclined to look for it in partial successes or in the improvements of the moment. But no one moment is the last term in the series. A man must go forward without ever stopping and this can be done only by not riveting one's gaze on any one point, by never allowing one's progress towards God to turn back on itself in satisfaction and contentment. A believer who does not feel on his lips the taste of life, who cannot enjoy in life what is good and beautiful, who lacks the simplicity to love men as they are—such a man is not a citizen of heaven making a short stay on earth. He is a deserter, a fugitive, and a coward. Yes, science is uncertain, happiness is fragile, and society unstable. But that is one more reason for contributing to progress. The illusion would be to think that after a few reforms, or even after a violent revolution, paradise would be established on earth. The idea of an end to struggle which would also be an end to our problems is a snare. Faith preserves us from falling victim to it. We must learn to struggle ceaselessly and indefatigably, for the twofold reason that perfection will always be an ideal, and that this ideal outside the world obliges us not to abandon the world but to save it.

What are we to conclude from these reflections? That a clear and vital faith does not come from a simple membership in a circle of believers. We are too prone to think that the mere fact of being baptized, going to Mass, adhering to what the Church teaches suffices to develop a spirit of religion. This is not quite the truth. Historians of religion know that even an archaic religion can harbor a very pure intention, can foster a perfectly sincere generosity. And, on the other hand, the follower of a more demanding religion can live it on a mediocre level. The religious consciousness, even when guided by a doctrine of holiness, is liable to laxity. It becomes the prey of laziness, of ease, of the temptation to follow the line of least resistance. A monotheistic religion, for example, is no guarantee that its adherent is monotheistic in all his devotional undertakings nor at every moment of his life. He can, on some occasions, behave like an idolater or a fetishist even though in theory he has a horror of such perversions.

Thus we can understand that Christians themselves do not always and everywhere uphold the high standards of the Gospel. Even while proclaiming that the Revealer of the God of Love is their leader, they are sometimes liable to live as if it were not so. This is but further proof that even an eminently spiritual religion, even one that is completely disinterested, can be lived within perspectives that do not do it justice—and this not only because the believer is also a sinner, but because his understanding of his religion varies as much as his practice of it. Taken in itself, Christianity is certainly the apex of religion, as Hegel saw. It is *the* religion because it is impossible to surpass the commandment of love. And yet this universal of charity is not always understood or respected by Christians. It is said that the early Church, despite the message of interiority proclaimed by Jesus, fell back into Jewish particularism. This is a tendentious remark that is perhaps true of some Judeo-Christians in Jerusalem, but is surely disproved in the case of St. Paul or St. John. Today, however, it is no exaggeration to say that some Christians are indeed living the New Testament in the spirit of the Old. A retrogression in mental attitude is possible, when one's intentions are pure, even when one is convinced that one accepts the fullness of the faith because one repeats the formulas with the scrupulosity of a scribe.

That is what happens, I think, when a Christian considers himself justified not by faith and the works of faith, but by the letter of faith. He has forgotten that the letter kills and the spirit gives life. He behaves, therefore, as a strict observer of precepts and rites, but he is mistaken concerning the source of salvation. He sees it in the materiality of expressions or of signs, which is the definition of superstition. Is it too much to ask such a man that he recover the true religious meaning by seeking God himself, who lies beyond his words, figures, and symbols? These fulfill an indispensable function; we must use them and then go beyond them. Faith is precisely this continual passage from the sign to the signified, from history to the spirit, from human situations and experiences to God.

If this passage is to be made correctly, however, it is much more helpful to teach how to acquire and preserve the sense of the transcendent, than to train people to be jealously attached to the body of religion and to defend it fiercely. Instead of trying to fit minds into a mold and freedoms into categories, instead of solemnly professing that religious instruction should appeal to the sensibilities and make judgment yield to the shocks of emotion (as they do who defend a "visceral and somatic" catechesis), we would no doubt do better if we tried to educate powers of reflection at the same time that we are trying to stimulate proper affective response. If we teach young Catholics that the quest for God is something difficult, something profoundly personal and never fully achieved, we shall make them less eager perhaps, but more balanced, more serene, and in the end more persevering. We urge them to the assault of every citadel, we point out the targets, we let them think that in the struggle between God and Satan they are the forces of good on whom the issue of the battle depends. But if the storms of life shipwreck this invincible Armada, we ought to understand that God has no more need of assault troops than he does of Knights Templar. The victories of the spirit must be bought with the weapons of the spirit, not with those of cunning or of force. It is easier to picket *The Devil and the Good Lord* than to reflect. It is easier to organize meetings and demonstrations than to uncover the needs of the times. It is easier to agitate for special privileges than to join in the national effort so as to assure the peaceful presence of an exacting but disinterested witness. Yes, it is always easy to be facile. But we have not been signed with the seal of Christ to play Philip II or even Don Camillo. We are Christians only to sow love, concord, and justice.

In the final analysis, the apostolate and the work of evangelization are not conquests, but witnesses to life. They have to do with preaching through attitudes and offering examples of dedication, not with the use of techniques of conversion. We have condemned constraint and trickery. We have asked that the believer judge his belief so that it may be not the love of a system but the love of God himself. This means making an appeal to critical discernment as opposed to a burst of enthusiasm and ardor. It means asking from reflection what one ordinarily asks from enthusiasm, from the mind what one expects from the heart. Perhaps it even means condemning acts of magnanimity that offend against clearsightedness. But if religion teaches us to love, it is because it supposes us to be capable of understanding. It would not teach virtue to anyone who was not able to make a judgment on it. We must do the same. Let believers give testimony of their belief before all. But let them wait until the unbeliever voluntarily opens his mind to their teaching. It is freedom's role boldly to forge its own course. One can suggest that it take this or that direction. But in the end it will follow only those paths it has laid down for itself.

II.

Immanent Reflection
and Transcendent Faith

1. THE LIVING GOD AND THE GOD OF PHILOSOPHY

God is affirmed first of all not by philosophical thought, but by
spontaneous thought. Mankind had myths and religions very
early, but metaphysics only much later. This is evidence that the
needs of life, of psychology, and of society precede, and by a
long time, methodical awareness of ideas and their ordering and
classification. Criticism is always a fruit of maturity. There
would be no consolation in seeing it born late if one did not
know that, kept dependent on life and held in its wake,
criticism is capable of participating in life's movement and
profiting from its vigor. It would not be difficult to show that
philosophy became sterile each time it separated itself from the
living creations of the spirit in the sciences, the arts, or religion;
or to show the contrary, that philosophy enriched itself each time
it drew near to them. Through reflection on concrete contents, it
has prospered; through abstraction or purely formal deduction,
it has been endangered. This is a sufficient reason for asking it
to maintain contact with the spiritual life in all its forms,
especially its religious form. In the West, for example, it would
be a sorry mistake to propose removing philosophy from the
influence of Christianity. Moreover, such a proposal could not be

70

followed, given the long exchange of categories between faith and reason.

One fact, however, is surprising: in the areas where faith and reason have been given separate domains, their conflicts become more embittered. Instead of allowing them to get along as spontaneous thought and reflective thought, one seems to take pleasure in hardening them, in opposing them to each other. It is thus that the great monotheistic idea has broken apart into two rival notions: the one remaining on the side of religion, the other limiting itself to the plane of abstraction. What is pejoratively called the *God of philosophers* has become the antithesis of the God of revelation, or at the very least its replica or noticeably impoverished double. By perpetuating this misunderstanding, we excite the spirit of polemicists in both camps. But it seems this renders service neither to religion nor to philosophy. Perhaps Pascal had his reasons for humiliating the Cartesian God before that of Abraham, Isaac, and Jacob.[1] His eloquence must not keep us from realizing that the fault is shared both by those who seize the notion of the Absolute for mysticism and those who confiscate it for rationalism alone.[2] In fact, the antimony of the God of the learned and the God of the naïve has its origins in a confusion concerning the responsibilities incumbent on the philosopher and the believer. It is advisable to reëstablish the order of competencies in order to restore harmony and union.

The philosopher, first of all, must be aware that his discipline is only a reflective technique applied to lived experience. He does not supplant the concrete subject, the thinking and acting man. Only the latter is really engaged and brings values into play. Only he does a free act; only he effectively conforms the means at his disposal to the end he pursues. The philosopher

---

[1] Before Pascal, St. Augustine had used this formula, but he preferred that of Exodus 3:14, *Ego sum qui sum.* See *Sermon* VII, n. 7. Commented on in F. Cayré, *Dieu présent dans la vie de l'esprit* (Paris, 1951), p. 96.

[2] "Neither scientism nor false mysticism," Maurice Blondel liked to say. (See *La Pensée*, II, Paris, 1934, p. 135.)

is always dependent upon the man and remains his pupil. He must clarify man, but not substitute himself for man. This is to say that philosophy always comes after life; it is a recovery of life; but it cannot be identified with life. Philosophy is, if you like, the word of life, it is not life itself.

By saying that philosophy is reflective, do we imply that human life is or can be reflective only because of philosophy? Here it is necessary to agree on the meaning of the words. Human life is conscious of itself; it is thought in act; it is light as well as liberty. Thus there is a word immanent to life, even before this word is raised to the level of philosophical discourse. In fact, man never acts without intentions. His practice is always directed by some theory. Hence spontaneous consciousness, or living and concrete spirituality, is mediated by ideas as well as by values. In this sense, man thinks and even reflects. But in a very broad sense, for this reflection does not know itself as reflection. It remains tuned to the practical behavior it guides and regulates. It holds to a straight course in the service of action; it is prospective, not retrospective. To become properly reflective, to be aware of itself as reflection, it must move to another plane, detach itself from the immediate, become both systematic and disinterested. If one prefers to call *reflection,* in the strict sense, this second act that returns to spontaneous thought in order to recover it methodically, he will contend that lived experience, even illuminated by the thought that it contains within itself, remains *non-reflected,* or, in the terminology of certain authors, pre-reflective. In this case, even though life remains a thought in act, only philosophy will be called reflective. At the same time we see what relation is established between philosophy and life: the first is related to the second as the reflective to the spontaneous, knowledge to the concrete, judgment to being. There exist, consequently, two planes that must never be confounded: the *speculative plane* and the *concrete plane.* They are distinct, yet interdependent. Reflection lives on concrete life. For its part, the concrete would never become "reason" and system without an ordering through a technical ordering.

If the preceding is correct, the so-called God of philosophers risks being an illusion. The philosopher, having nothing other to do than criticize the products of spontaneous consciousness, is mistaken when he believes that he fabricates ideas, no matter what they may be, and imagines that he gives them value. He only recovers ideas and defines the conditions under which the subject may acknowledge that they have value. The philosopher points out to the subject what responsibilities he must assume; but only the subject is capable of assuming them. The critical function does not take the place of the practical function; it uses the practical function and refers to it. But criticism neither eliminates nor dispenses with practice. These remarks have special value with respect to the idea of God and the scope proper to it. The philosopher *encounters* this idea; he is not the author of it.[3] He must therefore seek to know what it signifies and what role in life can be assigned to it. But he is not to mold it as he pleases nor turn it to uses which do not answer to the fundamental aspiration of the subject.

In these conditions, the God of philosophers is from the start a theft and a blunder. One pretends to believe that the idea of God is the property of philosophy, whereas it is borrowed from the religious life. One makes it the point of departure of a series of deductions, whereas it is a principle of conduct. One confiscates it for the benefit of supposedly autonomous operations, whereas it has been removed without discretion from spontaneous thought. How could it be surprising that the idea of God, so treated, becomes unrecognizable? One severs it from life and also would like it to return there: an untenable proposal. The God of philosophers fails because of abstraction. He will never be more than a substitute product, an alibi for concrete

[3] The idea of God would indeed languish if it were sustained only by logical reasoning; on the other hand, it is vigorous when proclaimed by faith and instilled by worship. Practice serves it better than dialectics.

theism. In life the God of philosophers or of non-philosophers does not exist. There is only one God,[4] and the idea of him prompts definite actions, while offering itself and those actions to critical reflection. We should not speak of a God peculiar to philosophers, but of a God that religion worships and that philosophy must take into consideration as it does any other value. In any case, the affirmation of God is a work of free and spontaneous consciousness. The work of philosophical reflection is to state in what way this affirmation is coherent and obligatory or, on the contrary, vain and superfluous.

If there is no God of philosophers, neither is there a God of tradition who is inaccessible to reflection. Here the illusion does not come from the philosopher, but sometimes from the defender of religion.[5] The latter is correct in thinking that the affirmation of God rises from spontaneous consciousness, especially in

---

[4] At the very least, one sphere of the divine.

[5] In an historical context where positive religion dreads naturalistic contaminations, and above all in an academic setting where it is essential to distinguish truths of faith and truths of reason, there is opposition to the philosopher's taking for his own the notion of the living God, since he would thus appear to be arrogating the benefit of revelation to himself. Consequently, he either remains docile and appropriates for his natural theology only those elements which the theologian declares to be rational; or, taking as a pretext the poverty of thought left to him, he sets revelation up as a principle and reduces God to an axiom. Rationalism is already germinally present in the mistaken segregation of religious and metaphysical evidences. If in actual fact the philosopher is not free to examine the idea of God as a function of the whole of human experience, including religious experience, he will set out from fragmentary initiatives and distorted evidence and will be able to discover only a mutilated or burlesqued notion of it. The apologist who would force him into such a situation is not entitled to reproach him with it later. Man's experience cannot be divided either *de facto* or *de jure*. It is easy to understand that one problematic should be employed to situate both that which calls attention to human powers and that which, on the other hand, proceeds from a special initiative of God. This problematic is indispensable to the theologian in one form or another, and, as method requires, the philosopher necessarily affirms its complement in his domain. Still, we should not conclude from this that the quest for God is not imposed on the philosopher as a function of the concrete life of man, of the *whole* man. Religion belongs to this concrete life. Thus, it cannot be left on the margin. It would be an exaggerated paradox to enjoin the philosopher to seek the idea of God wherever he sees fit, but stipulate that he should steer clear of religion.

its religious form. But it is wrong for religion's advocate to confound the object of this affirmation with the modalities of the affirmation; it is wrong for him to believe that the transcendence of the divine mystery is extended to the materiality of the expressions that it takes on in human consciousness. And it is even more seriously wrong for him to consider that his own particular problematic is canonized by this transcendence. Some religious people seem to think that their logical instruments, and the frequently contestable manner in which they employ them, are rendered divine by the God they worship. This is as flagrant an abuse as that of the monopolistic philosopher who, shut up in his specialty, is ready to reduce the content of life to his own capacity for interpretation.[6] If the religious man judges God to be transcendent (a question that the philosopher in turn must ask himself), this is not to say that the representations he makes of this transcendence, and the procedures he employs to connect them, are essentially different from the modes of ordinary thought. Faith is undoubtedly a singular perspective on God, a unique intention. But when it formulates itself, its

[6] Nothing is more puzzling than the mutual distrust of the philosopher and the believer (sometimes in the same individual). The former reproaches the latter for giving himself an extra dimension, for being "more than man." The latter reproaches the former for wishing to naturalize everything, including the divine. Each denounces a prejudice to the other. Many distinctions would be required to reconcile them; we will pursue the question elsewhere. But one thing can be said to the philosopher, and another to the believer. The philosopher who leaves religion aside, under the pretext that it is the affair of specially endowed minds and superhuman faculties, is not a rationalist. This abets the false mysticism which pretends that the means of expressing faith (I do not say faith itself) transcend humanity and belong to another world. Thus, the philosopher who regards religious experience and thought as taboo actually plays the fanatic. On the other side, the believer should not defend the object of his faith as if it were a meteor fallen from the sky. Even in the Christian religion, where the notion of revelation determines everything, it is necessary to discern an element of human construction. In these conditions, religion can be examined as a factual given, elaborated according to certain human procedures which can be grasped by criticism. Neither God nor grace is threatened by it. Alain, following Hegel, says that religions are first of all natural facts. We would agree with this, except to add that immanence is quite able to shelter a transcendence.

categories and schemes are taken from a logico-rational context upon which the philosopher has the right to bring judgment. This is why, even if religion has its own manner of posing God, the philosopher does not exceed his authority by demanding to verify this approach. In this sense, the God of tradition serves in no way as an antithesis to the supposed God of philosophers. Simply, he serves as spontaneous evidence for a critical attention that will try to study his content, to determine his meaning and scope. If there is an antithesis (not antinomy) anywhere, it is between the plane of lived theism and that of reflected theism. But this is not an antithesis between the God that is worshiped and the God that is demonstrated.

Thus the plane of religious theism is delivered up, in its entirety, to criticism. Is it not to be feared that it will be dissolved or absorbed by reflection? This fear is groundless if it is understood that reflection is derivative from life and that the latter remains, first and last, irreducible. Criticism begins from life and returns to life. It is only a reflective detour, the time of methodical judgment. It never suppresses that which nourishes it. Moreover, the philosopher will take care, in criticizing concrete theism,[7] to respect its specificity. Otherwise, he would be able neither to understand it nor to appreciate it at its proper value. To the extent that he nowhere confounds his role and that of the living subject, the plane of reflection and that of lived experience, it cannot be seen in what way he could mutilate the religious object. We acknowledge willingly that it is a delicate matter to treat the religious object, but we do not believe that it is impossible. For, by right, reflection is co-extensive with the total range of human action. If it were otherwise, there would be no philosophy of religion. There would be no philosophy at all. Lived experience, whatever it is, is always "transcendent" to the

[7] By concrete theism, we refer more to the living intentionality that leads to the affirmation of God than to the academic schemas about God. These schemas are as relative as any rational problematic. In contrast, the intentionality of which we speak coincides with the dynamism of the spirit and is as unchallengeable.

reflective plane. In this respect religious reality is in the same position as all other "lived experience." It is worthier of attention and respect only because it involves affirmations of greater consequence. In any case, it could evade criticism only by desiring to avoid reflection, and the result of this would not be an increase in nobility, but rather a lapse into intrigue.

We no more admit separatism in favor of religion than monopolism in favor of philosophy. The first is an activity of man; the second, an analysis of human initiatives, excepting none. The philosopher should not uproot the idea of God from the natural context where it germinates; nor should he monopolize it, pretend that he invented it, or manipulate it, as he would a formal concept empty of all spontaneous content. He should, from his point of view, reflect on it, criticize it, judge it;[8] after which, if he considers it reasonable, that is, *affirmable* and practicable, he must put it back into the hands of the living subject, who will regulate his choice according to this instruction.[9] Thus the problem of the God of the philosophers will

---

[8] This situation is not unique to contemporary philosophy; it is found constantly in the history of doctrines. Plato and Plotinus, Augustine and Thomas Aquinas, Descartes and Spinoza, Malebranche and Leibniz, Kant himself, Bergson and Blondel utilized and criticized the religious capital of their epochs. Christian writers sometimes call the thinkers of antiquity the "pure philosophers." This is an equivocal manner of authorizing the Christian revelation. Theology itself admits that the idea of God is rational. But it has always germinated in a religious context before being taken up by the philosophers, including those of antiquity. A. E. Taylor calls Plato "the creator of philosophical theism" (*Plato: The Man and His Work*, 4th ed. [London, n.d.], p. 493). In fact, his role is limited to giving philosophical status to a religious idea.

[9] This is said, obviously, of the subject capable of understanding the lesson given by the philosopher. In fact, religion remains the great educator of millions of minds. It succeeds in directing them by itself. It often does better than learned reflection because the skill proper to the latter is not conducive to the presentation of transpositions, or even approximate adaptations, of the true. Religion has the secret of satisfying the obscure regions of consciousness, those concerned with feeling and the practice of life in common. It captures unsuspected energies and orients them towards a spiritual ideal, of which it invents various representations ordered to the diverse levels of concrete subjectivity. It enlists the whole man; it engages all his powers.

lead to no embarrassment at all; it will not even have taken shape as a problem. Its solution is found in realizing that it is an error to pose it.

On its side, the problem of the God of tradition will present no obstacle to criticism. For tradition is integral to life, and the latter lays itself open to reflection from beginning to end. There is, then, properly speaking, neither the God of the philosophers nor the God of tradition (in opposition to the former). There is *God,* affirmed by spontaneous consciousness (in its religious *élan*) and, by way of this affirmation, criticized by the philosopher. Philosophical theism is only concrete theism passed through the screen of criticism;[10] it is reflective appreciation of a spiritual act that is performed on the plane of effective engagement. Thus it is never a double of, or substitute for, lived theism. Philosophical theism is the methodical awareness and rigorous ordering of concrete theism. But only the subject relates himself to God, even after the philosopher has disclosed the valid conditions of this extremely intimate relationship. We do not imply that the philosopher's reflection does not maintain its independence or possess its own laws. The contrary is true. Philosophy has its own economy of a strictly rational order. Moreover, not being content to reflect what happens on the concrete plane, philosophy judges it. Philosophy not only describes; it *prescribes.* It demands that the subject conform to his decisions; otherwise, he may choose beyond limits imposed by reflection, and thus choose badly. But ultimately, choice and concrete engagement revert to the subject. The philosopher limits himself to stating

[10] Moreover, religious theism mixes reflective elements with those of feeling. All, or very nearly all, religions have had sacerdotal castes to intellectualize the myths as well as to regulate the cult. Christianity itself arose in a cultural world where the old myths were already purified and partially rationalized. Because it subsequently developed in the environment of Greek metaphysics, its doctrine incorporated many philosophical notions. The result is that rational criticism finds in it an initial arrangement of categories. It is a question of profiting from this and pushing the effort of elucidation to completion.

the rule for choice, the meaning and scope of engagement. Then it remains to choose, to act.

2. THE PROBLEM OF GOD: A
CONTEMPORARY CRITIQUE OF TRADITIONAL THEODICY

The religious soul comes to God through faith, hardly at all through dialectic. This is not to say that the man of faith does not have recourse to numerous and subtle reasonings if ever he attempts to think his faith. But faith itself lies nonetheless on a plane more profound than any reflection. Thus we can say that it belongs to a separate order. The act of believing in God is a *sui generis* venture; to study it as such, it would be necessary to make a general critique of faith. We will be occupied with that in other works, the present chapter has another object.[1] It is simply to state what happens when the idea of God, incorporated into belief, falls under the regard of philosophy.

On this very point, observation discloses an almost constant procedure that is extremely revealing. It seems that the philosophy's only task concerning God is to *prove* his existence, which is peremptorily affirmed by faith. Reason is asked to establish by its methods, what religion achieves, at less expense, on its own. Everything happens as if faith, which has its own certitude, had need either of being reinforced by reasoning (which is not at all specifically religious) or of being persuaded that it sustains infinitely more than reason (and this is not of much profit to the latter). In both cases, there is something strange about the process.

Certainly, it can be understood that faith, since it penetrates the totality of consciousness, involves a rational plane. Belief

[1] The reason our study of concrete theism does not lead to a critical exposition of the notion of *religious faith* is that it is impossible to define faith critically inasmuch as the principal objects on which it bears cannot be examined.

in God presupposes, in this respect, reason's adhesion to the idea of God and the equally reasonable conviction of his existence. For most Christian philosophers, the possibility of a rational discourse on God is founded on this point. Natural theology exposes the rational elements integral to belief. It organizes and appraises them, although in a way different from that of faith. However, even that procedure is not without some drawbacks.

In the first place, this process of bringing to light the rational elements included in belief seems legitimate only if it remains subordinate to faith. Using the medieval formula, we can say that it remains meaningful for those who put philosophy in the service of theology. If the philosophical demonstration of the existence of God could not be taken up and transcended by belief in God, it would be manifestly impossible to bring the affirmation of reason in accord with the affirmation of faith. The moment one seeks, in the name of reason, to undermine the foundations of belief, natural theology becomes the operation of bringing into focus that element of belief which permits it to lay claim to rational proofs.[2] Methodological considerations make it clear, however, that this procedure is acceptable only to someone who previously admits two things: first, the division, into two sectors, of truths of faith and truths of reason; second, a philosophical autonomy circumscribed within the limits of the exigencies of dogmatics. Those who, to the contrary, refuse all dualism (or even the risk of it) between faith and reason, as well as any attempt to limit philosophical inquiry to a restricted area of truths,[3] can only advocate recourse to other approaches.

There is another more serious disadvantage to enclosing natural theology in the frame we just described. If one holds that intimacy with God is achieved only through faith, whereas God's existence falls within the scope of demonstration, he becomes the

---

[2] In this sense, natural theology is apologetics. By turning their objections back on them, it prevents unbelievers from advancing a prejudiced rejection.

[3] See *Critique et religion,* Chapter III.

victim of a logical device. He projects on God a distinction of perspectives that was conceived[4] only in order to maintain two sources of truths, the one transcendent and the other immanent; in return, it is forgotten that the "transcendent" truths come to expression within immanence. But how is God able to divide himself into the God of faith and the God of reason? How can he become simultaneously, or by turns, the locus of mystery and the object of demonstration? One of two things must be chosen: either he is mystery and no explanation of it can be produced; or he is object and explanation triumphs over, but also dissolves, mystery. However, does this not confound two orders of questions, one concerned with what God is, the other with the fact that he is? It can be answered that if it is important not to confuse these questions, it is also important not to separate them. Now they are inevitably separated when they are related to processes as different as those of spiritual freedom in the order of belief and those of intelligible necessity in the logical order. Faith does not sever them; hypothetically, faith is assured of revelation concerning both the nature and the existence of God. As for reason, how could it establish the existence of a being if it were ignorant of the conditions under which it is able to be, if it is? It is easily understood that a theologian seeks to found in reason the existence of a God whose prerogatives he knows through faith. For him natural theology amounts to finding an argument that refutes the principal denials of the unbeliever; that is a useful tactic and it is impressive. But the philosopher finds himself in a completely different situation. He raises simultaneously the question of the *quid* and the *quod,* of the nature of God and his existence; he considers the two questions to be indissoluble.[5] Thus the philosopher, if he poses the question of

---

[4] Perhaps this distinction was made primarily for academic convenience, so as to classify theology and philosophy according to different objects.

[5] Brunschvicg is right in saying that the manner of establishing the proofs of the existence of God is dependent on the idea one has of his nature. "Not only the modality of the proofs that we will endeavor to establish in favor of his existence, but also their legitimacy, are dependent

God, will acknowledge the right of posing it only with respect to God's existence or non-existence, that is, his mystery. He will not say that God exists, as an object exists, nor that he is this or that, as an object is this or that. In a word, the question of the existence of God and the connected question of his nature are carried beyond the plane where their disjunction renders the first soluble by simple objective explanation and the second soluble by the fixed determinations of faith (it being forgotten that their character as determinations necessarily refers to a discursive power of reason). That shows why criticism cannot ratify a system of representations that leads to thinking of God as divided within himself,[6] his depths being confided to faith, his existence offered separately to philosophical demonstration.

Moreover, the dualistic systems become tangled in their own problematic. On the metaphysical plane they hold that in God essence and existence are one, and on the methodological plane that his existence is demonstrable without his essence being clarified by reason. This inconsistency is aggravated by another, typical of the same systems: that of first establishing the existence of God and then launching forthwith a determination of his essence, without saying how the passage from existence to essence is able to follow upon their initial disjunction. Then comes a third contradiction which attempts to make up for the other two: since it is important to limit the determination of essence, for fear of crossing the threshold of mystery, one divides, if we may say so, the divine essence into two parts, one penetrable by reason, the other reserved to faith. If one retraces these three procedures—disjunction, then reunion of essence and existence, and finally division (at the second degree) of essence—they will be recognized as artificial schemes that are tainted with spatiality: the scheme of extra-position, the scheme of juxta-

on the idea, more or less pure and intellectual, more or less true, that one has of him" (*De la vraie et de la fausse conversion* [Paris, 1951], p. 123). In the language of criticism, the value of God is the value of the mind that conceives him. Each one has the God he deserves.

[6] This is to treat God as a thing or a solid, as an object in space.

position, the scheme of superposition (supernature).[7] Is a natural theology, developed in terms of these schemes, anything other than a logical contrivance?

This is why we prefer another manner of resolving the difficulty. Can the same object be known and believed at the same time and in the same respect? St. Thomas answers no, St. Bonaventure answers yes.[8] Undoubtedly, this opposition would be transcended if it were held that the line of demarcation passes, not between faith and reason,[9] but rather between *living spirituality* and *critical reflection*.

With this we are approaching the solution: it consists in saying that belief is entirely on the side of the concrete subject, whereas knowledge belongs to criticism. But both belief and knowledge have to do with the same reality, the God of living spirituality.[10] The phantom of a notional Absolute is not reintroduced on the reflective plane. From the start, the reflective plane refers to the living Absolute, as reflection refers to the plane of lived realities. The reflective plane defines the conditions under which the free subject can hold that God exists and

[7] We will see how the positive aspect of the scheme of supernature can be preserved. See *Philosophie de la religion* (Paris, 1957).

[8] Texts cited and discussed in E. Gilson, *La philosophie de Saint Bonaventure,* 2nd ed. (Paris, 1943), p. 91, and *Le Thomisme,* 4th ed. (Paris, 1942), p. 29 (English translation by L. K. Shook, C.S.B., *The Christian Philosophy of St. Thomas Aquinas* [New York, 1956], p .17). St. Bonaventure holds that if it is a question of an object transcendent to human thought, it is necessary to know it and believe it at the same time. Because knowledge and belief together are not too much for thinking an object which transcends each of them singly, they must associate their efforts, and even admit that man *in via* is not able to perceive the divine mystery in its true light. On the contrary, St. Thomas holds that when knowledge decides on the basis of first principles, faith should not intervene.

[9] We do not say that faith and reason are not distinct; we affirm and repeat that they are. But it is still necessary to understand what distinguishes them. To be content with a mutual compatibility—faith-reason (or theology-philosophy)—is insufficient; faith, in order to express itself, borrows from philosophy. Furthermore, this dualism leads to disguising God in the masks of the *God of reason* and the *God of religion*. And thus one returns to the false problem of the God of philosophers and the God of simple believers.

[10] Knowledge thereby directly sanctions mystery and yet maintains its character of rational criticism.

under which he can serve him religiously. We no longer need to pose the problem of the relationship between a *knowing* and a *believing* which divide up, so to speak, the reality of God. Knowledge deals with the whole extent of belief, of which it formulates the *a priori* conditions. In other words, criticism no longer has to affirm that God exists, while leaving intimate communication with him to the subject. It simply states what is demanded of the subject in order that he, without betraying the imperative of reflection, can acknowledge the Absolute in his existence and in his mystery. It is no use proving that God exists if we do not indicate at the same time the necessary value he has for man. Indeed, the problem of his being and that of his value are one. This is to say that criticism must achieve knowledge of belief rather than of an object that is excised from a belief, than dealt with on its margin. Otherwise, one inevitably reverts to a God of philosophy which is not that of religion. This difficulty is overcome if critical reflection limits itself to recovering the affirmation of living spirituality in order to disclose its meaning and its norms.

Does this point of view make natural theology less reliable? Does it weaken the classical arguments? We will see that it does just the opposite. It does not burden faith with the worry of proving that God exists, as if reason were incapable of taking a position on this matter. By giving criticism the mission of verifying all the affirmations of practice, we do not encourage fideism; we elevate reflection, giving it universal jurisdiction. It remains true for us that reason has the capacity to prove God,[11] and in a more complete sense than is ordinarily granted to it. For the judgment it will produce on the reflective plane is a *categorical* summons, addressed to the subject, to come to a decision. But in doing this, reflection will not pronounce in favor of an Absolute situated on its plane; it will refer to the only Absolute worthy of the name, that which the subject can discern in his mind and obey in his conduct. In fact, philosophy's task is

11 We will see how.

less to prove God than to establish the subject in the rational and moral dispositions through which the notion of the Absolute will prove itself. Or, if philosophy is able to construct the proof of God, it is because God is, from the beginning, immanent to the reason and to all the powers of the concrete subject. Criticism only transposes and makes rigorous a norm that *remains implicit* but *is really operative in all consciousness.*[12]

Thus the sole duty of the philosopher is to examine the meaning and value that the idea of God bears for living spirituality. He converges on an actually lived intention, without having to take the place of the concrete subject and pursue it himself. If, on the contrary, the philosopher severs the critical function from the content of life, if he isolates it, if he sets it up as a self-sufficient system, the notion of God will become for him something quite different from what it is for spontaneous consciousness. It will take on the characteristics of the *God of philosophers;* in other words, its own face will be hidden by this mask. Certainly, it is understandable that the professional philosophers abstract from the positivity and particularity of the religious traditions; knowledge of these traditions is only one specialized branch of philosophical criticism. But it is incomprehensible that a philosopher would study the idea of the Absolute without

[12] Unfortunately, the role of philosophy is not always understood in this fashion. It is confused with thought in act, with the reason or reflection of the concrete subject, although it is only the technically ordered awareness of it. Blondel put it well: "reasonable reason underlies rational reason" (*La pensée,* I [Paris, 1934], p. 178). This leads to innumerable verbal misunderstandings. If we say, from our point of view, that the task of philosophy is neither to invent the idea of God nor to construct arguments in the void, some will understand that we are dispossessing reason of its rights or even that we leave it to mysticism to be occupied with God. We hold, on the contrary, that philosophy is nothing other than reason, but reason become fully conscious of itself, master of its criteria; it borrows ideas and values from living consciousness (thought in act), then it systematizes and judges them. In this respect, its intervention is decisive. Without the *moment* of philosophical reflection, spirituality would remain as spontaneous activity. God would be lived but not truly thought. In order to reach the critical plane, theism must, like every spontaneous movement, pass from the plane of life to that of reflection. This expresses the indispensable role that we give to philosophy in natural theology.

referring to spiritual experience, that is, to the process of conversion that initiates, independently of cultual determinations, the religious attitude in general.[13] If he fails to proceed in this way, it is hard to see what could support him. The prejudice of relating essences, disconnected from their attachment in reality, is not a satisfactory foundation; rather, it is the refusal of the only normal and legitimate foundation. Consequently, if the philosopher ends up with an abstract God, a God-axiom, a God-law, or even worse, a God-thing, he has only himself to blame. No one has ever worshiped such a God, for he hardly transcends the cunning of the one who constructs him. He is not even raised to the level of the living spirit, inasmuch as it is creative subjectivity; he is confounded with a product of thought, with an object that one attempts to circumscribe. Far from being an Absolute, he is a determination—the highest perhaps, but posed in a manner similar to the others. He is found in the prolongation of no real aspiration, of no sincere adherence, he is simply conceived as an intellectual opinion, as a logical possibility, and, in the extreme case, as a fiction.

Everyone with any feeling for the concrete will agree that this result is disappointing. The most astonishing thing is not that this capacity for distraction is found in thinkers of only slight religious temperament. The greatest scandal is that religious minds believe it is necessary to transpose the problem of God onto the plane of a criticism without interiority. This concession to formalism becomes a betrayal. Once engaged in a purely notional matrix, it is only a matter of evoking the adventure of the idea of God. Under the pretext of rational selection, of demonstrative proof, one lapses into a veritable thing-ism.

[13] All religions suppose a movement of inner conversion (the scope varies according to the requirements of the given religion). A similar process, by which consciousness attempts to rejoin the Absolute or the Divine, develops beneath, or rather in the heart of, the structural ensembles. This process, this effective advance, is the concern of "reflection"; the philosopher must determine its meaning, control its orientation, and test its value.

3. THE RELIGIOUS ROOTS OF PHILOSOPHY

Everyone agrees that religion is older than philosophy. Few authors add that the philosophy of religion is as old as philosophy. It is nevertheless absolutely true.

It is customary to place the beginning of philosophy with the Ionians (Asia Minor) in the sixth century B.C. One suspects that this decision is somewhat arbitrary. Did man pose the problem of his destiny only after he learned that the world comes from water, air, earth, or fire? In fact, man's concern about man is always older than its proper formulation, and *a fortiori* older than the first statements of it that have reached us. If Western history looks upon the Greeks of the sixth century in so favorable a light, it is because the Greeks of the fifth century preserved their work (at least in part), and because we have agreed to see in Plato and Aristotle the best judges of the matter. We call the Milesians, Ephesians, and Eleatics "pre-Socratic" to emphasize that Socrates is the philosophic messiah who decides all things, giving direction to the future and re-ordering the past around himself. But this nomination of Socrates as a frame of reference is necessarily a choice. The terms "pre-Socratic" and "post-Socratic" correspond to historical reality only insofar as we determine they should: Socrates is the center of the history of philosophy; the Socratic method is the patron of all philosophical method; in a word, the Greek way of philosophizing is the only possible way.

But things are not quite so simple. From Thales to Jean-Paul Sartre, there are less than 3,000 years out of a human duration that counts several hundred millenniums. That means that the history of our philosophy is very short. It is true that time does not affect the matter, and that quality does not depend on quantity. But has this very quality met with so few occasions to make itself known? Could the Hellenic world be the only "chosen people" of the philosophical idea? Do we not display an intolerable conceit when we claim that only the West has conceived, engendered, and perpetuated philosophical reflection? Experts in Chinese and Indian culture have every reason to denounce such provincialism. Not only has the East produced "wisdoms" comparable to ours, but it preceded us in time. It also succeeded in making them flourish, not among the élite, but among entire groups and in very extensive communities, which was not the case among the Greeks. And it did so less through school training or formal methods, than by more concrete and direct procedures. Paul Masson-Oursel points out that Eastern civilizations have had a genius for getting the masses to think through rite and religious gesture. (Judaism used the same means.) Besides, contrasts drawn between oriental and occidental thought prove to be artificial. Today this has been shown on the historical level: the two cultures have communicated with each other from earliest antiquity. We can tell them apart, but we cannot make them exclusive one from the other. They have come into contact with each other on many occasions in the course of history.

Therefore, to attribute to the Greek world alone the formation of philosophical ideas is simply to show either prejudice or ignorance. The truth is that the Greeks were the inventors of a certain formalism. They perfected methods of reasoning that have no equal for introducing order into thought, and continuity into action. Perhaps their logic does not include all logic but it does possess an undeniable precision, an effective rigor. Moreover, it is indeed to Socrates that we owe the discovery of philosophy as the discernment of self, or rather, as attention to the universal in the self. No doubt, he did not secularize philosophy as much as we commonly maintain. But he did rescue it from the confusion of Ionian polymathy. He preferred self-knowledge to knowledge of the world. In this sense, he really founded philosophy as Western humanism understands it.

However, it would be a mistake to believe that he became the leader of Western philosophy without drawing upon work already accomplished. His initiative was not an absolute beginning; it was a point of culmination. It is one with efforts undertaken before his time, even though it was able to react against them. Now, even if it is impossible to go back beyond the School of Miletus, we can still see that the thinkers of this school concentrated particularly on the cosmogonic myths which were included in the religious traditions. It is unfortunate that Aristotle and his disciples should have become interested in Thales, Anaximander, and Anaximenes as physicists and meteorologists. This is why, to this day, we look upon the Milesians less as philosophers who were rethinking and recasting the archaic myths than as naturalists about to stammer the first rudiments of geological and astronomical sciences. In fact, they represent at once the infancy of science and the infancy of philosophy, but both as they sprang from the religious cosmologies which came to the Greeks from Mesopotamia or Egypt. In this light, religion appears truly the mother of all thought, even among the Greeks. It furnishes science with a choice of images with which to establish a first representation of the world; and it provides philosophy with a sense of the infinite (Anaximander remembered this), of the just and the unjust, of the perishable and the imperishable (Anaximenes did not hesitate to divinize the primordial substance). Each of these notions transcends the scope of simple positive observation.

Similar observations suggest themselves concerning the thinkers who came later. Pythagoras and the Pythagorean School constantly interrelated religion and philosophy. The School of Crotona (ancient Italy or Magna Graecia, c. 530) was a religious association modeled on the Orphic associations much more than a philosophy club in the modern sense of the word. It formed its votaries and initiates for the happy life. Yet unlike the Orphic religion, this philosophical school combined the methods of purification which gave immortality, with a mathematical symbolism whose significance was other than that of rite and other than that of myth. It was in this respect a pre-philosophy of universal harmony. The discovery of irrationals limited its ambition; it could not stem its inspiration. Pythagoreanism constituted the remarkable precedent which would prevent Greek philosophy from becoming totally "laicized." Offspring of the East but well received in the West, its influence spread everywhere and brought it about that Greek thought preserved a religious dimension even when it was most positivistic.

Heraclitus, who lived in Ephesus towards the end of the sixth century, showed greater contempt for popular beliefs. He rejected the Orphic mysteries and denounced Dionysian practices. But his cosmology remained as mythical as that of the Milesians. He claimed to prefer what is seen to what is said; he sought to make intuition superior to tradition. The theories he expounded were aimed at determining rationally the measure of every combination, at discovering the formula, the *logos* of reality. They nevertheless preserved a continuity with the preceding representations of the world. The theory of opposites (prototype of dialectics whose moving power is internal conflict) has the same intellectual age as the Manichean structures; and we know that their origin is lost in the night of time (even Babylon, whose civilization was flourishing eighteen centuries before Christ, did not invent them). The theory of the fundamental unity of things, despite transformations and endless transmutations, proceeded to moderate the first theory. It is considered less ancient; yet that is not certain. Dualism and monism could be two complementary positions; we already find them interwoven in the myths that ancient man developed. At the very least the theory of unity recalls the earlier derivation of all things from an original element, as so many of the Milesians maintained. As for the theories of the perpetual flux of all things, of opposites which are both unforeseen and controlled, these also recall the tone of the primitive cosmogonies. It was through them, or at any rate thanks to them, that they presented change as a disconcerting but fertile becoming, impetuous yet "numbered." In a general way, one can say that Heraclitus marked an improvement on the spontaneous myths. He emphasized the law, the orderly pace of change. But we must add that the force of his theory continued to depend on the mythical foundations he claimed to have surmounted.

Parmenides (Elea, sixth and fifth centuries) also merged two ideas. He was a pupil of the Pythagoreans and wrote in imitation of Orphic models. He opposed permanence, the identity of being to the mobility that Heraclitus extolled. In this sense, he is the father of rationalism. But he knew how to reconcile the research of truth in a mathematical way with the apprehension of the sensible in a mythical way. Parmenides admitted two functions: "dialectic" on the level of ideas, imagination on the level of opinions, beliefs, and affective needs. Plato was later to recall them. Moreover, this union of idea and myth, this intimate collaboration between concept and image seems to be the very condition of philosophy. It is indeed the natural food of the life of the intellect. The rhythm of the latter never consists in purely abstract reflections. It is the mutual, alternating promotion of word and life, meaning and the senses.

It does not serve our purpose to describe the other presocratics: Zeno, Empedocles, Anaxagoras, Leucippus, Democritus, and so on. Some were religious and others not, some were physicists and others moralists. All of them made use of the foundations of the Ionian thinkers. The original myths continued among them in varying degrees. It even happened that they bore fruit at the very moment that they were being attacked. (The atomism of Democritus, despite its mechanistic, non-qualitative character, is still a myth, and a scientifically fruitful myth.) Only the sophists assumed a general scepticism with regard to the past. But this was only a pose. The great sophists took upon themselves the mission of saving art and culture, which means that they did not reject *a priori* any heritage. Their humanism was mainly a guide to social life. They discovered the existence of virtues in the political order, even though they did not know how to define them properly. This led them to neglect religion.

(Too obscure a subject, said Protagoras, for men whose life is too short.) But they did not neglect ethics, which they frequently and willingly preached. We must not judge them by their less able followers who ended in cynicism and verbal fatuity.

Of Socrates (470–399), who wrote nothing himself, and whom (like Jesus) we know only through his disciples, we often make a simple moralist. He had, however, taken the precept of self-knowledge from a maxim inscribed on the pediment of the temple of Delphi. He was convinced of his mission as a religious teacher by a reply from the oracle at Delphi. His personal "daemon," moreover, was a religious inspiration and not a secular intuition. The astounding thing about him is that this communication with the divine absorbed him in a profoundly interior life, a withdrawal from which he emerged only to deliver a message of self-mastery. Socrates' religion has no particular ideological content and no ritual. Or rather, unlike the Sophists, Socrates appears to have respected the religious customs of his time, just as he respected the laws of the city. His freedom of thought and his freedom of speech (which cost him his life) were put into practice when there was a question of defining ideas that involved everyday conduct. His quiet irony then became the most exacting, the most purifying of criticisms. In the presence of Socrates, no one could correctly define temperance, courage, piety—ample evidence that self-integration, the coherence that is no longer notional but personal, cannot be reached at the level of discourse; and proof that self-knowledge fails on an objective level, on the level of language, so that we may be led to acknowledge that conscious ignorance (the "knowledge that we know nothing") is the only virtue.

Must we see in this a culture of skepticism with regard to reason and concept? Certainly not, at least Plato held the contrary. We must see that reason is a mediator, that a concept does not end with itself; that every idea goes back to another idea, and back to still another, interminably; that taken as a whole, ideas do not suffice; they return to man, to the subject who produced them and who, in knowing them, would be wrong if he thought that through them he knows himself. The mystery of self, mystery itself, still perdures, and remains intact even after dialectical scrutiny. The latter, however, is not in vain. Only discussion, the constant effort at definition, allows us to see that the theoretical discussion is endless, whereas practical reform cannot wait. It is interesting that this lesson—that theory should be subordinate to practice, ideas to the Good, essences to freedom—which was accepted and extended by Plato, should later be occasionally overlooked. We must reassert the specific character of ethics and its primacy over critical philosophy. Yet, we must insist that it is critical philosophy which brings out and justifies that primacy. Only "learned" ignorance, only practice which is epicritical and not precritical is fully justified.

Were we to extend these remarks to religious criticism, we should learn the useful lesson that it is the interest of every philosopher of religion to take Socrates' attitude as his model. Like Socrates, he must take the position that theory never exhausts practice, does not replace it, and yet plays an irreplaceable role with regard to it. In this way, the criticism can apply its analyses wherever it pleases, follow its own laws, and be mistress of its own domain. But it is very careful not to reduce the mysterious, irreducible world of acts and conduct to its system of ideas. Criticism can be, and ought to be, the *word* of practice. But it is not practice. In this sense, philosophy of religion is to religion what criticism is to practice. This is why religious values—which only the religious man can discern and appreciate as lived values—cannot be dissolved even by a radical and unreserved criticism. These conclusions evidently go beyond the historical case of Socrates. What we know of him is too general and too indefinite. But it is certain that his example turns reflection in this direction: we must reason, argue, and define *in order to act*. And when we have reasoned, argued, and defined well, the integration of the self remains to be established at the level of action, in the privacy of our conduct. These instructions have often been lost and again recovered through the ages. Sometimes they have been reborn without reference to Socrates. But since we have seen that he is their author, it seems only honest to recall them under his name, to return them to his patronage.

Plato (427–348), Socrates' most illustrious disciple, reaffirmed his teacher's position and considerably enriched it. It is not the place, in this short summary, to offer an exposition of Platonism. But it is important to note at what point Plato's philosophy is bound up with factors which are religious. This is first of all in its form, since it rejects neither mythical expression nor the information of the experimental sciences. Thus it recovers the sense of complexity and totality which characterized the ancient Ionians. Secondly, religious notions are involved in its very basis: Plato, like Socrates, speaks of divine inspiration and of demonology; he holds that all knowledge should lead to contemplation of the Good; he specifies that the contemplative act should concentrate within itself all the powers of the soul. It is not always easy to bring together the theory of ideas, the dialectic of love, the cosmology, the ethics, and the politics contained in the *Dialogues*. For Plato's thought evolved; it renewed itself at different periods of his life. In any case, we cannot deny that the submission to the unconditioned Good, to the Good "that is not a being, that is beyond being," together with the primacy of the practical already affirmed by Socrates, testify to a genuinely mystical impulse. At times we think that this impulse has little to do with logic and epistemology, whose technical subtlety seems more like an academic exercise, the refinement of an academician. According to Plato, however, science and mysticism mutually pervade each other, so much so that the destiny of the soul, its immortality, becomes a condition of the possibility of science. For the same reason myth, which could have been only a pedagogical device, quickly became an auxiliary representation of the idea. Myth was auxiliary but original—of irreplaceable assistance.

The Platonic myths baffle the modern reader, particularly the Christian reader, because they have neither the same foundation nor the same structure as the typology to which the Bible has accustomed us. They are even too perfect from a literary point of view to be taken with the same methodological seriousness as the primitive myths of the ancient Hellenic cosmogonies. They are nonetheless instructive, however. Except in a few passages of the *Timaeus,* Plato expounds only anthropological myths. These myths concern the whole history of the soul, its preëxistence and its future life. They involve genesis and eschatology, which is classical enough, but with the particular difference that their imagery is often taken from the scientific, geographical, and astronomical material that Plato had at his disposal. Genesis and eschatology are precisely the points to which concepts cannot be applied, for there is no actual experience of origins and endings. This explains why religions are so anxious to fill the lacunae of reasoning. Every man would like to know that which remains essentially unknowable, and Plato was fully conscious of this. However, unlike modern rationalists, he did not refuse to portray, to *visualize* what it was impossible to think clearly. Why did he consent to doing this? We could answer that it was an act of condescension or weakness. But this answer seems to be wrong. If, in fact, myth is not a proof but is generally introduced after proof—if, as Plotinus would say, it is only a projection into time of that which is timeless—it is nevertheless the only form of thought that can impregnate consciousness at certain of its levels. Besides, it is not a substitute for the idea, a kind of confused idea that takes the place of a clear idea for less enlightened minds. Plato did not invent myths to assist those who could not understand conceptual argument. He presented them as a philosopher to philosophers. The myth in his eyes is not a substitute for the idea, not its degraded replica, but rather the paradoxical radiance of the idea in the density of consciousness— paradoxical radiance, for it illuminates indirectly, it proportions or adjusts its light according to the degree of receptivity of the lower levels of human subjectivity.

When, for example, Plato has souls preëxisting, when he attributes to them a choice before the fall, he had no intention of positing a time that preceded time, or an option which preceded effective freedom. He did not betray the idea (were he to betray it, his philosophy would contradict itself); he simply exposed it to the imagination, diffusing it according to the needs of sensibility and affectivity. In doing this, he safeguarded it. He succeeded in acclimatizing it at the very point where formal evidence would not establish conviction, in that psychological dimness where the fantasy of images must be controlled if we wish the spirit at its zenith freely to dispose itself to contemplation. From this point of view, the myth is intended to "grasp" the lower levels so that the upper plane remains protected from their counter-effects. The grasp is no doubt on the order of an incantation, and it may be that everything mythical functions at certain levels as a charm. At all events, this charm, this art of mastering the imagination, enables the idea to give expression to its self-affirmation without fear of the counter-offensive of sensible evidences, of the illusions of the psychological self. In fact, Plato accomplishes his ends. He does not lead us to believe that the soul preëxists, that it decides beforehand. Through the myth of preëxistence, foreknowledge, and pre-choice, he teaches that our present life, our present knowledge, our present choices are determined by us alone. A valuable and effective lesson, this refutes the thesis of a constraint anterior and exterior to the workings of conscience. Joseph Moreau has written with good reason: "Reminiscence (insofar as it is a myth) expresses in terms of becoming and historical succession, the *a priori* character of knowledge. Following a method of exposition which will be employed in the *Timaeus,* the myth expresses through a chronological anteriority what is an anteriority of principle, a transcendental relationship."[1]

[1] *La construction de l'idéalisme platonicien* (Paris, 1939), p. 372.

What weakens the Platonic myths is that their author consciously elaborated them like a man constructing a fable. He knew their explanation before composing them. But this objection is not entirely justified. The myths, whether genetic or eschatological, anthropological or cosmological, are almost all derived from suggestions and outlines which are older than the *Dialogues*. In fact, they are as old as culture. Plato took them over from a tradition which already existed, remodeled them and touched them up; only rarely did he create out of whole cloth. We may say, therefore, that even in his hands they conserved that spontaneous, "global" character they had when they first appeared, and which corresponds in man to his first mode of grasping values. He poured off some of their contents and stylized them, but this did no harm. This simplification or adaption made it possible to see more clearly how he linked them with the essential idea, or rather, how the mythical developments of the idea are still properly an integral part of the original idea. "In this respect," continues Moreau, "it [the myth] is by no means allegorical; it is an intrinsic moment of scientific representation, as indispensable to physics as figures are to geometry."[2]

Within this perspective, the magical explanation changes in significance: the image is not only made subordinate, but the orientation imposed on it acquires the effectiveness of a plan; henceforth, it conveys the idea, or rather, it makes the idea "develop" in the symbol. It makes the idea live in the symbol.

In a word, Plato taught us authoritatively that philosophy should not be afraid to confront mythology, to integrate and even to make use of mythical structures. It is both strange and regrettable that this was later forgotten, and that so many historians of philosophy continued to treat the Platonic myths as by-products of his work, even as an element apart.

We shall not mention Aristotle (384–322) except as a reminder. For the works of his that have come down to us con-

<hr />

[2] *Ibid.*, p. 419, n. 1.

tribute very little to the object of our study. A logician, physicist, metaphysician, naturalist, and moralist, Aristotle had a multiplicity of interests. That is why, when his books became known in the Middle Ages, his influence could extend into the most varied domains. Doubtless because of his positive turn of mind, a truly mystical inspiration played only a restricted role in his works. Yet he affirmed the primacy of contemplation and developed a theology of the unmoved Mover, of the pure Act, which is also "the thought of thought." This sober and uncluttered theodicy was revived by St. Thomas Aquinas in the thirteenth century, with many changes and additions. Because of the kind of philosophy it was, it could condition the posing of the religious problem, but it did not itself pose it. Aristotle's God, in his immutability, is necessary for the equilibrium of the world, for its finality, and hierarchical order. But knowledge of it or contact with it seems to be denied to man. In this context, we think it would be excessive to seek any definite aid for a philosophy of religion.

The Platonic tradition was revived by Plotinus (205–270 A.D.). Like the Epicureans, Plotinus escaped the tragic universe of religions and myths. Although he was influenced by the Stoics, particularly in cosmology and psychology, he remained immune to their theology and piety. Despite all this, he was undoubtedly the most religious of the philosophers of antiquity. Beginning with Pseudo-Dionysius the Areopagite, Christians did not miss this fact. To this day, when Christian mysticism seeks to express itself, it spontaneously repeats a lesson learned in the *Enneads* and handed down through Dionysius, Augustine, Eckhart, and John of the Cross.

Plotinus, however, dissociates mysticism from all prayer or cult. He does not deny them a certain efficacy, but he fears the superstitious illusions connected with them. He seeks salvation only through the mediation of the intellect. At the same time, he insists that the intellect acknowledge itself as dependent, that the passage to the intelligible is only a stage (although an indispensable one) towards the One, towards ecstasy. Since the One is transcendent, the final ecstasy presupposes a grace. Only those who link "the idea of grace to that of contingency," remarks Jean Trouillard, can dispute Plotinus's having professed a mysticism of gratuity, of divine liberality. Once we admit the transcendence of the One, we should see in the Plotinian ecstasy a religious experience beyond the intelligible order. This is tantamount to accepting philosophy as a mediator between two presences of the One to the spirit: a hidden, unperceived presence that constitutes the source of all spirituality; and a known, willed presence that in the light of meanings and of speech consummates the marriage of the intelligence with the Absolute. This is the unique case of an intellectualism that requires a mystical flight, and which conceives of it as an access to pure liberty. In the fifth book of his *Ethics*, Spinoza made a similar attempt. But he did not indicate so clearly the distinction to be made between intellectual effort and entrance into the supreme indetermination.

On leaving the Hellenistic period, we enter a Christianized world. Henceforth, culture will pose the relationships between philosophy and religion in an entirely different way. Now the relationships become those of reason and faith, or philosophy and theology. This new way of thinking belongs roughly to the entire Middle Ages as well as to modern times, and this despite the variety of positions taken by various thinkers, believers and non-believers. For this reason we can content ourselves with a general view. I have intentionally laid stress on antiquity. We are too willing to pass over in silence the fact that Hellenic or Hellenistic thought has always contributed moral and religious concerns to philosophical research.

The Middle Ages could approach the religious problem only in terms of Christianity. But Christianity, which is derived from Judaism, is an historical and positive religion. There is not a single case of a Christian teacher—and, until Hegel, not a single case of a philosopher—who attempted to recapture the meaning

99

of Christian positivity with the help of rational reflection. As a result, this positivity has been placed outside the philosophical field. It has become the exclusive property of the theologian. The rather unexpected result has been a growing disaffection on the part of philosophy for religious questions. Augustine, Erigena, and Bonaventure neither foresaw nor desired this rationalism. St. Thomas, with astounding boldness, accepted it. He sorted out truths of reason and truths of faith, attributing the former to the philosopher and the latter to the theologian. Certainly, he welded these two subjects together; he distinguished them by their material object and by their formal object only to bring them closer together. But in relegating the philosopher to an order of truths apart, truths called natural as opposed to the supernatural truths reserved to the theologian, he decided the fate of modern philosophy. Philosophy became less and less concerned with its companion discipline, to the point of cutting itself off. St. Thomas is not responsible for this divorce: he enjoyed the twofold competence of philosopher and theologian. Even Descartes is not responsible for it; his dualism never went so far as a formal break. Malebranche could still claim Descartes' authority even while rejecting this very dualism. Nevertheless, it cannot be denied that Thomism had a double effect. It sanctioned the autonomy of the philosopher, which was a good thing. It also, and in all innocence, gave certain minds an opportunity to appropriate the title of philosopher without maintaining any link with those professionally trained in the religious problem. Now this is not necessarily a good thing, for the dialogue with religion, which was carried on under various forms throughout antiquity and the Middle Ages, has not ceased to serve as a stimulant for the philosopher. This is so true that the most unorthodox thinkers (Spinoza, Kant, Hegel, Comte, Renouvier, Brunschvicg, Alain, and others) have themselves experienced the need of renewing the dialogue. Unfortunately, they have tended more and more to pursue it from the outside, in a negative or polemical manner. They have not often shown a desire to understand religion in the sense that the religious man practices it. Apart from Hegel, they have never succeeded in reintegrating the problem of the positivity of Christianity into philosophy itself. That is their most serious lacuna.

In their defense it must be said that they had an excuse. Since the Middle Ages it had been understood that only the theologian had any authority over this positivity. It was proper, then, that it be left to him. As an exegete, the former pupil of rabbis, Spinoza wrote a criticism of the Judeo-Christian Scriptures. Indirectly, he was led to define the ideas of revelation, prophecy, religious history, rite, institution, and the like, only he ultimately destroyed them more than he clarified them. At the end of his examination, Christian positivity was neither understood nor well-founded; it was considered unworthy to receive philosophical status. This refusal by Spinoza was well motivated, and his exegesis is far ahead of that of his contemporaries. It would be unjust to consider his hesitations as a simple condemnation. He nevertheless maintained that religious positivity, as an historical expression and doctrinal or cultic determination, cannot be assimilated into a philosophical reflection. From this it is only a single step to the suggestion that it has no meaning, that it possesses coherence only for the theologian. And this suggestion, incidentally, is not overly displeasing to the theologian. Like any specialist, the theologian looks askance at anyone who ventures into his territory.

Such boldness is necessary, however, and the philosopher ought to have it. He cannot admit of reserved questions. The jurisdiction of reason is universal or it is not—on the condition, of course, that the method employed is adapted to its object. If the philosopher abandons religious positivity to the theologian, he relinquishes one of his own duties, as Blondel rightly reminds us. The theologian accepts the positivity of religion as a fact, he does not recapture it rationally as a right. The Christian theologian takes Scripture and tradition as sources and as objects of faith; from the outset they have a revelatory value. They serve to establish a religious experience, to promote it, and to control it. But they themselves are never called into question, nor do they have to be. Theology begins with an act of faith; it stimulates and develops an understanding of faith, for which purpose it makes use of rational middle terms. These react on the principles of faith and enable us to draw rational conclusions from them, but only so far as we maintain our adherence to the faith value of these principles. In a word, the theologian uses his reason to understand his faith, but always remains dependent on faith and works only within its light. That is why it remains —and this is no threat to the theological enterprise—another task to apply a properly philosophical reflection to the religious datum. Without denying *a priori* that Scripture and tradition could have a revelatory significance for the believer, there still remains the task of submitting them to a strictly rational criticism. This amounts to returning the whole of religious positivity to the domain of the philosopher so that he can examine its very foundations from a point of view which does not in itself imply the act of faith—a bold, delicate but indispensable undertaking. If it is not attempted, religious experience will continue to be suspect. The philosopher will continue in the impression that he is mistrusted, and will become mistrustful in his turn.

Hegel deserves to be considered the first philosopher of Christian positivity, the first philosopher of religious institution. Because of his moralism, Kant neither understood the specific character of the mystical in relation to the ethical, nor admitted the connection between faith and historical structures. Schelling's interpretation of myth and revelation was often very rich, but he maintained that the positive and the institutional was always secondary in religion, and that the first religious form was natural in essence and mythological in expression (in the pagan sense), not intentional and voluntary. This seems questionable, since it supposes that man can live as a human being before being a giver of meaning. Hegel escaped this error. For him,

positivity, at least the desirable kind (for there exists an undesirable kind which has no possibility of ever *knowing* its
meaning), is a necessary moment of dialectic. Every spiritual
experience and every human enterprise, in order to be coherent
and complete, leads to expression, to concrete realization, to
mutual communication. This detour through exteriority is evidently not the term of the process. It must return from the outside to the inside just as it passed from the inside to the outside.
The reintegration closes the cycle, and closes it effectively by
the fact that the experimental, after having expressed the ideal,
knows that it possesses it in expressing it. This conception remains somewhat abstract and artificial in its formulation. But
reduced to its essential scheme and relieved of all excess, it is
certain that it lays the foundation of positivity. It recognizes in
positivity an expressive value which is not accidental but necessary. Restored to this context, historical religion of the revealed
type is no longer a fact which the philosopher cannot assimilate.
In virtue of its law of expression, it is an authentic figure of the
Absolute. This is how Hegel understood it. There would be
nothing to redo in his interpretation if historical expressivity,
instead of translating the reaction of man to a transcendent
Absolute, did not seem to involve a necessity for the Absolute
to become directly the subject of history; and if, besides, religion
did not appear to recover its meaning from the philosopher, the
only faithful interpreter of the dialectical movement. These
inadequacies prevent us from remaining content with Hegel's
philosophy of religion. But it would be useless to try to understand religious positivity without having at least "been introduced" to this philosophy.

We had to wait for the contemporary period for the development, in the wake of Husserl's phenomenology, of a philosophical understanding of religion with a goal other than the
condemnation or the surpassing of religion. Husserl himself did
not apply his method to religion. Some disciples did it for him:
Scheler, with a minimum concern for positivity, and van der

Leeuw, with his constant concern for restoring the religious phenomenon to its historical perspective. This approach consists in describing positive religion just as it appears (Maurice Blondel did this), accepting the significance it claims for itself, but abstracting from the values the believer finds in it for his life. One by one the religious structures (dogmas, rites, and so on) are subjected to scrutiny, analyzed only from the point of view of preserving the meaning of each part within the axis of the whole. (Without this axis, the religious phenomenon would be treated not as religious but as moral, social, political, economic, literary, or esthetic.) The advantage of such a method is to understand, without having to accept or to refuse, the ontological efficacy of the ideas under consideration. Religious phenomenology thus gives evidence of respect, although it is true that this is due to a suspension of judgment.

Many authors go no further. They describe, but do not decide. To judge, however, remains the right and the duty of the philosopher. In order that religious phenomenology may become a philosophy of religion, therefore, there is a place for adding a judicial opinion to the description. We personally believe that this is possible, desirable, and even necessary—on one condition, that critical philosophy keeps strictly to its role. It is quite all right that it take the initiative to discuss everything and to evaluate everything, but it must also become conscious of its presuppositions and postulates. It should make sure that its conclusions, like its premises, are all of a piece. It must recognize the specific character of practice, and the fact that practice cannot be reduced to criticism. It has to determine the conditions of the possibility and the validity of the religious act. But it should not reduce the act itself to these conditions; it should not absorb it or dissolve it in its theoretical elucidation. A lesson in ethics is not the same thing as an ethical life, although the one clarifies the other. In the same way, the philosophy of religion is not religion in action, although it clarifies its meaning and defines its type of effectiveness. This should be a useful recall to modesty for those who may be inclined to confuse *knowing* with *doing*.

The only objection that would touch the faith would be a proof of the illusory and illusion-producing character of religious values. But who can mount such a proof? The unbeliever does not possess these values, and thus he cannot pass judgment on them. The believer lives them, and lives them as original, as distinct from every other kind of values. And he lives them without being able to objectify them. Were he to objectify them, he would by that fact destroy them, for he would be depriving himself both of the joy of living them and of the ability to testify in their favor. The truth is that we can criticize the expression of a lived experience and therefore the stated objective toward which it aims, but we cannot grasp this lived experience itself except by experiencing it. The existent is not proved, it is experienced. If we do not experience it, we must keep silent, and neither complain nor condemn. Otherwise, we would have to accept the blind man's denial of color, the boor's profanation of art, the fool's criticism of the role of the scholar. Such an attitude leads to an absurd, albeit picturesque world, but who would wish to identify such a world with the world of philosophy? We offer to criticism a rather fair share, so that it may not ignore anything that can really be criticized, apprehended, and evaluated by it. If there is anything inconsistent or incoherent in religion, criticism will know how to find it. If religion itself, which does not exist without reflecting itself in a language and showing itself in a behavior, is only a parasitic activity, the fruit of fear or of oppression, criticism will know how to find this out and how to tell it.

At any rate, no one will deny that ours is a time when philosophical discourse has learned anew to nourish itself with ideas that for centuries had awaited in vain their rational development. Judaism invented the categories of history, revelation, faith, sin-transgression, and the like. It was Judeo-Christianity that gave a place of honor to the categories of incarnation, person, witness, charity or pure love, and so on. But the philosophical development of these categories had hardly begun before the nineteenth century, and several of them have been reinstated by philosophers only within the last thirty years. When historians and commentators suggest that we are going back to the pre-Socratics; when rationalists protest that since Kierkegaard, the existentialists, and the phenomenologists, myth or religion is making a reappearance within the temple of reason (at times in borrowed vestments), they are not completely wrong. But we must convince them that the natural climate of philosophy is not the rarified air of the study. It is the atmosphere of life, of life under all its forms: scientific, moral, esthetic, and religious. The system of ideas, which some scholars have ingenuously confused with the chain of reasons which they have locked up in their books, has nothing to do with the logic of the schools. It is identical with that tremendous effort of history and culture. No one can isolate the system of ideas or separate it and say that it begins here and ends there. To grasp its meaning we must listen not only to the melody of this or that discipline, but to the symphony of the whole cultural world. We cannot mention one single idea that does not stand out against a background of myths and religions. The most refined concept still clings to an imaginary vein, which remains its only evidence of belonging to the human complex. That is why we should rejoice and not allow ourselves to become indignant over the need for wholeness which is felt so strongly in contemporary philosophy, even if for a time it stirs up no little confusion. Things will eventually settle down, and classification will begin again. An anthropology with a scope equal to the dimensions of the world is worth more than an algebra of ideas or a residue of abstractions. I say this not to give agitation a primacy over lucidity, but so that reflection may know itself and will itself be co-extensive with human experience.

It is possible that this will to accept everything and to integrate everything without constructing anything on the border of life may exhaust forever the inspiration which built up the great metaphysical systems. But who will regret it? Without remorse and without futile nostalgia we must return to philosophy its pure critical function. The philosopher always arrives on the scene after the event, after life, after history, after the datum. He can only recapture what is already there, the meaning already proposed and already established. Whether we like it or not, we can continue philosophy only as *culturalists* and *institutionalists*. The time has passed when culture could be considered the extension or slightly altered transposition of nature. Indeed, such an attitude was an illusion even on the first day of what we call civilization. Man knows nature only in humanizing it; he knows only a nature that is already humanized. Even members of primitive societies could not dissociate the natural from the cultural, since they could live only by arranging time and space to their convenience. Let us set before us, then, the fact of language, of the great collective myths, of the arts, the sciences, and the religions. To study them, to analyze and judge them is the task of the philosopher. It belongs to him to give an account not of ideas alone, but also of institutions, understanding this term in its broadest sense. Religion is one institution among others. We do not see why the philosopher should scrutinize all save that one. Resentment or false respect have nothing in common with an attitude of reflection. If we turn again to religion with an unprejudiced eye, with sympathy and complete independence, we will give to one side an example of objectivity and to the other an example of intellectual courage. To both we will give a lesson in calmness and integrity.

4. PHILOSOPHY OF RELIGION AND THEOLOGY

All theologies have the following characteristics in common: theological research is carried on in the light of faith; it relies on Scripture and on its authorized commentary, tradition; and finally, from the Middle Ages on, it has consciously undertaken to mediate the experience of faith with the help of philosophy.[1]

These three characteristics stand out quite clearly when compared with the opposite procedures of philosophy. It would be worth our while to make this comparison point by point.

(1) To reflect while enlightening one's judgment in the *lumen fidei* is not necessarily to be more than a man, as Descartes maliciously suggested, for faith itself is within man. Nevertheless, it is to admit that, on a certain plane, man can dispose himself to enter into the mystery of God and assume the obligation of affirming nothing or doing nothing that would harm his participation or this communion. Doubtless, this participation is obscure. It escapes direct analysis, and cannot be reduced to any other experience known and described by science or by philosophy. It is specific and defies all reduction. Despite this act, or rather because of it, it is an experience to be respected. Those who do not have it have no right to say it does not exist, since others have experienced it and attest to its existence. To deny faith as an attitude or experience *sui generis,* on the pretext that we cannot obtain it at will and that we are unable to obtain it *in order to see* would be, *mutatis mutandis,* tantamount to denying the esthetic experience because one has not experienced it himself and cannot call it up by simple command. One might object that, in the case of the esthetic experience, there are at least works of art as objective signs. Yes, but the exterior evidences of religion are just as obvious everywhere. These also could be the sign that numerous individuals and entire groups, in the most varied situations, have experienced religious values. Before saying that such people are laboring under an illusion, it is necessary to study

[1] In our times, there are some exceptions to this last-mentioned rule. They are not necessarily happy ones. The fathers themselves had at least an implicit philosophy. To return to them without returning to their philosophical presuppositions, whether to assume them or to criticize them, would be to interpret them in a manner different from that in which they understood themselves.

their experience such as they claim to live it and in the sense in which they say that they live it. Thus the philosopher of religion can seek a sympathetic understanding of religion, at the same time he is trying to establish its legitimacy under certain conditions. Thus also the philosopher of religion cannot object to the legitimate effort of believers to "reflect" their own experience starting from their central conviction which is, as it were, the creative intuition of their style of life and thought. For believers, to reflect in the light of faith is simply to recapture the totality of their particular beliefs in the unity of their prime intuition. Although there are many articles of faith, there is only one creed.

Besides, the *lumen fidei,* which we can picture to ourselves as an illumination superadded to intellectual illumination, is not a new object in the mind, but a new mental apprehension.[2] This apprehension or, to use Husserl's language, this *noesis,* is evidently linked to an object, to a *noema;* but the latter does not remain within psychological immanence. It remains outside, in the world and in history. Faith is related to certain facts that it interprets; it is not subjective, but objectifying. However, its objectification is unparalleled in kind: through certain fact-events or accounts of events, it perceives the mystery of God as present in humanity. The *lumen fidei* is thus not an additional faculty or organ attributed to consciousness, but a *perspective opened towards a situation.* That is why, as we shall show, the theologian who is guided by the light of the *lumen fidei* necessarily refers to the Bible, to Tradition, to the Church, to everything that determines a common situation and experience, by letter or by word.

The philosopher is deprived of these resources. For light he has only that furnished by his reason. And he endeavors to give an account of all that concerns man without making use of any

---

[2] This corrects the schemas of exteriority: one apprehension is not superadded to another; it transforms it from within.

special intuition that would provide him with new modes of perceiving and evaluating. Likewise, he does not intend to place himself *a priori* in a privileged situation that would serve as a key to all human situations. Nor does he profit from the collective assistance of a society which, in pursuing the same values, serves as a guide and support to all its members. In short, the philosopher, as philosopher, assumes his responsibilities without any assistance foreign to his own reflection. The rest depends on the idea we have formed of philosophy—whether as a method of critical discernment or as a dogmatism having jurisdiction over a sector of truths. We have chosen the first formula. If philosophy is to be universal it must remain reflective. This does not imply that it should remain an empty framework, purely ideal, without any grasp on a concrete given. On the contrary, philosophy has a content, one that is so extensive it cannot be monopolized by any particular object. Its content is life as a whole, human activities in all their variety and their totality (not excepting religion). It includes everything, which precludes the choice of any one type of activity or of reality as its own special subject matter. Otherwise, it would be only one particular science among others. It would then be like theology, which specializes in the criticism and development of certain values to the exclusion of others because of an order of evidence which is reserved to it alone. Of course, this privilege restores a certain universality to theology since, as St. Thomas says, faith can judge all the sciences from the point of view of the needs of salvation, even though it cannot establish their principles. This we maintain philosophy can do, for it possesses the epistemological sovereignty that St. Thomas also mentions,[3] even though theology retaliates by claiming for itself the soteriological primacy on the level of faith.

(2) A second difference between philosophy and theology is equally clear. The philosopher applies his reflection to the whole

[3] Q. 1, a. 6, 2.

110

range of the human given,[4] as we have just seen, but in order to elucidate its meaning on his own responsibility, without drawing from a deposit in which this meaning may have been inscribed or might be preserved. The theologian, on the other hand, thinks only while in contact with Scripture,[5] and if he is a Roman Catholic, while in contact with tradition and the ecclesiastical magisterium.[6] As M. D. Chenu says, "theology is the science of a book, the book of books, the Bible"; it has a text for its basis. This, we believe, has promoted the parallelism we mentioned before between theology and rational science. As the philosopher studies nature or the order of creation in terms of the sensible world, so the theologian has undertaken to study supernature or the order of grace in terms of that spiritual universe which is the Bible. The correspondence that the authors of the Middle Ages established between Scripture and nature, the book written within and the book written without, is not simply an ingenious comparison founded on the laws of symbolism. It is a methodological procedure according to which Scripture is to be to theology

[4] He accepts it as properly given only in returning to that which produced it, that is, to the conditions that allow one to understand it and evaluate it correctly. Just as philosophy, according to Hamelin, begins by eliminating the thing in itself, so we might say that the philosophy of religion begins with the elimination of a given that is only given, that is, a reality which reason must admit without being able to recapture its laws of constitution.

[5] "Sacred teaching or theology," writes E. Gilson, "properly exists only as *included* in Sacred Scripture; it is only when we wish to conceive of it in itself and cut off from its scriptural source that the problem of their relations becomes inextricable" (*Le thomisme,* p. 21, n. 1). That is why there is no opposition between theology as the word of God and theology as a science of the faith. Through Scripture, they coincide.

[6] From a Catholic point of view, tradition and the magisterium only interpret Scripture. As the product of the religious community, Scripture remains at its service; the community has authority over it. If the community does not modify it this is, as we have said, because the Church of the second century recognized in the text of the Scriptures the exact expression of its faith. Protestants object that once the definitive form of this text was decided in the second century, it should be adhered to literally. To this the Catholics reply that to adhere to it, even literally, involves promoting the religious attitudes defined by the letter; thus there exists dogmatic growth without modification of the deposit of the faith.

111

what nature is to philosophy. Yet the difference becomes apparent immediately: nature offers itself to the senses and to the reason without their having to choose it as object, whereas Scripture offers itself to the faith on a religious plane only insofar as the faithful discern it as matter or medium of faith. Read by an unbeliever, the Bible is a text like any other, like a dialogue of Plato or a *Upanishad*. Read by a believer, it becomes revelatory in the strict sense, the bearer of divine revelation. Thus faith alone discovers in the depths of the written word a specific spirit that no profane eye can perceive. Consequently, the bond between Scripture and faith is entirely different from that between nature and reason, not only because they do not belong on the same plane of consciousness, but also because Scripture, instead of being an inductive starting point for theology as nature is for philosophy, is in reality a deductive starting point. The theologian does not begin with Scripture until after he has recognized it as the bearer of the Word of God. In other words, he first places it in the order of faith, thus giving it authority over his intelligence, and then has only to draw out the consequences of its teachings. His method is *hypothetico-deductive*:[7] it consists in discriminating the given with which he will begin —giving it a privileged status and raising it to the order of evidence at which he wishes to establish himself[8]—and then proceeding from it to draw consequences all of which are of the same sort, all of which involve faith. This is a legitimate method, considering the ends it pursues and the services it renders.

The fact remains that the theologian, unlike the philosopher, imposes a limit on the investigation of his point of departure. He does not attempt a radical reassessment of his foundations. By

[7] George Gusdorf noticed this hypothetico-deductive characteristic. See *Mythe et métaphysique* [Paris, 1953], p. 166. But we may find him a bit austere concerning the use of reason in the service of the faith.

[8] This movement by which we raise ourselves to the level of the faith could be an inference, inductive knowledge through signs (beginning, for example, with the Judeo-Christian religious fact). But once faith is born, the dialectic becomes a descending process.

the act of faith he decides the general meaning of the given which he receives. Then he exploits this given and searches its implications in detail while remaining in strict accord with the general sense. The paradox is that this given, whether Scripture or tradition, has been developed by man.[9] Yet the believer and the theologian read in it direct divine inspiration. Nothing is more characteristic of this method than that it does not stop at intermediaries but goes straight to its goal. The religious consciousness employs mediations but it wastes no time in finding out who fashioned them. It hastens to make use of them so as to grasp that which they mediate. An analysis of this phenomenon can help us to understand in what respect the philosophical mind and the theological mind remain very different.

Let us suppose that a philosopher and a theologian are studying Scripture. The task for the former is long, while for the latter it is short. The theologian contents himself with affirming that the Scripture is the Word of God and therefore that it brings us his message. Thus we ought to accept Scripture and conform our behavior to it. The philosopher, as a philosopher of religion, cannot proceed so quickly with his task. His purpose is not to sanction a religious tradition as such but to understand and evaluate rationally the matter in hand. Now it is obvious that the synthetic judgment: Bible = Word of God, which is a simple premise for the theologian, is an extremely complex conclusion in the eyes of the philosopher—so complex that once the analysis is complete, he acknowledges that of himself he cannot effect the synthesis. Since he has to take apart the mechanism of belief piece by piece, the philosopher advances laboriously towards a point to which the theologian arrived with no difficulty in a single flight. The Bible appears to him as a witness to a religious experience lived by a group. It sums up a long cultural and spiritual evolution, and bears the traces of different moments in this evolution. It is homogeneous in the sense that the religious

[9] This does not minimize its transcendent origin through the immanence of human situations and human awareness.

evolution which it relates progresses towards a determinate end, but it is not homogeneous either from the point of view of its composition or of its schemata or structures of thought. At any rate, it exists only because men, a select few submerged in the masses, took the initiative of certain moral and religious attitudes. Of these attitudes it is the expression and witness. It is worth whatever the perspectives of faith formulated with it are worth. If these had not seemed admirable to the group, they would not have been recorded nor preserved. A living faith was required to begin the process of composition and the same faith was required to carry it on. It was faith that dictated and faith that respected, honored, even adapted and interpreted what was fixed. Thus we return to the religious experience as lived in history, which is the source of all the products which have remained faithful to it. However, this first experience could have been lived only according to the familiar processes of sacred symbolism and mysticism which the history of religions and critical philosophy can restore in their authenticity. Thus the philosopher understands what the theologian expresses in an abbreviated form; thus he understands the meaning of the anthropomorphisms: Word of God, revelation, inspiration, and the like. He understands that these are ways of representing the theandric relationship, which remains spiritual in nature. Better still, he understands that these categories or schemata tell the story of actual steps humanity had to undertake in an area of the Near East in order to find a purer religious style, in order to create higher religious values.[10] The theologian will continue to speak the language of divine immediatism. The critic, on his part, can speak only the language of historical immanence and human mediatism. In fact, for him who is able to situate the two points

[10] The critic is inclined to become a relativist when he notices that Judeo-Christianity derives from a tribal religion and takes up a few millenniums in a history that perhaps includes more than five hundred. In truth, however, neither time nor geographical limitations have anything to do with the matter. There could have been more philosophy in Socrates' head and more religion in Jesus' heart than have ever existed in any part of the world. It is a question of quality, not quantity or amount of influence.

of view, the same meaning underlies both terminologies. But the philosopher is the only one who knows both sides, and thus we can understand how it is that the theologian, who considers himself betrayed and misunderstood, very often cannot help suspecting the philosopher of profanation or irreligion.

The theologian takes short cuts to arrive at God, just as the believer does. The way he uses Scripture and Tradition, taking them as the starting point of his reasoning without seeing that these notions are themselves the results of the constructive efforts of spontaneous thought, proves how much theological discipline depends on anticipation in the service of religious experience, rather than on retrospection in the service of critical thought.[11] This is by no means a reproach. No one can take it ill that faith should wish to promote faith.

(3) However, despite all the differences between the behavior of the theologian and that of the philosopher, theology assumes a definite form and is truly systematized only when it borrows its logical apparatus from philosophy. Now, this seems to involve a wager on the theologian's part, and raises several problems. Since we can touch on them only very lightly, we shall be satisfied with pointing out some methodological difficulties. First of all, there is a problem involved in passing from an article of faith to a theological conclusion. There is also a problem in passing a scriptural formula to an abstract idea, and from a personal and interpersonal (ecclesial) experience of faith to a methodical systematization that involves particular philosophical choices.

The passage from an article of faith to a theological conclusion is not the theologian's only pursuit, nor even his primary one. His first concern is to grasp the given of faith as a whole, to note each of the affirmations which it involves and to bind them harmoniously together. All this can be effected, if not without

---

[11] It is evident that if the theologian is also an historian or a critic, he is aware of the "constructed" character of Scripture and Tradition. Nevertheless, it suffices for him as a theologian to know that revelation is the word of God.

reflection,[12] at least without incorporating a particular philosophy into the theological given. But on the contrary, once we try to recoup this given through rational propositions, as when we attempt to make a minor react to a major premise, we seem to be trying to clarify transcendent truths with purely human truths. From then on, do not the premises become heterogeneous? And is not the resulting conclusion overdrawn? The theological reasoning would then be tainted or strained by definition.

Theologians do not agree on the solution to be adopted. Some hold that the theological conclusion remains in the order of faith; others, that it is essentially rational. We ought, it seems, to agree with the former, for it is difficult to see how an evidence of the faith can transform itself into an evidence of reason.[13] But the difficulty only appears again. The philosophical minor premise we added to the major premise of faith could not validly take hold of it unless it was assimilated by it, that is, unless it changed its nature and ceased to be philosophical. We must admit then that the philosophy used by the theologian loses its autonomy and even its intrinsic quality. From a metaphysical reason it becomes a theological one. This does not mean that it ceases to be true, but rather that henceforth it is considered only from a soteriological point of view. In fact, we can attest that theologians use philosophical ideas very freely, and for their own proper purpose, namely, to guide men towards their salvation. We may thus consider that to pass from articles of faith to theological conclusions, *via philosophiae,* is not to rationalize the faith but to order it discursively with the help of middle terms which serve as guides, and which have been borrowed from philosophy but which were immediately transposed and assumed into an extra-philosophical perspective. In other words,

12 The least *auditus fidei* requires a minimum of *intellectus fidei.*

13 It is certain that a non-believer could try his hand at drawing correct theological conclusions. But this would be a purely formal effort, since only an effective act of faith opens the religious mind to scriptural formulas or dogmatic propositions.

what is borrowed from philosophy plays only a functional role. It is a technological tool, which helps the mind to grasp the given of faith by explicating it in successive propositions, but which adds nothing substantial to it.[14] Furthermore, and on the same grounds, the philosophical middle term thus employed is not strengthened in its metaphysical truth by the fact of its theological use. The theologian sanctions it as *useful* but he does not make it any more philosophically. Only a philosophical demonstration verifies a philosophical assertion.

The passage from a scriptural formula to an abstract concept is indeed delicate, but less difficult to explain. It poses only a problem of language and translation. Chenu has posed this problem very well in an article entitled "Vocabulaire biblique et

[14] Nevertheless, a certain relativity is introduced here. The recourse to philosophy involves a risk of error that recourse to faith could not involve in the eyes of the believer. It is not without utility to point out that this recourse to philosophy is often effected implicitly, even where it is not mentioned. When the theologian seeks to gain understanding of his experience of faith he attempts two steps: (1) he endeavors to clarify the interchange between the experience of religious values and the historical features of tradition or of institutions—features whose interpretation, one way or the other, conditions the access to orthodox faith; (2) he connects his experience of the sacred with certain rational hypotheses, which he must use to think discursively. Thus a twofold relativity creeps into the theologian's research, either in the way he decides that signs are perceived (according to the theory of knowledge he adopts), or by the way he establishes or links his theological affirmations together with the help of rational principles more or less critically founded (depending on the ontology or epistemology that he uses). At any rate, there is the *choice* of a philosophy, and from this choice there flows the tonality and even the solidity of each theology. If the theologian keeps in mind that the rigor of his system is established within the limits of his philosophical hypotheses, no one can object. But it happens that he takes his methodological point of departure as an absolute, and on the whole comes to believe as much in his philosophy as in his faith. This is a misunderstanding of the two orders. We can find in Ulrich de Strasbourg (see E. Gilson, *La philosophie au moyen âge*, 2nd. ed., Paris, 1944, p. 517) this conviction that the articles of faith are substantiated by their rational first principles, which are universally valid. St. Bonaventure took an exactly opposite stand, which George Tavard has summarized as follows: "After the exposition of faith, theology undertakes to prove it not by an appeal to rational certitudes, but by having recourse to faith itself" (*L'Année théologique*, 10th year [1949], fasc. II–III, pp. 212–213).

vocabulaire théologique."[15] Its solution was already given in the thirteenth century by the theologians who had to transpose the scriptural metaphors into Aristotelian concepts.[16] It consists roughly in this: the formulas from Scripture provide the starting point and because of this remain regulatory.[17] Beginning with them, we can search for corresponding ideas in human disciplines. If we find any, we are permitted to adopt them, remodeling and adapting them as need requires. The indispensable condition for passing from one to the other is that each idea can be clearly formulated and a precise relationship be established between them. The theologian endeavors to establish a semantic comparison[18] and to find out if a particular biblical idea and a particular philosophical (or scientific) idea can exchange content. This involves some risks but, since faith is supreme, it is in principle sufficiently perspicacious to control the transpositions from language to language.[19] As a last resort, there is the magisterium to settle any dispute.

Nevertheless from the philosopher's point of view, this procedure remains unusual. The biblical categories are drawn from a mentality totally different from the philosophical mentality. The religious man who expresses himself in the Bible is the pre-reflective *homo loquens,* while the religious man who expresses

[15] *Nouvelle revue théologique,* 84th year, t. 74., no. 10 (December, 1952), pp. 1029–1041.

[16] As a matter of fact, the Councils had already formulated the dogmas with the help of philosophical concepts: substance, person, nature, and the like, which cannot be found in this form in Scripture. Their initiative furnishes the proof that the passage from spontaneous language to learned language without detriment to the native expression of faith seemed possible to them.

[17] St. Thomas explains why they express the spiritual under the guise of corporeal things. He refers to Dionysius the Areopagite, but at the same time, appeals to his theory of abstraction (see q. 1, a. 9 resp., trans. cit., pp. 54–55).

[18] We only wish that this comparison were founded on a preliminary critique of all language.

[19] Faith has proved this in the Fourth Gospel, in which it successfully united the ideas of *messiah* and of *logos.*

his thoughts in theology is the reflective *homo sapiens,* the man of philosophical epistemology. Hence the question arises as to how the reflective can be substituted for the pre-reflective without betraying the latter. To this we must reply that only an abstractive and ultimately unreal rationalism dissolves the human "situations." A philosophy that is respectful of the real and attentive to the structures of incarnate consciousness and its projective mechanism is on guard against any reduction of the formulations through which spontaneous thought proceeds. It preserves such structures, understands them and saves them. For once there is human experience, however crude, spiritual values are already present and can be refined and recovered. It is true that rational investigation of myths attempts to distinguish their form from their content, and this might lead to the belief that one can be separated from the other. But in reality, no such disjunction is possible. The whole meaning is attached to that which expresses it and cannot be disincarnated. At most it can be transposed, provided that its original expression be assumed and transmuted without being destroyed or contradicted. No schema and no image, however poor or awkward it may be, is devoid of value when it is taken on its own level, in its own function and in its own context. The passage from the biblical element to the conceptual element in theology is one of the best proofs that mentalities and cultures are fundamentally homogeneous. Perhaps we can see in this an illustration of the forgotten truth that the language of life and the language of science (in the broad sense of the word) are but two ways of recreating the natural world, and of establishing a cultural universe in which man can find himself everywhere at home.[20] Wherever there is

[20] Gaston Bachelard's method of relating the symbolism of the sciences to the myths of the natural elements is well known. They are two aspects of a single "function of unreality" which allows consciousness to free itself from things to the extent that it engages itself with them. See Jean Hyppolite, "Gaston Bachelard ou le romantisme de l'intelligence," *Revue philosophique,* t. CXLIV (1954), pp. 85–96.

a man, there is meaning; and whenever there is meaning, man can always recognize himself in it.

* * *

The theologian says that Jesus is the incarnate Word. The philosopher and the historian, for their part, cannot make this equation. If they do not reflect on what this dogma implies, what intellectual, moral, and religious presumptions it supposes, they will not understand what the theologian means to say. Perhaps they will congratulate him on his gift of second sight, but they will remain a little baffled by it. To make matters worse, the theologian will not always know how to explain to them in their language the why and the wherefore of his position. The conversation will be a dialogue among the deaf, and the discussion will not get very far. The philosopher of religion, on the other hand, as a critic, can show that Jesus obviously could not himself profess the Christology of Ephesus and of Chalcedon, but that the Christian consciousness was gradually led to understand that, if Jesus is truly the Messiah as the Synoptics believe and the *Logos* as the prologue to the Fourth Gospel asserts, then he is truly God present, living, and incarnate among us (Emmanuel has this same meaning). Why is the Messiah, the *Logos,* God rather than his delegate, his representative, or his minister? Because for the religious mind there can be no difference between the God who reveals himself and the Revealer of God. The problem, in short, is no longer to prove that the Revealer of God is God (this conclusion is here self-evident), but rather to know if one will or will not choose Christ as the revealer. The choice in this matter is free; it can be affected only by a personal initiative, by an understanding in depth which recovers the connection effected by the apostolic community between the fact of Jesus and its messianic or sacral interpretation. Supposing that Christ is deliberately acknowledged as revealer, his history judged as holy, his attitude theophanic (it is important to note that these affirmations are made only if the life of Jesus is considered to admit of such a meaning, which means that it already contains it), the judgment that *Christ is God* will follow after a more or less lengthy development. Evidently, the series of equations which maintains that Christ is the revealer of God and that the revealer is God revealing himself could have been formulated in a culture other than Greek metaphysics. In fact, however, it was formulated there. Christology then spoke a language that was substantive rather than functional and empiricist rather than spiritual, and Spinoza was confused by this fact. But the phenomenologists of religion who are undertaking to prove that the incarnation of the Word and theophany, revelation and hierophany[21] are basically interchangeable categories, help us to understand what the reworking of the fact of Jesus by the New Testament and the Fathers means. It is nothing but the recognition of Jesus as the revealer, and of the Revealer as the manifestation and presence of the Revealed himself. In order to take this step, even informed pre-critical thought quickly has recourse to schemes based on contingency and to chronomorphisms (preëxistence of the Word, incarnation subsequent to the accident of the fall, and so on). But these are only auxiliary procedures which can be reduced, transposed, defended, and retrieved. I would demonstrate this fact if this were the place to do so.

As a further example: the theologian wants us to demonstrate the existence of God and at the same time declares that God is transcendent. The philosopher asks himself how it is possible to combine this insertion of God within a chain of formal reasoning (God then becomes one determination in a series of determinations) with the divine transcendence and simplicity, not to mention the fact that the idea of a transcendent immediately evokes a spatial imagination of height, as Brunschvicg has pointed out. But the philosopher of religion could, it seems to

---

[21] Of course, the Christian hierophany extends to the end of the process. It is capable of individualizing the theophany and of bringing about its culmination at the very moment in which it involves something which cannot be surpassed and which is normative.

me, offer two explanations. On the one hand, transcendence is a schema, an index, a raising of one's sights and not an attribute or a predicate of which God is directly the subject. On the other hand, if it is legitimate to require the formulation of every attempt to grasp pure Unity or Freedom as the term of an intentionality too rich to be enclosed within the immanence of determined values, there will be less risk of reducing God to an idea similar to others or to an ultimate determination. If God exists, he can be only the One, rigorously simple, bare of any determination, pure energy, perfect spontaneity, aseity. Thus we may seek to know how consciousness can aspire to him. No doubt, we will come to see that it can only be as a radical Presence, so radical that it is not numerically distinct from the spirit in which it plants itself, but rather posits that spirit in allowing it to posit itself, creates it as self-creative. At all events, consciousness will not intend God as an object, nor as a thing, nor as a concept. Ruyssen himself was wrong, I believe, in confusing the problem of God with a simple investigation of psychic schemata, indeed of psychoanalytical instances, which consciousness can discover within the problem and which it uses (with more or less success) to explain to itself its quest for the Absolute. The question is not so much the aggregate of procedures employed for this purpose, but rather the very fact of a spiritual need which nothing can satisfy—the power man possesses to challenge everything—nature, his own limitations, the entire order of the finite. This is also the reason why proof of God ought to be neither formal nor positive, but intentional, active, and negative (apophatic). The theologian as well as the philosopher will have reason to be satisfied. But on the condition that the philosopher of religion intervene in order to transpose into his critical register what too many theologians ambiguously maintain on the borderline between religious research and an entirely unexpected rationalism.

I have presented these examples merely as suggestions while refraining from any involvement in the numerous side issues which it would be worthwhile to describe in detail and develop, as I shall do elsewhere. There are always surprises in store for the critic in these matters, and they fairly swarm with paradoxes, not the least of which lies in the fact that religion holds at once for a formless God and for an Absolute of dialogue. I cannot dwell on this point, but I hope I have convinced the reader that the theologian's language baffles philosophers only insofar as they are unable to discover in what the theologian is saying, what he means to say. As far as he is concerned, the theologian knows very well what his words mean to his own practical activities and to those of believers. He does not always know his meaning critically, nor need he. The philosopher of religion, for his part, understands the game *without substituting another meaning for the religious meaning held by the theologian.* He can clarify this meaning methodically and critically. Hegel had this idea and we would be ready to adopt his position were it not that he believed that religion philosophically understood was worth more than religion actually lived, indeed that the former could dispense from the latter. For us, all things being equal, to understand and to practice religion is worth more than to practice it without understanding it. But if it is to be understood, it must first of all be a living act. The formal transcript is only a representation of it. It does not take its place, and as a copy it cannot be superior to the original. The philosopher of religion can no more eliminate religion than the idea of action, as Blondel has pointed out, can replace action. It throws light on it, however, and that is not unimportant. But if it unravels its meaning, it does not establish its value, even when it defines the conditions of its validity. In a word, it is not religion. Religion continues to carry on its operations at the level of spontaneous thought, prior to reflexive recovery—or rather, subjacent to any reflexive recovery.

However, the very idea of a philosophy of religion is not as yet wholeheartedly accepted. Theologians are suspicious of it because of unfortunate precedents. Philosophers themselves are skeptical and take it for a theology in disguise. Was not Hegel accused of attempting an apology for Christianity? Actually, the theologian has nothing to fear from a criticism of religion which seeks to understand, and not to dissolve the religious object. And the philosopher would be wrong to consider impossible a rational treatment of the categories and schemata of religion. This would suggest that reason does not have universal jurisdiction; that it can reach all save certain activities of man. It would be more sensible to let the philosophy of religion proceed at its own risk and to judge it by tests and by evidence. In such a case, I believe, we would see at least one happy result. Theologies which are falsely metaphysical and falsely scientific would gradually disappear. The philosopher would denounce their collusion as confusion. At the same time, the totalitarian rationalistic systems, which cannot distinguish between reflection and action, formal and concrete thought, abstract determinations and values in act— these also will retreat. The philosopher of religion will not fail to show that *homo religiosus* is never eclipsed by the *homo philosophicus*. For the latter can meditate only on the creations of spontaneous man, on the initiatives he takes and the values he posits. Thus neither theologian nor philosopher will deviate from his role. Each will see more clearly and judge that much more soundly.

By this very fact, the discussion of religious matters will be facilitated. Few professional philosophers read theologians, and indeed, in some cases, they are unreadable for philosophers. Theologians understand each other, but to an uninitiated philosopher they always appear to make gratuitous or arbitrary assertions.[22] For their thought to be comprehensible and their

[22] We should never be in a hurry to say that an author is making affirmations without any reason. Theologians formed in the scholastic method are intellectual strategists of the first order. Their positions are firm, and always very logically deduced. Within their specialty, they are perhaps to be preferred to supple and brilliant minds who dilute their ideas in place of defining them and gathering them into a system. The great theologians have sometimes been portrayed as palaces of abstraction—solemn, but empty and useless. This is exaggerated and unjust. Their dialectical vigor is undeniable

demonstrations plausible, a constant restatement of the question, a change in register is necessary for the sake of philosophers. Only the critic, only the philosopher of religion can effect these transpositions. It is true that for him this is only a part of his work. The essential part of his effort should bear on the religious object itself. It should be geared, not first and foremost to the religious sciences whatever they may be, but to the living religious man. It is only by beginning with him and by remaining in contact with him, that the philosopher will understand the meaning of cultic *believing* and *acting,* and the system of representations derived from them. Philosophers, scientists, and intellectuals will usually do better to consult the results of this work of elucidation than to read theological treatises, which they often understand badly. Frequently I hear non-theologians speak ironically of theological ideas which in all good faith they objectivize and distort. For their sake, it would be useful first of all to present these ideas in their proper light in order to be able to appreciate them correctly. Otherwise, they will continue to think that original sin is an affront to personal responsibility, Christian soteriology a worn-out myth of expiation by blood, the sacraments a bit of magic, the eucharistic communion—it has been so described—a cannibal piety, and so on.

Nevertheless, the air of the philosopher of religion is not to write a catechism for unbelievers nor to get atheists to ask for baptism. He is neither a theologian, nor an apologist, nor a recruiter. It is just that before coming to any decision he wants to understand and to make others understand. And when he has

---

and, more than that, they are a mine of ideas. For the man who wishes to make use of them, these systems become extraordinary conveyors of intuitions or of arguments. It is well known that German philosophy has almost always developed against a theological background. To a lesser degree, this is also true of French philosophy. Following Plato, Plutarch had already recommended that rational teaching be drawn from the religious traditions. This is proof that theology, taken in its most general sense, can offer immense services to philosophy. It is possible that, in scorning theology, many intellectuals remain ignorant of how much their thought owes theology. The seminary of St. Sulpice, Renan used to say, knows what religion is, but the Ecole Polytechnique never will.

understood, he allows consciences to decide freely for or against on their own responsibility. The act of faith is obligatory only for those spirits who declare on their own initiative: *credibile,* hence *credendum.* But these two steps are not within the province of the philosopher of religion. His independence remains complete, like that of any other philosopher.

5. PHILOSOPHY OF RELIGION AND ITS METHOD:
IMMANENT REFLECTION
UPON THE EXPERIENCE OF THE TRANSCENDENT

There is no doubt that Blondel understands the idea of the supernatural to be taken from Christian tradition. The philosopher does not invent it, he receives it. It is the theologian who teaches him of it. That is why Blondel declares that he is talking of the supernatural as defined by orthodox Christian tradition. By what right does he take such an acquired, borrowed and imported idea out of its original context in order to transplant it into philosophy? That is the point to be clarified here.

At first sight, Bondel seems to have accepted the idea of the supernatural because it corresponds to a felt need. It expresses a human aspiration, and gives a name to a need felt for something over and above[1] the natural. But we shall see that we must avoid any psychological interpretation of these formulas. It is not sufficient to examine consciousness in order to find in it the demand of the supernatural.[2] The majority of men would fail

[1] Blondel, *Lettre, Annales de philosophie chrétienne,* vol. XXXIII, October 1895–March 1896, p. 610.

[2] It is useless to try to establish empirically that there is a "trace of the supernatural in man purely as man." This is not the philosopher's task, and introspection is uncertain. As to the interpretation of exterior signs, this has to do with the subject in a particular situation, and not with a reflection on the necessary. The only thing the philosopher can properly do with such a problem is to graft on to the experience of insufficiency (such as we shall analyze it) a theory of a possible surplus, in order to try to free action from the predicament into which it has fallen. The

to undertake such an examination. Furthermore, to do so would be to go outside the realm of philosophy, for the full discernment of the supernatural is reserved to faith alone. We must take on the eyes of faith if we are to decipher it in consciousness. Besides, the believer himself does not resort to such direct procedure, since it would not be without equivocation. It is through the Church, in listening to its message (*ex auditu*), that he becomes conscious of the amplitude of his destiny, of the full extent of his action. The external act, if we adopt the language of Cardinal Deschamps, precedes the internal act. When these come together, faith is born. In other words, the testimony serves to clarify religious concern, to *decipher* it, qualify it, and make it fruitful. There could be nothing more pretentious or more vain than a subjectivism of the religious inspiration which would also be a psychologism of the faith, that is, a state of belief without any universal criterion, an impressionist fervor lacking both control and stability. But if the believer himself, looking as it were with naked eye, does not discern within himself his vocation to the supernatural, how could the philosopher directly observe the signs of it?[3] Blondel

---

philosopher can do no more than this, nor is it his task to do more. It remains for the living consciousness to do the rest. To ask ourselves why we find ourselves confronted with an action that experiences the insufficiency of everything, and not with an action that finds its sufficiency in the natural order, is simply idle. Our world raises enough problems to keep us busy. It is useless to resolve those of another world, except to point out the contrasts that would help us to understand our own. But the fact remains that action, as it expresses itself to reflection, necessarily calls for a philosophy of insufficiency and a philosophy of a possible surplus. That is why Blondel holds that reflection on action, if it is developed according to this double necessity, legislates for all individuals, whether they know it or not and whether they consent to recognize it or not, the factual reality of a supra-human assistance. "There is no philosophy but that which precedes, includes, and surpasses these distinctions" (*Lettre, Annales*, XXXIII, p. 612).

[3] There are many signs of the presence of the supernatural, but they are signs inscribed in history and not in subjective psychology. Besides, even these signs have a double meaning (*Lettre, Annales*, XXXIII, pp. 345–346). This ambiguity of the sign does not destroy its value. Quite the contrary, it stimulates consciousness to rise to the level of evidence that the

never claimed for philosophy a perspicacity of this sort, for this would be the worst possible naturalization of the supernatural.[4] On the other hand, the modern philosopher comes after centuries of Christianity. He lives in the midst of a civilization permeated with Christian influences and ideas. He cannot, therefore, be unaware of the idea of the supernatural. The fact is that he sometimes repels it, distrusts it, and declares it null and void without being able to prevent its being already there, around him, in him, pressing upon his thought. He is asked to consider it and examine it carefully lest he distort it. It is unnecessary to ask him where it came from. The answer has already been given.

Thus the question of origin is settled. Far from deriving the idea of the supernatural from its roots by psychological analysis, the philosopher receives it from Christian teaching. All attempts to show that Blondel studies man in the concrete and discovers this idea in him because *de facto* man is destined for the supernatural are thus misguided.[5] They are based on texts which deviate from the main line of his thought.[6] The truth is that even historical man, considered in his real essence, does not by virtue of this essence bear within him any evident trace of the supernatural *on the psycho-empirical level.* For no purely sensible or purely objective mark of the supra-sensible exists. On the contrary, if we take man "in situation" within the framework of our civilization; if we grasp the ties of his psychology and the whole of his cultural context; if we realize that what he knows or even what he is arises from what is revealed to him day by day by a reflection nourished by a thousand social influences (of

---

intended object allows. Ambiguity is here a summons to purify oneself, to adapt oneself, and to fulfill the conditions of an authentic knowledge.

[4] "Were we to draw the supernatural as a forced conclusion from natural premises, as the condemned doctrine of semi-rationalism tried to do, we should no longer be orthodox" (*Lettre, Annales,* XXXIII, p. 470).

[5] Actually, as we have explained, philosophy for Blondel does not deal with the question of fact (*Lettre, Annales,* XXXIII, pp. 609, 613).

[6] Under the influence of certain theologians and to ward off certain attacks, Blondel finally came to hold this thesis. He betrayed his own method, however, by including an element of fact within the philosophical analysis.

an intellectual, moral, and religious nature) and governed and dominated by a personal intention; and if, finally, we understand that the orientation of his life depends on everything that is thus revealed to him, and that he must judge everything, all that comes from within and all that comes from without, in order to decide how to act; then of this man, who is neither an abstract essence nor a concretely and completely determined nature,[7] but who is our very self, a conscious and free being, civilized, informed, and heir of the conquests of western thought,[8] then of this man, I say, we can declare in all justice that he possesses the notion of the supernatural.[9] Did he acquire it? Did he invent it? Both, for in the interaction of the cultural and the individual, to receive and to understand, to accept and to discover are the same thing. It is man's historical situation, not his historical essence that communicates to the philosopher, through culture and language, the idea of the supernatural.[10]

[7] Human nature, through the presence of freedom, remains intrinsically "open," which makes it *deifiable*. This thesis of man's openness to the supernatural is only one implication or one moment in Blondel's argument.

[8] In fact, Eastern thought needs the message of the Church in order to recover the exact equivalent of our notion of the supernatural. Does this require that it assimilate our culture? No one would pretend that it does without reservations, since the faith and the human problematics which convey it are not of the same order. Nevertheless, we must not deceive ourselves: before the transpositions from culture to culture could be effected, Christian preaching would already have infused the East with a considerable number of Western categories. Yet the desirable transpositions remain to be made. Nevertheless, it is not a question of orientalizing the faith for the sheer pleasure of de-Westernizing it. Rather faith should be allowed to take on all cultures, without neglecting any one of them.

[9] The uneducated person, who possesses neither secular nor religious culture, and has heard no echo of Christian teaching, is necessarily deprived of it in his consciousness. His case is analogous to that of the pagan, whose choice of the supernatural is made implicitly. The same holds for the man who is mistaken in his idea of the supernatural and sincerely rejects it because he has misunderstood it. Blondel always held that the acceptance of the divine gift can be effected in a hidden, anonymous, or pseudonymous way.

[10] Only those authors who understand the *historical essence* of man to be what phenomenology calls *man in situation* could claim to discover the idea of the supernatural within his concrete essence. But this language is ambiguous. We should never allow ourselves to think that man deduces from

Without the fact of Christianity, and without the Church, the historical situation would be different. But it is not our task to imagine a situation that does not exist; our job is to become aware of the present situation. Blondel always confronts the Christian fact as already constituted. Thanks to the soft and secret action of the Christian spirit,[11] philosophy has given up its totalitarian hegemony, its claims to be on a par with objects, life, and transcendence. Under its influence philosophy has learned to respect the irreplaceable initiatives of the spirit and the Absolute. Similarly, it is only because Christianity spreads through the world its teaching and belief in the supernatural that these can become a problem for the philosopher. In a word, for Blondel the idea of the supernatural results neither from a psychological experience nor from a psycho-metaphysical analysis. It is a datum furnished by religion.[12] However, we ought to reflect on this datum because philosophy, once it is aware of its own reflective nature, owes it to itself to reflect on religion as on all other activities of man.

Why now declare *necessary,* on a philosophical plane, this idea that the philosopher borrows from the theologian? Simply because "philosophy considers the supernatural only insofar as the notion of it is immanent in us."[13] The notion is "immanent," that is—let us mark it well—not placed in the mind as a witness to a supernatural experience, but rather inserted in the sequence of ideas that philosophical reflection must scrutinize in order to find out if they are coherent and capable of clarifying our action. *Immanent* is here the opposite of transcendent, and means that in any case the *reality* of the supernatural is a question apart,

---

his nature, even his actual nature, what he receives through social and cultural interchange. Or else we must make it clear that we identify the natural man and the cultural man, or better still, nature and nurture.

[11] *Lettre, Annales,* XXXIV (April–September, 1896), p. 346.

[12] Would the philosopher have discovered it without Christianity? This is a question that should not be asked. The only thing we have to say is that Christianity taught it to him.

[13] *Lettre, Annales,* XXXIV, p. 341.

belonging to another order, and transcendent to the idea we have of it. The philosopher can and ought to examine this notion, because he does not claim to know if any real existence corresponds to it. As we have mentioned, he takes his stand on an ideal plane, which can never substitute for the plane of actualizations. We need not then fear that philosophy will exceed its competence and postulate the supernatural as fact. This can neither be asked of philosophy nor accomplished by it in the real order. Philosophy is content to understand and to affirm the supernatural as a necessary idea.

What are we to understand by this last statement? Simply that philosophy cannot help establishing the supernatural as a hypothesis (a necessity for posing the problem), nor fail to recognize that this hypothesis is coherent (logical and formal necessity). In fact, as we know, at the end of its course, action nowhere finds its equilibrium in the natural order. It is important, then, to furnish it with a new idea as a working hypothesis or suggestion towards solution. If action is unable to bring itself to completion it becomes the philosopher's obligation to ask himself under what conditions its efforts could be brought to a close. Thus the philosopher comes to understand that God alone in his generosity could communicate his pure freedom to man, free him from his limitations and, in a single stroke, transport his *élan* to the infinite. The idea of the supernatural consists precisely in this. The philosopher henceforth assimilates this notion as representing and defining exactly what will bring the movement of action to completion.

In this the philosopher does nothing but what he does at each stage of action. Why, for example, must he place sensible intuition in the ideal series of conditions for action? Is it because sensation is a reality? Not at all, and we can explain why. Sensation, cut off from the psycho-spiritual experience, has no being in itself and is not a reality. It is only a partial condition, an aspect of the total act of the subject. Isolated from other aspects or from other conditions, it disappears. Its effectiveness lies ex-

131

clusively in the concrete subject who performs the total process which, through intermediaries, links sensation with the Absolute. Taken alone and reflected upon separately, it is only an abstraction. And nevertheless, this "abstraction" must enter into the series of conditions for acting, for on its own level, it can contribute to the understanding of action. The process employed here is analagous to that used in modern phenomenology. We put the question of being in brackets (but in Blondel's case the brackets will eventually be removed); we do not know whether sensations have or are being, or even whether sensations in fact exist. We retain only their structure, that is to say, the relation they necessarily express if they *exist*. Likewise, the thesis in *L'Action*[14] will examine sensible intuition in a structural, and

---

[14] Blondel himself sees a relationship between the content furnished by real sensation and that provided by effective revelation. Philosophy considers only the ideal structure of the one as of the other, structure being understood as the conditions which reason will require of them in order to recognize them as valuable if they exist. "Pure of all alloy, then, philosophy consists, no longer in the heteronomous application of reason to a matter or to an object, whether it be given [*really* given and not simply as an idea] by sense or by revelation, but in the autonomous application of reason to itself" (*Lettre, Annales*, XXXIV, p. 257). This "autonomous application of reason to itself" defines very well the method of immanence. For Blondel, every idea and every structure, whatever may be the object which might correspond to them in fact, properly belong to the immanence of rational reflection. (In the sense employed here, every object is called transcendent, that is—as Blondel explains in *Lettre, Annales*, XXXIV, pp. 142, 143— "heterogeneous" and "transcendent" to "the knowledge we have of them," and to "the reflective or philosophical view we have of them.") For "the immanent affirmation of the transcendent, even if this be of the supernatural, does not at all prejudge the transcendent reality of the immanent affirmations." This position, which we have met before, amounts simply to this: to affirm an object—we might better say to scrutinize or analyze the idea of an object—is not to prejudge either positively or negatively whether or not the idea in question corresponds to an effective reality. Here Blondel makes us think of Husserl with his two reductions: the eidetic, which allows us to examine essences independent of facts, and the phenomenological, which frees the subject of its pre-critical illusions and raises it to the level of authentic comprehension. Unfortunately, Blondel, who in certain areas surpassses Husserl, still uses a terminology which is insufficient and still impregnated with psychologism. (See *Lettre, Annales,* XXXIII, p. 606, where Blondel, like Husserl, dreams of a "technical" philosophy, a texture of the "phenomena" of thought and of action, while all the time continuing to speak the language of introspective psychology.) This is all the more

not in an ontological manner. And the philosopher, as philosopher, will never know whether sensation has a real content nor which content. But man, the living subject, will experience this content. Yet the philosopher will have one advantage over the ordinary man. The philosopher will know what conditions a sensation must meet if it is not to be adulterated, illusory, or false, while the subject will never know this unless he initiates a reflective process similar to that of the philosopher. Obviously, this distinction between the philosopher and the man appears tenuous and perhaps even ridiculous, for, after all, the philosopher is himself a man. However, unless we make this distinction, it is impossible to define each one's competence. The philosopher then risks going beyond his role as reflective witness to assume that of the agent or experimenter. It is easy to imagine what the consequences of this confusion would be. In the one case, the reflective attitude is compromised (pragmatism), while in the other, life dissolves into its representations (idealism).

With regard to the supernatural, *mutatis mutandis,* an analogous process of reasoning is appropriate. As a man (because he is in fact a believer), Blondel recognizes the existence of the supernatural. As a philosopher, he ignores it and ought to ignore it.[15] What he examines is the meaning, the coherence, and

---

deplorable since Blondel rejects, with reason, any psychological method for religious philosophy (see *Lettre, Annales,* XXXIII, pp. 467–477). On the other hand, as Maréchal recognized, Blondel surpasses Husserl in that he poses the ontological problem at the proper moment. See *Mélanges Joseph Maréchal,* vol. I (Paris, 1950), pp. 181–206, "Pure phenomenology or a philosophy of action?" The author concludes: It is necessary to join "the rigorous analyses of M. Husserl" with the penetrating views of M. Blondel concerning the "dynamism which underlies formal thought" (p. 206).

[15] This amounts to saying that Blondel ought to find the technical means of approaching the supernatural as idea, leaving aside every question of fact. Now this means is known to philosophers, at least since the invention of transcendental analysis: confronted with a given (real or fictitious), and leaving ontological problems aside, philosophy scrutinizes the ideal conditions that determine the intelligibility of this given. Faced with the given of Christianity, Blondel has tried to apply to it (not without adaptations) a method of this kind. He suspends the judgment of existence and of value (which, according to him, belongs to living consciousness, to the man totally involved) and examines the given as a philosopher in order to see

the content of a notion. He determines what conditions the supernatural, if it exists, must fulfill. He therefore studies it as an ideal structure, and not as a concrete reality. And he cannot put off this study because action, which cannot be completed in the natural order, obliges him to investigate whether a solution of another order would succeed where naturalist solutions fail. It is, as it were, the last chance open to him. He must take it deliberately, consciously, *inevitably.* Why? Because the inability of action to content itself with any purely human salvation could be an indication that there is something in it which secretly responds in advance to a supra-human intervention. However, in the light of what we know about the ambiguities of psychological consciousness, we must be on our guard not to interpret a sign of this kind according to empirical procedures.[16] Before anything else, we must submit to a rigorous analysis this idea

---

under what conditions it would be reasonable, normal, and obligatory to adhere to Christian salvation. Once these conditions have been considered, the suspension of ontological judgment can be removed. For man is sufficiently well informed in regard to what, in the name of reason, he ought to demand of religion. This method of putting off the ontological question in order to pose it better at a later moment may seem to be artificial. It is, in fact, a purely methodological procedure, but legitimate and indispensable. It is the price one pays for the "detection" of essences, as Husserl has proved anew. Moreover, in the case under consideration, it is the only way to oblige the unbeliever to raise the religious problem without demanding that we have faith (which would be a vicious circle) and to compel the philosopher to scrutinize the *idea* of the supernatural without waiting for a light superior to that of reason.

[16] On the contrary, once the mind of the subject has been prepared through reflection and has disengaged universal norms, he may and indeed should take the initiative in interpreting certain signs. These will be objective signs of external facts, since the consciousness of the subject cannot be an indication *which is seen,* but only an indication *which allows us to see.* Blondel, unfortunately, came only later to the idea of motives which were "illuminating rather than illuminated." Only this idea allows us to understand how it is not a question of discovering things within the intimacy of the subject, but on the contrary of disposing the subject to receive a new way of looking at things, new eyes for discerning the supernatural within objective and historical witnesses. It is well known that Rousselot, in his *Yeux de la foi,* definitively established the truth that this interior fact is apperceiving and not apperceived.

of a supra-human intervention, of help from God himself. Thus, we examine the Christian notion of the supernatural as the one most capable of defining properly this call to a gratuitous surplus. The hypothesis of a divine gift, as it is presented in positive religion, thus finds its way into the analytic course of reflection. The purpose of this procedure is to see what would happen if this hypothesis were to be realized. Once this is determined, the philosopher can only urge consciousness to investigate in a practical manner whether this hypothesis is a factual reality, enjoining consciousness to adopt it should it exist. In this way, the philosopher will have come to the end of his task. He will have demonstrated the impossibility of shutting action in on itself in the natural order, and he will have posed, on the critical plane, the necessity of examining whether the "flight upwards," which becomes imperative as a hypothesis after the failure of naturalism, would not produce better results. Thus after having rejected various false clues, Blondel shows that there is good reason to try this last one, and even that it is necessary to do so. A philosophy of defeat thus succeeds the defeat of philosophy. At any rate, whether the supernatural solution or the religious clue proves to be the right one or not, only the concrete subject, on his own responsibility, can decide. Philosophy reflects and orders one to choose, but the choice alone decides.

We have said that action is not only incomplete, but naturally incapable of completion. In fact, it is not primarily because Blondel observes the final defeat of real human action that he appeals to the supernatural. For him, the method of direct experimentation or of practical verification belongs exclusively to the free consciousness. But the indirect method of reflection, of understanding and of theoretical judication, is properly that of the philosopher.[17] It does not allow the philosopher to *do*,

---

[17] Philosophy "proceeds by an indirect path in successively determining solutions which remain incomplete" (*Lettre, Annales,* XXXIV, p. 340; see also *ibid.,* p. 338).

but only to say how we do and how we ought to do. In the case of the supernatural, it does not simply observe that man fails to be complete himself naturally; an empirical observation of this kind does not remove all doubts. It *demonstrates* that man cannot but fail, that he can neither maintain his position of immanentism, nor procure by his own means a transcendent plentitude. Philosophy "shows—this is its twofold role—that man cannot do without nor by himself obtain possession of that life which is for him necessary and impracticable."[18] And it shows this fact, or rather it demonstrates it with conclusions that have "an apodictic value,"[19] for, setting aside the order of realities, it is interested only in the ideas that man cannot fail to

[18] *Lettre, Annales,* XXXIII, p. 345. Here we might calm certain fears: "man cannot do without it with impunity" implies: "in case the supernatural really exists." If it exists it can only be obligatory, for it is impossible to implant it in man (a free infusion) without making it his ultimate concrete end (and hence the practical obligation). The phrase "this necessary and impracticable life" is equally ambiguous. (It is repeated in *Lettre, Annales,* XXXIII, p. 608.) The phrase recalls an analogous, but even less determinate, one from *L'Action:* "It is impossible not to recognize the insufficiency of the entire natural order, and not to feel a need beyond it. It is impossible to find within oneself the wherewithal to content this religious need. *It is necessary,* and *it is impracticable*" (*L'Action,* p. 319). In these statements, no distinction has been made explicitly between the *idea* and the *reality* of the supernatural, and we should not make use of them without altering or completing them implicitly. Nevertheless, the citation in question from *Lettre* is taken from a passage in which the intention of the author is plain. We will quote the immediate context (a part of which is already familiar) and underline the phrases which seem most important for our purpose here: "In this philosophy agrees with theology, that *philosophy could not pretend to cause the faith to arise within a soul.* Reduced to human means and natural paths, philosophy shows—this is its twofold role—that man cannot do without nor by himself obtain possession of that life which is for him necessary and impracticable. As long as philosophy does not have to invest the supernatural even with the type of certitude it confers on everything which it affirms, *it need not make pronouncements on the question of fact.* Its task is simply to determine the dispositions of mind which *prepare* the understanding of facts and the practical discernment of truths proposed from elsewhere" (*Lettre, Annales* XXXIII, p. 345).

[19] *Lettre, Annales,* XXXIV, p. 341.

consider if he wishes to examine the full scope of the problem he is to himself.

*   *   *

Blondel's position comes to this, that the idea of the supernatural is proposed by Christian teaching, but it can be integrated with the philosophical dialectic. The reason is that for the Christian this idea denotes a living experience of which it is the direct expression and from which it cannot be dissociated and yet, since the Christian is also a conscious and reflective being, *once one analyzes the immanent logic of his faith* this idea is also a moment in his process of thought, a link in the series of ideas that binds his rational certitudes to his religious convictions. In this case, either this series of ideas is fully rigorous for him or it is not. If it is not, his experience is worthless and holds no interest. If, on the contrary, there is no break in the chain, this means that there necessarily exists *continuous intelligible structure* which can certify that faith itself, when it surpasses reason, does not cease to be reasonable. In other words, unless we are to imply that faith is absurd and without any foundation or meaning, there must be, in some way or other, underneath the states of pure reason and the states of faith, the same notional skeleton, the same intelligible fabric, in virtue of which what we believe remains coherent or compatible with what we know. In short, if to believe is not to talk nonsense, the mental organization which the Christian attitude involves is, *from a notional standpoint,* all of a piece. The notions, ideas and determinations that compose it form a single identical determinism.[20] Hence, once this logic has been restored to its intelligible rigor, it is possible to treat it as a whole, as an aggregate of representations which has its own unity and internal

[20] This word should always be taken in its technical meaning of "a series of determinations."

relations. Brought to life in the Christian by an act of faith which is a free act, it has a salvific value. But once it is abstracted by an artifice of analysis—which the critic has a right to do from a strictly methodological point of view; once it has been taken from the living context of the believer and considered only as an "ideal order" presented to reflective thought before being presented to obligatory choice, its only value is intrinsic coherence and formal rigor.[21] That is why, in the hands of the philosopher, the logic of faith can become an ideal framework and a structure-type, capable of serving as a reading-pattern, or as a "function of intelligibilization" which helps us better understand the obscure aspirations of human activity. That is precisely what Blondel tried to do.

However, we must not see in this ideal determinism, of which the idea of the supernatural is only one of the links, a simple heuristic structure, or merely a means to decipher the enigma of our destiny. In reality, the order of notions underlying the act of faith is nothing but the necessary rational foundation which requires the religious initiative if it is not to be arbitrary. Without this "order," however, the religious initiative would be short-lived—neither structured nor structurable. Doubtless, in the consciousness of the believer this ideal order must be considered as a theological rationale, for it serves to mediate an experience of faith. But this does not exclude—rather it requires —that from another point of view the notional series be a philosophical logico-rationale. In other words, even before the theologian intervenes, and in order that he may intervene, we

---

[21] Speaking of faith and reason, Blondel writes: "Even when their affirmations seem to cover each other at least partially *sub specie materiae seu objecti,* they remain fundamentally heterogeneous *vi formae.* And perhaps we ought to conclude that even rational truths verified or sanctioned by revelation have, in their theological aspect, a very different import from what they have in their philosophical aspect. . . ." (*Lettre, Annales,* XXXIII, p. 608). Likewise: "In this sense, even in that which touches upon the natural order, theological doctrines have an import and a meaning entirely different from the philosophical theses on which they seem to be precisely superimposed" (*Lettre, Annales,* XXXIV, p. 256).

must presuppose an intelligible structure without which the religious experience would be as it were completely devoid of reason. It is therefore legitimate and even necessary to distinguish here, beneath the theological rationale,[22] a structural conditioning which has its own economy before being theologically informed and which, for this reason, will be retrievable for the philosopher and recognized by him as being simply rational.[23] Or if you prefer, the logical progression that the theologian makes use of for his own purposes and according to his own sense, could equally well be used by the philosopher in another context and for other purposes. This is normal and even inevitable. For if the theologian can use the ideal order of which we speak, it is because this order is first of all a system of relations in order to become a structure of experience. Suppose this order were not present. Not only could the theologian no longer think or express his faith but, what is more important, faith would lose all its rational substructures, that is to say, everything which constitutes its very *conditions of possibility*. Thus, in its formal rigor, the ideal order is not a contribution of faith to reason, but rather a contribution of reason to faith. It is *that by which* faith has been able to assume a human intelligibility, that is, to develop along lines of theological reason. And it is *that without which* faith would have had no hold, no reasonable foundation in man's mind. We may therefore legitimately conclude that the series of ideal notions, before it allows itself to be taken over by theology, is of a rational

[22] We should not forget that, in the present discussion, we are considering only the bond between the idea of the supernatural and other ideas. Blondel is concerned with finding an "intelligible communication" without which the supernatural order will remain entirely extrinsic and thus, from the rational point of view, "as though it never existed" (*Lettre, Annales,* XXXIII, p. 603). But it must be noted that there is no question here of rationalizing what is properly dogmatic. Blondel wants to determine the notion of the supernatural, but certainly not its content.

[23] ". . . it is necessary to try to distinguish that which is of faith, or consequent to faith but based upon it, from that which is of reason, or antecedent or consequent to faith but based upon reason" (*Lettre, Annales* XXXIV, p. 260).

texture. Indeed, no one will contest the assertion that without this series the conditions for the possibility of faith would not exist. Now, the investigation of the conditions of possibility of an object is always the province of philosophy, whatever the object in question. By declaring that the order of immanent notions belongs to philosophical criticism, Blondel is only restoring to philosophy what is its due.[24]

The following conclusions can, I believe, be drawn from our discussion: A critical analysis of the "integrated sequence" of the Christian's intellectual and spiritual states allows us to distinguish underlying those states an ideal determinism, a series of logically homogeneous and formally continuous notions. Furthermore, it permits us to recognize in this determinism and this notional articulation a rational structure, *stricto sensu*. It thus confers on the philosopher the right and the obligation to recover in his own way this "order" of determinations and connected system of affirmations. Consequently, the philosopher should verify whether or not he is really dealing with a truly consistent determinism, without fault or break. He should determine especially (for this is the whole problem: the intelligible union of rational requirements with the notion of the supernatural), whether the idea of surplus tallies exactly with *the*

[24] In one sense, all of Blondel's doctrines were born from the desire to discover the true link between philosophy and religion. Blondel believes that he has discovered it in a twofold necessity, which basically is only one: *a necessity for reason to raise the problem of the supernatural and the necessity that the idea of the supernatural conform to the demands of reason.* He has established that there is no formal incompatibility between reason and the notion of the supernatural. Indeed, he has proved that there is formal compatibility between the two, that is to say, that they are united by an intelligible link, an ideal necessity. The problem of the supernatural is thus in all justice incorporated within the most autonomous philosophy. Nevertheless, since philosophy remains reflective and critical, and excludes in principle the question of being, the *real continuity* does not follow from the *formal compatibility* (*Lettre, Annales,* XXXIII, pp. 610–611). The method of immanence thus succeeds in formally linking philosophy and religion without confusing natural and supernatural realities. These only action unites in itself, because it is not simply theoretical but practical, not merely reflective but free.

conditions of possibility that reason imposes. This requires, for example, that he prove that the gratuitous character of the divine gift and the free character of the act of faith fully correspond with the *a priori* requirements which the philosopher establishes as norms of validity for *every possible religious experience.*[25] But assuming that this be done, assuming that the idea of the supernatural be clearly recognized as consonant with what philosophy has the right to demand, then the critical conclusion has been reached: the religious solution of the problem of action is revealed as reasonable. More than this, it is declared to be the only authentic solution, for the supernatural that it sanctions appears to reflective thought as the only idea which is reconciled and which can be reconciled with the other ideas of the regulating order. Thus the truly decisive point is to establish that the idea of the supernatural can be and should be integrated with the internal logic of action. Once that is done, the case is clear: the hypothesis of a supernatural contribution is the only plausible hypothesis, that is, unless it is to deny itself, action allows of no other effective solution than that which meets the ideal requirements of reflection. But after all this, as we know, a choice remains to be made. Only this option can fill up the empty framework of the supernatural ideal by giving it a concrete content: "It is not really a question of the mind's theoretical adherence to a dogma exterior to us, but of the practical introduction of a life-giving truth into our heart and into our be-

---

[25] Auguste Valensin has most aptly written: "For Maurice Blondel, a Catholic philosophy is not a special philosophy. It is properly the philosophy which, by the exclusive use of its own methods, succeeds in pointing out, through an adequately delineated void, the place that revelation should fill. To formulate as clearly as possible the problems that is its *raison d'être*; to expose the conditions which any solution of the problem must satisfy; and finally to reveal by rigorous demonstration the powerlessness of reason to determine this solution in a positive fashion—these are, according to Maurice Blondel, the province of philosophy and its task. This is what makes philosophy, as it were in spite of itself, 'catholic,' whatever the 'system' in which it expresses itself may be and whether it is aware of it or not" (Foreword to *Maurice Blondel,* collect. "Les Moralistes chrétiens" [texts and commentaries], 2nd ed. [Paris, 1934], p. 11).

havior."[26] For reasons that we know, philosophy cannot pass beyond the threshold of practice; only a living and free consciousness can make this decision.[27] The role of philosophy is limited to naming the conditions and the guarantees of the choice. Once these have been defined, the choice cannot be put off. Reason commands, in the very name of the necessity that binds together the links of the ideal order.

[26] *Lettre, Annales,* XXXIV, p. 338.

[27] We expressly said: "a living and free consciousness" as opposed to the critical reflection of the professional philosopher. True enough, as we already explained, reflection prescribes choice. It expressly determines the conditions to which it must subscribe in order to be valid. But in the final analysis only freedom in act takes the initiative of the choice. It is liberty's place to maintain its decision within the limits determined by reflection. Once this is done, we know that the choice does not run any risk of arbitrariness; reflective judgment becomes its guide and acts as an immanent norm for the practical judgment. These observations, important as they are in ethics or natural philosophy, are still more so when a decision in the supernatural order is at stake. A choice without law, a choice without discernment would produce a clear case of fideism.

III.
A Philosophical Critique
of Revelation

1. THE ULTIMATE PHILOSOPHICAL REDUCTION:
THE ONE AS SOURCE OF THE CREATIVE PROCESS

How can we treat the idea of God without lapsing into objectivism? Is there a means of providing valid arguments in its favor without measuring it by a standard suitable for things? Yes or no—after so much beating about the bush, can the existence of God be proved, and is it possible to search for what his nature is or is not? Certainly there is a means; it is suggested, we believe, by religion or living spirituality, whose witness the philosopher must criticize. By retracting the spiritual movement which, in fact, leads to God for all those who endeavor to discern his presence, one can bring to light certain secret incentives, certain intentions whose efficacy is indubitable. It is this movement, this process of conversion, that we are going to describe. It is situated less in the order of notions than in that of values. Even if we speak a technical language, it will be understood that we refer to attitudes and initiatives of the naïve as well as the wise.

The procedure we want to develop is not at all original. Husserl named it "reduction"; we will call it that ourselves.[1]

It could as well be called *apperception,* a word borrowed freely from Leibniz. If we use these terms, it is not in order to innovate; it is to serve the spirit of the tradition and to avoid betraying the object of our inquiry. But what is it to "reduce" or "apperceive" with respect to God? Is it less than to demonstrate, thus involving a lack of certitude? Is it more, thereby yielding to the ontologist illusion? The mind need not abdicate its rights; God need not, to meet the requirements of demonstration, be changed into an object.

Reduction, in the technical sense, is an act, a movement that seeks to pass through the different levels of consciousness[2] in order to secure, step by step, their foundation. It is not a question of a homogeneous regression that would move uniformly from the outside to the inside or from the inferior to the superior. It has to do with a progressive discernment that, acknowledging the specificity of each plane, fashions its own approach; just as criticism, in order to get a grip on each reality, must discern its originality before being able to give a precise determination of its meaning and scope. The difficulty with reduction is that out of respect for the nature of experience, within which it works, it must maintain the solidarity (while distinguishing them) of subject and object. But if it remains faithful to this complexity, it is not long in discovering that the conversion of the subject implies a corresponding promotion of the object. There is not only parallel progress, but mutual progress. This is why both being and the world have the value of the act that constitutes them.

It is useless, for our purpose, to expose at length the differences which Husserl introduces between eidetic reduction, tran-

---

[1] However, merely by using Husserlian terminology, I do not adopt Husserl's system.

[2] The plurality of levels is well presented by P. Ricoeur in his translation of the *Ideen,* I (Paris, 1950), p. xxx.

scendental reduction, and the full act of constitution.[3] We make free use of the vocabulary and example that Husserl provides. The important thing for us is to bring into relief the path taken by the movement of reduction when we go with it to the end of its course.

At the outset, reduction tries to isolate the factual elements so as to consider only essences or significations. For example, it is permissible to take a thousand and one cases of imaginative creation—here the number is irrelevant. It would be a loss of time to focus on the picturesque in each case; the imagining attitude, the essence common to all these facts, is what counts. And we must go further. The signifying attitudes themselves must be appraised separately. When we have suspended in them what is only particular signification, the capacity of posing significations as such will remain. Pure consciousness, the transcendental Ego, constituting intentionality, will be disclosed facing the "world."

If we stop there, we post results that are interesting but insufficient: psychologism is conquered (and all forms of empiricism), the transcendental is established and, moreover, not isolated and separated, but referred to the world, reinstated in the concrete. Furthermore, that which in the natural attitude could only give rise to false meaning and contradiction acquires its true meaning; in particular, the meaning of being is seen, whereas it would have been premature to define it at an earlier stage. Nevertheless, has everything been said when the transcendental is attained? No, and Husserl himself concluded by suggesting[4] a hierarchy of three concepts of intentionality: psychological receptivity, noetic-noematic correlation, and finally productive and creative constitution. In other words, after disclosing the transcendental (whose acts are performed by the

---

[3] We have studied these notions in *Critique et religion,* chap. V. Complementary elucidations will be found in Gaston Berger, *Le Cogito dans la philosophie de Husserl* (Paris, 1941), p. 44 ff.

[4] See *Ideen,* I, trans. Ricoeur, pp. xxix and xxx.

natural subject, although the latter neither knows this nor even believes in an external cause of its perceptions), we must accede to a deeper plane. How can this be achieved? What will be our course? Undoubtedly, it will be an attempt to reduce receptivity to the limit, in the conviction that it is justifiable only when compared to an originary activity.[5] The discovery of this activity does not entail, however, a reabsorption of the receptive or the received. To make the act soar triumphantly over passivity would be to dissolve the latter and, at the same time, to deprive the act of its point of support. The inquiry then anticipates this act which denies itself an escape and, in the instant of execution, remains solidary with the inferior planes that are necessary to its exercise. In this sense, it can be said that the psychological I is required by the transcendental I,[6] or that the constituting activity in some way gives itself the frames of space and time in which to insert its representations. Secretly the act prescribes form and content, idea and sensation. It allows itself the luxury of strange misunderstandings when it no longer knows at the psychological plane what it gives rise to at the meta-psychological plane. The act demands what it receives and imposes on itself what is imposed on it. Ultimately, it chooses its complexity and merits its own facticity. We say "ultimately" because, although the transcendental is active in the psychological consciousness, it never emerges there as such. To know its visage, it is still necessary to learn through experience what its fundamental orientation is; only its products express on the outside what it is on the inside.

This last reservation seems to indicate a retreat on our part. For a moment, we were able to appear as timid on this point as Husserl deprived of Fink's audacious stimulations. It is nothing of the kind. To remain at the level of the second intentionality,

---

[5] It is known that this tendency belongs to Husserl's early philosophy, the so-called idealist period. But we have taken no position on the whole of Husserl's work.

[6] Certain authors, following Kant's *Uebergang*, would say not only *required*, but *engendered*.

to refuse to pass to the level of the third (the productive one), would be to hinder the movement of reduction from attaining its end. It has the right to it and demands it; for how can reduction be limited? It set out with a completely Cartesian goal: to find an indubitable which could only be both necessary and absolute. To reduce, then, will consist in tracking down the doubtful, exposing the dependent, the relative, the contingent. To the extent that, within a given, I succeed in discriminating variable elements and, in contrast, a common principle which invariably is found in all the cases, I am authorized to set the first aside so as to better exhibit the second. But this procedure, judged legitimate at the outset, cannot lose its legitimacy along the way. As long as something "reducible" remains, it must be reduced. Practically, as long as receptivity remains, we must progress towards a still more radical act. This is why no one can balk at coming to creative constitution, that is, to the level where, according to Husserl, intuition really gives itself its object. Can we stop there? Does there remain, at the level of this third intentionality, a receptivity or at least a passivity, a dependence or a multiplicity? In our opinion there does. Consequently, we postulate a fourth reduction.

In fact, what is this transcendental that is responsible for constitution? Each *Cogito* is capable of effecting its conversion by taking its own path. But it can then believe either that it transcendentally rejoins an impersonal principle, or that it finds, at its root, a singular intelligible. The first leads to a spiritual monism, the second to an intelligible pluralism, a noetic intersubjectivity. From the perspective of the reductive intention, these two results are far from equal in value.[7] An impersonal principle can individuate; it cannot personalize. That is, it can prescribe, by requiring the assistance of matter, multiple *psychologies* which will be provisional "modes." But it cannot found precisely what is in question: a *Cogito* that exists only

[7] We stress this problem of the status of the intelligible in *Philosophie de la religion,* Part One.

through the reciprocity of other *Cogitos,* a freedom that awakens and, in any case, opens out only through the mutual recognition of each and every one. But it will be asked if the *Cogito* and freedom are really that. Is there not a danger here of granting ourselves in advance what we want to prove? It does not seem so. For without even furnishing the complete justification of intersubjectivity at the intelligible level (we have done this elsewhere[8]), we can and must broach the problem in terms of the relationship of multiple consciousnesses to the transcendental.

Surely, no one denies the plurality of psychological consciousnesses. Some, however, hold it to be relative and finally void, the transcendental employing it as a means of expression, at once necessary and precarious. Now, even when the empirical is reduced and the particular significations are suspended, it is a question of knowing whether the *Cogito* retains its universal fecundity outside reciprocal existence with subjects that function as a worldly interference. We answer no, for the following reasons: (a) from the subjective point of view there is position only through opposition, life only through exchange, thought only through common reference and differentiation; (b) from the objective point of view there is determination only through negation, and this entails both a multiplicity of notions and a panoramic unity or horizon; and (c) from the functional point of view every determination refers to a determinant, and vice versa. Determinations as such imply system, but they can be conceived, compared, and unified around one determination (each in turn becoming the pivot) only if we pose conjointly a plurality of determining principles. The latter must be capable of being universalized through mutual openness, or of becoming, each from its point of view, the privileged center of the entire system. The differentiated multiplicity of the world of ideas has a correlate in the qualified diversity of the community of minds. In other words, there is no determination without a system of determinations (in which each one can be the starting point or

[8] See again, *Philosophie de la religion,* Part One.

head of the whole); but neither is there a system of determinations without an intersubjective college (in which each subject is at once a partner and a center). Thus the universal and the singular reciprocally balance and condition one another. Transcendental intentionality no longer says *I,* but *We,* although the plural must be attributed to each singular.

Does a unitary transcendental furnish a more economical solution of the difficulty? Nothing is less certain. If the transcendental were both monistic and impersonal, the plurality engendered below itself would be purely psychological, thus empirical. Intersubjectivity would be only a fall, an accident of fact, a contingent disgrace; it would be illusory and provisional; it would disappear in the light of the purifying reduction. This is why sorting the solutions to this problem imposes an option for one of them. The passage from the one to the multiple that leads from a transcendental monism to psychological plurality cannot be accomplished without loss. The psychological is nothing without the transcendental. If, then, the latter is not itself plural, intrinsically differentiated and singularized, the plurality of the former will only be borrowed, evanescent, and extrinsic. If, on the other hand, the singularity, or rather, the community of individual minds is founded only on the empirical plane, it will disappear with this plane. From the outset, it will be an illusion of an illusion, having only a phantom existence. To give it power, meaning, and value we must ground it in intelligibility itself.

At this level, the difficulties noted are removed. The multiple is the unity of a plurality of subjects and essences; there is, simultaneously, a college of minds and a system of ideas, a conjunction of universality and singularity. The passage from the intelligible[9] to the psychological is conceived in the following manner: subjectivity is really an order, an organic plurality, better, an intersubjective college, wherein persons have their

[9] In general, I prefer this term to "transcendental."

149

distinct attachment and their own singularity which they express through the diversity of consciousness. A certain fall is inevitable here; it can easily be seen in the everyday experience of the conflict between psychological individualities. At least, personal freedoms retain enough vigor to recover themselves, if they wish, from passivity or hostility. In any case, we see that the confusion of the natural attitude prior to reduction signifies not only a reaction to "mundane" objects (not bad in itself), but complicity with them, complaisance in them.[10] It is neither scandalous nor awkward that each subject has several orders of unequal dignity. The trouble begins when the orders are confused.[11]

However, understanding better the passage from the intelligible to the empirical only displaces our problem; we must still explain what the multiple is generated from. The genesis of consciousness is less disconcerting if it is true that it proceeds from the multiplicity of intelligible singularities to that of empirical individualities, the latter being the expression of the former. Plotinus remarked that plurality, even infinity, is introduced into the intelligible; and it can be held that there are ideas of singular things.[12] It remains, however, to throw light on the appearance of the first multiplicity. If we fail to do this, the question will be insoluble. There will be hope for nothing better than the incoherent thesis of a transcendental monism striving to sustain inconsistent "modes."

Now, the difficulty can be handled more easily than one would think. The intelligible, being both one and multiple, exhibits, if not receptivity (a term reserved for the empirical), at least incomplete unity. It is not totally one; it is one and

[10] As P. Ricoeur suggests, *Ideen,* I, p. xvii, there is contamination.

[11] Perhaps, as Plotinus thought, the sensible is only a cloudy perspective, a fog between the material and the spiritual; its ambiguity makes the psychological consciousness an unstable and confused, equivocal and transitory point of view.

[12] See *Enneads,* V, 7, I, trans. Bréhier (Paris, 1924–1938), p. 123. English translation by Stephen MacKenna, *The Enneads,* 3rd ed. (London, 1962), pp. 419–420.

multiple, the active liaison of a diversity, the community of a plurality. And just here the supreme reduction must intervene, leading us in the passage from the *one-multiple* to the One.

In fact, how could the intelligible pose itself as an order, at once subjective and objective (spiritual college and system of ideas), if no principle existed from which it could be derived? For whenever, in any given, an even tenuous discrimination can be effected by bracketing the variable elements and discovering the invariant, the reductive movement asserts that derivation is involved. Here the one and multiple, subjective and objective characteristic leads inevitably to critical discernment; it is necessary to reduce the staggered arrangement of the multiple and also the subject-object dichotomy. To perform this reduction is precisely to disclose the One as an absolute simplicity, as a truly radical spontaneity that transcends the whole of being and essence. Either one seeks to arrest the reductive effort at a given order (for example that of the *I*, or rather, the transcendental *We*) and is completely arbitrary, since the reducible remains. Or one pushes the purifying exigency the whole way,[13] and

[13] Maurice Merleau-Ponty writes: "The greatest lesson of the reduction is the impossibility of a complete reduction" (*Phénoménologie de la perception*, 3rd ed., Paris, 1945, p. viii. English translation by Colin Smith, *The Phenomenology of Perception* [New York, 1962], p. xiv). For the author this formula signifies that if particular objects are reducible, at least the presence of the subject to the world is irreducible. In reality, from our point of view, the world itself is reduced, for *to reduce* is not to suppress but *to grasp as relative*. The world is only the correlate of consciousness. In turn, the subject-object division and intersubjective multiplicity are reducible. In fact, all relation, all diversity, can be grasped as relative to an exigency for unity that is never satisfied. But this exigency, from the moment it is recognized, becomes the sign of a presence. It is not equivalent to the desire for what one does not have; for man, it is equivalent to the capacity for *really unifying*, although his consciousness remains divided and conditioned by the difference of level between subject and object. If man unifies without being Unity, it is because Unity gives him this power, without being confused with him. Thus there is, at the center of the spirit, a simple and infinite energy, an Absolute of liaison and unexceptionable spontaneity. The only irreducible, that which has no trace of multiplicity or passivity, is the pure Act. Precisely because an Act and not a supreme determination is involved, God cannot be discovered on the plane of notions, but only at the plane where the subject poses values. To reduce

establishes that it stops of itself only after going beyond all the orders and even the notion of order. God is not an order; he is that by which order can exist.

But does not this trans-ordinal character of God, which is equivalent to calling him the One, render insoluble the difficulty of the passage from pure unity to the multiple unity of the intelligible? Just the contrary is true. Reduction furnishes the proof that essence and existence must be surmounted in order to

---

here signifies that one attempts to lead the entire series of determinations back to the unity of a determinant, the free subject. But this latter, paradoxically, is one only by being double, and it is singular only by being plural. In fact, all freedom is exercised through instituting an order, a determinism, a series of determinations (thus there is duality between the free act and its order). And each personal Ego subsists, thinks, and frees itself only in association with all the other personal Egos (thus there is plurality in the Ego, a multiplicity of subjects, and an intersubjectivity tied to the objectivity of a common system of determinations that extends to all subjects). So for a double reason we fail to encounter a simple unity at the level of the transcendental Cogito. For better or for worse, the remaining doubling and redoubling to infinity in human subjectivity must be reduced. If that is done, if we suspend all determination (better, the whole order of determinations); if we in turn place the multiplicity of the determinants between parentheses (thus multiplicity attests that each subject participates in subjectivity without exhausting it, and it allows an objectivity to subsist as a divergence between each subject and all the others); in a word, if, within subjectivity and intersubjectivity, we reduce all the determined, the multiple, and the "objective" (and it must be done since each subject transcends determinations from the moment he discovers he is their author, contests the multiple from the moment he sees the non-me as relative to the Me, and surmounts the "objective" from the moment it exists for him), there remains, at the heart of human freedom, only a source of rigorously pure spontaneity. This constitutes a proof that God is really present in man. The proof is there as soon as freedom establishes its effective power to judge all determination derived, all multiplicity reducible, all "objectivity" transcendible. To challenge this proof would be to deny that the free act is trans-determinant. But if it is not, it is no longer a free act. Seemingly, one could be content with saying that the free act separates from the determinations in order to return immediately to them, for it remains situated even when it contests its situation. However, in admitting this "separation," one attests that the free act supports itself on an energy beyond determinations, and that is enough. If man does not escape the determined, although he surmounts it, it is because he employs the Absolute without being the Absolute. *Cogito, ergo sum; liber sum, Deus est,* would be the formula for exhibiting the irreducibility of the One. The proof by freedom, or by the exigency for unity that constitutes the dynamism of the free act, would be the application, pure and simple, of the reductive procedure.

attain the One. Consequently, the distinction between them applies only to the terms that proceed from the One, and not to the One itself. God is beyond being; he is not less, but more, infinitely more; he is its source. In these conditions, the appearance of the intelligible is also the appearance of being. And, as we saw earlier, this latter is possible only in correlation with the appearance of essence. At the outset, that is, at the tangential point where the One exercises creative motion, the coming to existence of a community of subjects coincides with the unfolding of a world of essences. Without a subject, no object; without a spiritual college, no system of ideas, and vice versa. In other words, there is no passage to be sought between the One and the intelligible plurality because there is no transition between what is simple and what is composite. God does not communicate something of himself, namely, being, to the intelligible (for God is super-being).[14] Rather, thanks to his radical unity, his pure spontaneity, he allows the intelligible to make itself exist, that is, to constitute itself simultaneously as being and essence, subject and object, one and multiple. God presents himself here as the founding productivity that guarantees and conditions the self-position of the intelligible.

The illusion might persist that a similar argument could have been produced in favor of a transcendental impersonal principle of the individual modes. But this attempt is contradictory. It ignores the transcendental's lack of metaphysical simplicity (from which comes the possibility of our fourth reduction). As for the rest, even if the transcendental principle were presumed to be one, it would have only a paltry fecundity; the multiple would appear only at the level of psychological, that is, empirical, consciousness. Consequently, the original unity would either communicate nothing of itself (like the One), in which case the derived multiplicity would collapse into pure psychologism; or it would communicate something of its being (unlike

[14] A. Sertillanges, commenting on St. Thomas, does not hesitate to call God *super-being.*

the One), and then the equivocation between the two orders would be not only a risk to be run, but an implacable necessity, a necessity of nature. Discernment between the empirical and the transcendental, that is, the very reduction by which the present question could be meaningful, would be rendered impossible.

* * *

If God is the One, pure simplicity, absolute spontaneity; if he is neither an order nor a plane, but that by which planes and orders are possible; if he escapes, by dominating it, the distinction between essence and existence, as well as the subject-object disjunction; if, in a word, he is not Being but, according to a neologism taken from Dionysian language, Super-Being,[15] it must no longer be said that the terms proceeding from him receive a part of him. They do not borrow from him the being that they are, because he is not. Strictly speaking, he communicates nothing to them. Thus, with respect to being, we can follow certain mystics and call him Nothingness or Nothing.[16] There exists no direct participation[17] between the One and beings; without correctives and expedients, that would lead to pantheism. The relation of God to the created cannot be defined by an ontological transmission, be it total or partial. Being, in

[15] I have already noted that Sertillanges used the expression "super-being." Maritain reproaches him for thus exaggerating our incapacity to know God. See *Les degrés du savoir,* 3rd ed. (Paris, 1932), p. 827 ff. English translation supervised by Gerald B. Phelan, *The Degree of Knowledge* (New York, 1959), p. 425 ff.

[16] Plotinus called God the *One* only because he lacked the term zero (see E. Bréhier, *La philosophie de Plotin,* Paris, 1928, p. 161, n. 1. English translation by Joseph Thomas, *The Philosophy of Plotinus* [Chicago, 1958], p. 157). Scotus Erigena called God *Non-Being* (see *De divisione naturae,* I, 3, in Migne, *PL* 122, col. 443 A-C; commentary in *Jean Scot Erigène* by Dom Maïeul Cappuyns [Paris, 1933], p. 338. English translation by Charleen Schwartz, *On the Division of Nature* [Quebec, 1961]).

[17] Maurice Nédoncelle presents numerous equivocal senses of this term in *La réciprocité des consciences* (Paris, 1942), pp. 29–34.

154

fact, need not submit to transfer and does not reside in God; it appears only at the level of the created and is found contemporary with the multiple, the finite, and the imperfect. Let us say then (a) that the One furnishes, to the term that proceeds from him, the capacity of being what it has to be, and (b) that the One is not. This reveals the One's mode of productivity and also the necessity for the immediately inferior term (the intelligible) to confer being on itself. The One cannot give derived spirituality, of any sort whatever, something of what he is, because he has nothing and is not.[18] The One can only give it the radical aptitude to give being to itself; in other words, to pose itself, to make itself. In this sense, the One creates by rendering self-position possible and participation impossible.[19]

To take the other side, if God were called *Being,* and not the *One,* procession would once again be ontological derivation, thus participation. Each derived term would imply the same act of

[18] Simone Pétrement observes that the "God who is not" risks, in a sense, favoring atheism, because "separated, unknown, detached from all," he "appears to be without power and nearly non-existent." But she adds, "in another sense, dualism is perhaps the only theism, because the 'God who is not' is perhaps the only God" (*Le dualisme dans l'histoire de la philosophie et des religions* [Paris, 1946], p. 120, n. 1). We do not see this dualism between the *God who is not* and *that which is,* for the reason that the first is not in series with the second. But it does seem correct to us to affirm that the super-being God, that of Plotinus and Pseudo-Dionysius, that equally of the fifteenth-century author of the *Nuage de l'inconnaissance* (see Armel Guerne's translation, "Documents spirituels," no. 6, *Cahiers du Sud,* [Paris, 1953]; *The Cloud of Unknowing,* ed. with an introduction by Evelyn Underhill, 3rd ed. [London, 1934]); that even of Lagneau (for whom being and existence are not proper to God, see "Cours sur Dieu," in *Célèbres leçons et fragments,* ed. Michel Alexandre [Paris, 1950], p. 250), is, so to say, more absolute (the only absolute) than the Being-God, who can be placed above determinations only by means of supplementary correctives. The famous verse, Exodus 3:14 (I am he who is), is not given as a metaphysical definition; above all, it expresses the refusal to name God. It can serve a negative theology as well as an ontological theology. In addition, let us recall that saying God *is not* does not insinuate that he is less than being; rather, it proclaims that he is more.

[19] Everything considered, supernatural grace is "participation" (in the technical sense defined above) no more than natural illumination (with different degrees of gratuitousness) is. It is preferable to conceive it as a passage from *self-position* to *Aseity.*

existing, which would restrict it in proportion to its own essence, this varying with the substances and serving to define them and establish a hierarchy among them. God could recover his transcendence only by the timely adjustments provided by analogy. He would become pure Existing and as such would be immanent to all existence. Yet, at the same time, he would be transcendent to it, since the essence added to the latter introduces the finitude by which resemblance and difference are mixed together in being. There is participation in the existent, but restriction as well; for participation is gradual and graduated, with beings set at intervals along a series in which a common element, being, is distributed at infinitely diverse levels. In any case, the opposition is clear between this *participationist* ontology and *processionist* ontology. In order to sum up the antithesis, it could simply be said that *ontology* has *henology* as its contrary,[20] defining them as follows: the first holds that the inferior borrows a part of what it is from the superior; the second holds that the inferior receives from the superior the means to be what the superior is not.[21] In the one, there is communication; in the other, there is literally position of self-position.

[20] I write *henology* with an *h* out of respect for the Greek etymology (Gilson, however, writes *énology* as one speaks in politics of *Énosis*). I believe that I have discovered a precedent in the historians of neo-Platonism who write *hénade*. In his *Vocabulaire* (5th ed., p. 397) André Lalande gives *hénothéisme*.

[21] Gilson has brought out this antithesis remarkably well in *Le thomisme*, 4th ed., pp. 193–200 (English translation, pp. 136–141), and *L'Être et l'essence* (Paris, 1948), pp. 38–45. This can be judged from the following passages: "The chief characteristic of the philosophy of Plotinus is that it is built upon a metaphysics of the *One* rather than of Being. To affirm that the One is the first principle of everything that is, is to admit at the outset that the One is not a being. . . . A superessential God is not, therefore, a being. Indeed he is much more than a being, and precisely because he is more than a being, he is not a being. This amounts to saying that God is a non-being, and that the *non öv* or 'what is not' is the supreme cause of all that is . . . the One, which precedes being, contains within itself all the being which itself is not" (*Le thomisme*, pp. 194–195; English translation, pp. 136–137). And there is more. "To speak of being *à propos* of God, is not to speak of Him but of His effect . . . being is but the revealing or manifestation of the One; in a word, its 'theophany.' As to the One, it remains *ante öv*: it is not entangled in the order of its participations"

2. THE ACT-LAW: MAN'S LIBERATION
THROUGH SELF-CREATED NECESSITY

Act-law is the name which we think should be given to pure consciousness, the consciousness which phenomenological reduction—or, if you prefer, phenomenological conversion—brings out. Psychological consciousness is only a derivative level, since it is reduced. The so-called transcendental or intelligible I, on the contrary, is originary. Doubtless, the ultimate reduction

(*ibid.*, p. 196; English translation, p. 138). "In a system in which being proceeds, not from Being, but from the One and the Good, one enters simultaneously into the order of being and into that of participation" (*ibid.*, p. 198; English translation, p. 139). Also, there is the following: "The One is not being, and precisely because it is not it, it can cause it. . . . The so-called pantheism of Plotinus is a perspectival illusion which stems from mixing two heterogeneous ontologies . . . it is not a question here of comparing two ontologies, but an 'ontology' with, one could say, an 'énology.' . . . In a doctrine of Being, the inferior is only by virtue of the being of the superior. On the contrary, in the doctrine of the One it is a general principle that the inferior is only by virtue of what the superior is not. In fact, the superior always gives only what it has not, since, in order to give that, it must be above it" (*L'Être et l'essence*, pp. 40, 41, 42). In the same passages Gilson gives the principal references to Plotinus and Pseudo-Dionysius. The rest can be found in Jean Trouillard, *La purification plotinienne* (Paris, 1955), and René Roques, *L'Univers dionysien* (Paris, 1954), or by reading directly *Enneads* V and VI and the *Divine Names*. The fifth *Ennead* is the strongest text in the whole history of philosophy in defense of the specificity of the intelligible. A careful reading permits the conclusion that Plotinus does not have the "floating conceptions" of the soul and the subject that certain authors attribute to him. Gilson, who put us in his debt by setting up the antithesis between *ontology* and *henology,* draws some surprising personal conclusions, notably that henology leaves existential ground in order to lead the subject to a plane of salvation through knowledge alone. This point of view is at least open to discussion, because knowledge in neo-Platonism does not have the partial and abstract character of a reflection cut off from life. In a Christian context, ontology has certainly been influenced by the *Ego sum qui sum* of Scripture. But this expression, which we spoke of earlier and whose meaning is periodically put in question (see A. M. Dubarle, "La signification du nom de Iahweh," *Revue des sciences philosophiques et théologiques*, XXXV, no. 1, January, 1951, pp. 3–21), can have only derivative philosophical importance. Henology retains the privilege of rigorously preserving the transcendence of God, the essential affirmation of the Judeo-Christian tradition.

presses farther and discriminates unity and multiplicity, thereby leading to the discovery of the One. But it is precisely the One, pure simplicity, which is the root of all order, without itself being order. The I is therefore truly the first order; first as the leader of the procession, and first also as constitutive of it. Determinations cannot apply to the simplicity of God. They can appear only at the level of the *multiple one,* that is, in the finite mind.

Thus in all consciousness, beyond the psychological plane and even beyond the rational plane (on which analysis reflects the unreflected), we discern a more radical plane: that on which the mind is *determining act.*

It is an act, for the One does not posit it as already made. This would be impossible, since absolute simplicity and pure spontaneity are indetermination or overflowing super-determination. It neither manufactures preëxistent material like the artisan, nor even acts according to a directing idea like the artist. Nor does the One conceive an idea beforehand and execute it like an architect's plan. It is sheer overflowing, without imperfection or ebb. If its aseity is at the beginning of the procession, we cannot tie it to the terms which proceed from it, either according to anthropomorphic schemes or according to material ones —although, as Plotinus realized, physical schemes have the advantage of betraying somewhat less the imprint of man. The One-source is the triumphant irradiation, the fiery furnace in full blast. Once the rays are intercepted and reflected in various directions, finitude is introduced. Thus we might symbolize the creation of minds. Infinite spontaneity allows itself to be intercepted, diffracted, "partialized" in secondary centers, which it freely creates. But even this comparison becomes misleading. It does not suggest strongly enough that the secondary sources transform the energy received into their own energy. The One remains trans-ordinal, whereas minds can act only by deploying an *order* of determinations. However, the Plotinian image can be taken over and adapted to our meaning: the ray emanated from the source can be grasped only as intercepted. Once it is intercepted, it is necessarily reflected (in the optical sense), and once it is reflected it is measured by an angle. Thus does it become determined, thanks both to the ardor of the emitting source and to the resistance of the receptor term. Thus the sovereignty of the One and the originality of minds derived from it are both respected. At any rate, we must admit that a trans-ordinal Absolute can diffuse itself only by collecting itself in secondary centers, the only ones capable of constituting *orders,* that is, of establishing multiple determinations. To be a center in which the Absolute collects itself is evidently the act of a dependent being. But to make use of the Absolute in positing oneself through positing determinations is the act of an active though dependent principle, or rather of a principle that is active because it is dependent. The mind does not come forth from the One already made and fully armed. It makes itself, it determines itself, it literally "breathes life into itself." It is an original reproduction, partial but inventive, of the energetic expansion of the One itself; it is the living bond of the procession and the conversion (of the irradiation and the "reflection"). It can therefore be defined both by the movement of going out and the movement of return, by creation and by ecstasy.[1]

Thus the name "act" can be properly applied to the mind. But a clarification is required immediately: the spiritual act is nothing if it is not determining, and even self-determining. Consequently, it is important to stress that this act is not an *actus purus* or *actus simplex,* but an *actus ordinans et determinans,* in short, an act-law. The operation and its determinations are thus united in the same formula, which describes at once its twofold aspect as constitutive and constituted, subjective and

[1] M. Maurice de Gandillac writes concerning Plotinus: "It is in becoming fully itself that subjectivity unites itself to the absolute" (*La sagesse de Plotin* [Paris, 1952], p. 85, n. 1). Nothing better explains how dependence upon the One remains the source of autonomy.

objective. From the start this description suggests that the mind is this very correlation. Thus through productivity and regulation, freedom and order, creativity and determinations—in a word, through act-law—the spirit directly presents itself as the *multiple one* derived from the supreme One. . . .

The act-law is the universal principle of position because it is auto-position. This is because it must make itself what it makes, create itself what it creates. The One is beyond essence and existence; it is strict simplicity. On the other hand, the act-law begins the cycle of being: in order to exist, it invents its essence. This means that, proceeding from the Absolute, it endeavors to return to it. Nevertheless, it can accomplish this return without denying itself only on two conditions: on the one hand, it must preserve itself from any absorption, and thus must adhere to the processive expansion instead of re-absorbing it; and on the other hand, it must make use of mediations in order that its conversion be an original and active renewal of the energy that has been communicated to it. The first condition is important: it prevents any pantheistic confusion and shows that the procession is never nullified. The second is also imperative: it forestalls any confiscation of the mystical by an equivocal anti-intellectualism. The unreflected (whether it be pre-reflective or supra-reflective) should be mediated by reflection, which does not mean assimilated or dissolved by it. It should be noted, in fact, that we are dealing here with mediations interior to the act-law, belonging to its order, and therefore in themselves beyond psychological consciousness, save when the latter distinctly uses them. They are intelligible or transcendental, not sensible, mediations. They are part of a system of relations that only the act-law, out of the source of its own initiative, posits and determines. Because this initiative is at the same time operative and legislative, we cannot at this level distinguish an axiological and a gnoseological viewpoint. Like the subject-object perspectives, the two viewpoints are interchangeable. They invoke each other, unite with each other, and clarify each other, while revealing two aspects of the same face.

Nevertheless, this totality of active mediations which flows from an actual initiative does not deploy itself in an intelligible space. It really exercises itself within the *Cogito;* consciousness carries it within itself and engages it in action and reflection. We can even point out the principal concrete activities through which the act-law expresses to consciousness its efforts of conversion: they are mathematics,[2] esthetics, ethics, and religion. Through these four functions of consciousness the act-law makes itself known, but the expressions that testify to its presence and its action on the psycho-empirical plane are only a rational or symbolic transcription of its hidden requirements. It is at the deepest, most basic level that the act-law commits and mediates itself. It never manifests itself openly, and we apprehend it only under the guise of discursive expressions which are often enough rather confused and which jumble together fragments of intuition, more or less coordinated reflections, and unverified empirical observations. Thus the act-law both asserts and hides itself in its quest for expression. It causes the burgeoning of all determinations (ideas, norms, values), establishes them and gives them life; guarantees their truth and supports their effectiveness in conscious thought and effective action. But it leaves to reflection, limited though it is, the care of recovering what it can of its riches for itself, once it is no longer a question of living them but rather of organizing them systematically.

We do not deny, however, that spontaneous thought suffices in practice to clarify its own course. For on the one hand, the act-law is by definition a judicatory operation, and on the other hand, its presence is implied in the activities of creative prospection. The four functions mentioned above, let us not forget, are

[2] Technology is simply the application of calculus to nature. In transforming man's condition it refers to the other three functions. It is never completely separable from the four activities enumerated. It depends upon them even without being aware of it, and must return to them.

161

prospective by nature; they reach the critical level only by a second step, passing from the pre-reflective to the reflective awareness which is, in my opinion, identified with philosophical consciousness. We thus admit: (1) on the intelligible level (that of the act-law), the *creation of an order* or *an ordered creation* of regulating principles; (2) on the plane of self-consciousness (in which the unreflected overflows the reflected) a transposition in two steps: first, a specification of ideas and values which are effectively thought and directly lived; and then a critical systematization[3] of these same ideas or values, this time apprehended reflectively. Practically speaking, were we to abstract from the categories and schemas that embody all determination in consciousness, we could fuse the plane of intelligible creation with that of living specification as it coincides with the pre-reflective *Cogito.* Only, the real specification cannot do without these categories and schemas—in which it is no longer creation but expression. Yet the intelligible realizes itself only within this specification. Thus it is advisable to affirm all the concrete inter-dependences and to maintain all the necessary distinctions. We must preserve the originality of the intelligible, for in one sense it is, by its creative power, beyond the conscious determination whence it takes substance. Yet we must also recognize that without conscious determination, intelligible determination would be nothing (it exists only in a present creation, which supposes a subject, and we know of no subject that is not at the same time act-law and self-consciousness). Finally, we must attribute to reflection the right and the duty of striving, not so much for self-consciousness (which is impossible in a direct way), as for *self-purification,* which consists in discerning the levels through which each living step passes in its accomplishment. Reflection then reveals to us that ideas and values are not objects but

[3] This systematization can be initiated by any somewhat sustained reflective effort. But we do not believe that it could be brought to a completion without the ways and methods of philosophical research.

creations, and that these creations are only the necessary consequences of self-creation.

This last observation leads us to understand that in ideas and values we ought to see not absolute entities, but rather mediating principles or subordinate norms. These principles and norms govern our vision of the world by assuring our grasp of it. At the same time that they allow us to transform things they also help us to transform ourselves. For no consciousness acts, even externally on matter, without adopting attitudes which fully engage it. The belief that creativity of essences or of norms leads to anarchy or to subjective fantasies is an unfounded fear. Such an excess is impossible in a philosophy of the subject where *self-position* is also, inseparably, a *position of laws*.[4] The act-law is self-governing; but to be a law unto itself involves mediating its union with the One. Now this relation with the Absolute, which constitutes the mind, is more demanding than any extrinsic norm. It calls for a fidelity all the more profound and demanding since to deny God in this context is to deny oneself. Literally, this would be to contradict oneself, to take up arms against one's own Source with the energy derived from it. We shall see later that the error is perhaps less the rupture of an essential bond than the misunderstanding or the ignoring of this bond through the excessive attachment of the Me to lower levels, which are inverted and derived expressions.

* * *

[4] That is why the objectivity of knowledge will finally be better established from our point of view than in systems of antecedent norms. The anteriority of the latter is only an illusory chronomorphism carried to the absolute. To establish the objectivity of knowledge, it is not necessary either to place the essences in God or to take them for things. It is necessary and sufficient that the human subject create them, and create them as *objective* (normative)—which he does according to intentionality—and that he cannot not create them, forced as he is thus to mediate his necessary return to the One. The foundation of the objectivity of essences is the intrinsic relationship of the mind to the Absolute, a relationship that has as its first and inevitable expression the projection (or creation) of essences.

Endowed with auto-position, singular as well as universal, the act-law can only be productive freedom. When existence posits the essence and the act the law, and when the choice is fundamental (initial and constitutive), the determinisms are only subsequent and derived. If the act-law engenders ideas and values (it sets up the whole noetic and axiological system, but in order to do so it makes certain ideas and values stand out), neither neutral determinations nor compelling objects any longer exist. Consequently, there no longer exists either subjective indifference or necessity to ratify.

Besides, both indifference in the presence of values deprived of any sign, and resignation in the face of an antecedent necessity imply chronomorphic schemata. These cannot withstand criticism and will shortly be resolved by our analysis of the notion of temporality. Nevertheless, these attitudes of indifference or of approving docility interest us in that they sometimes claim to rise to the level of reduction. In fact, however, they remain caught in the ambiguities of the natural man. To speak of indifference is to leave freedom entangled in the perplexity of psychological deliberation. But psychological deliberation is often only an academic, artificial, and approximative reconstitution of concrete psychological states. To speak of ratification is to harden the various principles of experience into objective, blind, and a-temporal necessity. Why do we harden them in this way? Simply because these principles cannot be directly observed. They are hidden from psychological consciousness and they likewise remain hidden from positive science, from its criteria and its decision to keep outside its frontiers whatever resists its grasp, or rather, whatever resists its definitive domination, for science's most cherished ideal is the repetition or reproduction of a phenomenon at will. In either case we act as though psychological consciousness were the whole of consciousness, or the scientist the whole man. Instead of keeping the limits of that which is limited, we extrapolate.

Even worse, we extrapolate in the wrong direction. We do not extend the facts along their own line; we prolong them arbitrarily. What right have we to project before ourselves an entirely objective necessity? Psychological consciousness knows only causalities of which its own choices could be the origin or indeed fragments of causality of whose beginnings and results it remains ignorant, or finally unjustifiable shocks of facticity. Never, except by abusive majoration or generalization, is it aware of a necessity at once intelligible and compelling. Similarly, the scientist discovers phenomenal connections and experimental concatenations. He supposes determinism wherever nature does not answer *no* to his questions, wherever the rigor of his calculus allows him to tie together the phenomena he wants to include into an operative whole. But never does he find himself in the presence of a fully constituted causalism. Order supposes an organizer. The experimental structures are those of the laboratory, that is, of man and his instruments, not of nature. Certainly, the establishment of order proves that the real can be utilized and, at least in part, mastered. We can even say that it allows itself to be rationalized. But the scientist is dealing only with a determinism of his own making (there is no determinism without a determinant). Or else he is dealing with phenomena which are still unclassifiable, "non-structurable" from his point of view, or more correctly "un-quantifiable." It would be pure whim and folly for him to attempt either to qualify them in themselves (we know the failure of qualitative physics), or to bring them together outside the control of mathematics (for example, according to a superstitious symbolism). It thus seems established that no type of purely objective necessity exists. It is only a figment of an inordinate imagination that goes beyond psychological as well as scientific observation.

It remains for us to understand how the schema of necessity has arisen from the same error as objectivism, by making affirmations outside the laws of the constitution. There is no order without an organizer, and no determinism without freedom—this is the conclusion of critical reflection. For minds inclined to stoicism to give the name "necessity" to the face of destiny,[5] they had to transport outside of subjectivity its own product, namely, the system of determinations. They superimposed it on things and projected it into them. Consciousness immediately became submerged in a necessity whose origin it had forgotten. It no longer knew that destiny is still an attitude of freedom, an attitude of incomprehension and of resignation. Seen from this angle, necessitarianism is nothing but fatalism. It is the subject's abdication of himself, the reification of consciousness, a complicity in the torpor of things, and a masochistic acceptance of the strokes of fate.

Why is the freedom of indifference generally more highly thought of than the freedom of ratification? One is tempted to answer that the fault lies with the professors. The free act is a lesson, a matter for exposition. But there is no easy explanation except by external or psychological description. In order to describe freedom, one begins by describing decision and deliberate choice. In other words, one starts by taking the wrong subject: in place of freedom, which is creativity of essences and values, one studies the psycho-empirical expression of this initiative. And since one ignores the pre-reflective presence to the self which makes a free act carry its own self-consciousness, one brings the reflective analysis to bear on an anterior (or future perfect) state. That I can choose between this and that really means: what will happen, good results or bad, when I will have chosen this or that? This involves an estimation of two terms with an unreal anticipation. The ruse is evident. Shall we nevertheless say that to weigh possibles is to experience contingency, and therefore freedom? The objection stems from a misunderstand-

[5] It is not certain that this criticism touches historical stoicism. Perhaps the authentic stoical thought, like that of Plotinus and Spinoza, envisages something beyond the categories of necessity and liberty. The way would be open to radical autonomy. The lesson of stoicism would consist in the process of contingent schemas.

ing. On the one hand, possibles are only imaginary realities; we inevitably construct them from realized realities, which are, of course, the only real ones.[6] On the other hand, contingency as indifference to being or not being and as neutral possibility is only an hypostatized fiction; it describes nothing concrete. Are we to apply it to an object? An object is always dependent on a subject. But the subject, endowed with auto-position, assigns to each of its creations a logical place in the ordered unfolding of determinations. The object is therefore no longer contingent in the sense of being fortuitous or irrational; it is prescribed.[7] Shall we apply the notion of contingency to the subject itself? If we mean that no objective, that is, extrinsic and causal, explanation of the sort applied to things can justify it, the subject is indeed contingent. Yet this is to speak equivocally, for the idea of contingency is often taken from another point of view and used in another context. It joins together *contingent* and *possible*. The subject then becomes the one playing heads and tails, the gambler. He credits himself with causing rents in the web of the real, and with inserting into it at will this or that causal series. He insinuates freedom into the gaps of determinism. But in this procedure, one comes again very quickly upon the case we have already encountered of retroversive anticipation. One imagines contradictory causalities as already played out, busily excluding each other alternatively. Thus one is doubly mistaken. First of all, one steps over into the future and supposes to have happened what has not happened. Indeed, one even supposes

[6] If we are to speak of virtual and actualizable possibles, where shall we put them? The henological Absolute resists them. The act-law itself has an essence only through auto-position. Thus the possible is always measured by the actual real. Or again, every possible is realized, for every existence confers upon itself the essence it requires to be what it is. In a word, the act-law posits the totality of what is or will be, of what is done or will be done. It is only chronomorphisms which confuse the natural man on this point.

[7] We are speaking of the phenomenal object; for in fact no other exists for consciousness.

167

as having occurred opposing causal series, of which one could not take place without excluding the other. Now this is to deny temporality and to imbue it, if only experimentally, with irreconcilable elements. Secondly, one reduces the future to the past, submerging it in the past through the grammatical ruse of the future perfect tense. One changes a logical ability into an ontological maneuver destined to abolish the irreversibility of time. We shall understand this better when we study the duration of consciousness. At least we have said enough about it to warn against the concept of contingency advanced by possibilist schemata.

The sole fact of believing in gaps within determinism betrays an objectivist falsification. For determinism—a postulate for positive science and a strict consequence for every philosophy of constitution—always refers to the act of freedom, to the determining initiative that instituted it. Thus freedom is in the connections, and not in the gaps of determinism. Besides, where do such gaps come from, if indeed there are any? Simply from an operative control whose extent is limited. Thus through the expression of a practice that sometimes fails, the relational network presents solutions of continuity. We objectivize these logical discontinuities by projecting them into the things; we transfer to the real the responsibility for limitations which should be imputed to scientific or philosophical problematics. We refuse to consider an instrumental insufficiency, an error in our calculus, or an inability to disentangle a particularly complex skein of conditions—an inability that is often an incapacity to change our methods, to vary the attack, to remodel the logical structures we use or to create new ones. We find it more reputable, and above all, more convenient to blame things and to attribute to them one's own insufficiency—a familiar procedure of which Brunschvicg, Bachelard, and Piaget have been incisive critics. Let us not speak of ruptures or interruptions within determinism but simply admit our theoretical or practical blunders. Is not science the history of mistakes rectified? If determinism seems to have gaps, this does not mean that reality is flawed by them. Rather, it means that the determining principle, when it ought no longer unfold the system of ideas in an idealist fashion, but rather express it in an aggregate of categories (even pure ones such as mathematics)—and with even greater reason apply it to the transformation of the sensible (physical science) or the transformation of self (ethics)—encounters resistances with which it ought to combine. Descending the levels of consciousness one after the other, the subject-object opposition diversifies and becomes more serious: the irrational in mathematics, the unknown in physics, heredity or passion in biology are so many deviations or characteristic tensions between subject and object. We do not have to analyze them; this job belongs, as the case may be, to the logician of sciences or the epistemologist of normative sciences (for there is also a criticism of ethics). It suffices if we understand that in these domains even the failures have their secret laws. Nothing is a-logical, Blondel used to say; there is also a logic of inconsistencies. Nothing, however, neither a hostile world nor the threat of annihilation, can justify the human subject's renunciation of his initiative and his responsibilities through timidity or laziness.

Nowhere shall we lay down the burden of freedom. Neither indifference[8] nor submissiveness will allow us to resign. The

---

[8] Still other schemas are involved in the notion of a freedom of indifference or in the ambiguous experience of deliberation. These are the substantialist schemas, which here I only recall since we have examined the case for substantialism. The intellect and the will (to which is added the emotions) are assimilated as accidents of the soul-substance. They interact as rivals which influence or neutralize each other from without. This is gross reification. It allows for precise academic dissection but involves an arbitrary atomism repugnant to the spirituality of the subject. When history is ignored and the act of faith is analyzed with the aid of schemas of this sort, the believer becomes a consciousness in episodes. To an intellect deprived of evidence we add a will capable of making the intellect *believe* what it cannot *see,* and this through a grace which is created and finite, but of which we do not know (the question is debated) whether it supernaturalizes from the beginning that which leads to the faith (including natural reason) or whether it is content to baptize after the fact the adhesion of reason to religious truths. The intentions of these problematics

only kind of neutrality there is must be regarded as suspect and blameworthy; and the only kind of submissiveness, false and deceitful. This means that freedom implies an irreducible dignity, even in the midst of dishonesty, error or imperfection. It has the amplitude and intensity of auto-position; it is noetic and axiologic creativity. It is limited by nothing, since its very failures still suppose that it accepts them, even if only to get rid of them. Now we must clarify the meaning of the fact that the act-law proceeds from the one, and that it derives from Aseity without being this Aseity.

The fact is that those who place God and man in competition for the creation of values are thinking of a God-object, the place of eternal truths, the subsisting Good.[9] Once order (or the constellation of ideas and values) is identified with God,[10] productive human freedom is finished. If the issue were pressed, the Absolute would be presented as ready-made, eternal and static, which would prevent the activity of man from creating and inventing. How then can we dream of *doing* good? As Sartre would say, it is useless to try; it has already been done, and God has done it.[11] To man would remain the possibility of doing evil, for evil is outside God and opens before man as a new path to be cleared, a new road to be trod. Evil does not imply anything positive, and thus man is endowed only with a negative freedom.

---

are certainly pure: they wish to respect the transcendence of the divine mystery and of human freedom. The error would be to canonize these schemas of common sense and to pretend that they can adequately hold the spiritual act and the gift of God. No one would make such a claim, at least in theory.

[9] In *L'existentialisme est un humanisme* (Paris, 1946), Sartre directly likens God to an intelligible heaven where values are to be found.

[10] We should, however, avoid criticism without reservations. According to Malebranche, for example, order is indeed in God (the Augustinian Word, place of ideas); but the divine transcendence remains unchanged, because of the fact that Malebranche distinguishes between the "substance" of God, which he "engenders by the necessity of his Being" and his "work" which he "produces by an entirely free action" (*Méditations chrétiennes,* IX, par. X, Gouhier ed., p. 174).

[11] See *Le diable et le bon Dieu* (Paris, 1951), p. 89.

Either he does what is good, and must then be satisfied with sanctioning the order inscribed in the divine essence; or he does what is evil, in which case he invents, but in a void. One way or the other, he is the loser, for neither adherence to something ready-made nor meaningless adventure leads to any effective freedom.

We can solve the dilemma if we exclude the Absolute that alienates man from himself. Once God is rejected, man regains possession of creative prerogatives. He himself will trace the path of freedom without any concern other than avoiding any relapse to the level of things. No longer are there objective goods or evils. No longer is any norm of value anterior to the creative choice which freely establishes the laws of existence. No constraint, consequently, burdens an autonomy that has finally been equipped with all its powers. Man, conscious and responsible, is henceforth the maker of his own destiny. He does not escape the domain of ambiguity in which his situation traps him, but it is precisely this freedom that preserves his ability to react despite the limitations or rather because of them. The rejection of limits, their active negation and their irrealization become the most exalted fortitude. It is in this struggle, in this defiance, that man assumes his subjectivity, and undertakes the transformation of himself and all else.

It is easy to see what we accept and what we reject in a position of this kind. We admit and affirm a creativity that is just as inventive, just as effective. For without human productivity, humanism would no longer exist.[12] But we so readily endow man with creativity because we believe we would offend the divine transcendence were we to project on it the system of determinations. This does not belong to the One but to the *multiple*, to the

[12] *Christian humanism* is only too often a spurious concordism. It combines a causalist—and therefore anthropomorphic—theocentrism, with an anthropocentrism of ratifying adherence, that is, of conformism, and not of inventiveness.

171

act-law.[13] Far from being driven to atheism in order to preserve noetic and axiological productivity, it is theism that imposes on us the creation of ideas and norms. Once we admit a henological transcendence—the only way theism can escape the criticisms properly leveled at causalist and spatial schemata—we must also admit a creationism of essences on the human level. Nor is such an attempt unheard of. In my opinion, Plotinus had an idea of it. And it is because subsequent philosophy failed to explore the idea, that it has continually oscillated between an objectivist theism and an antheistic humanism.

Nevertheless, one may object, how does an henological Absolute change things? Are we not always restricting man's autonomy, whether we are dealing with the One or the first Cause? If God is the source, it makes little difference what mode of presence we attribute to him. He remains the eternal intruder, the *Other;* and that makes two subjects in consciousness. The otherness-duality sanctions the regime of alienation.

There are not two subjects; there is not me and the *Other,* or rather me and the divine *Thou.* These are reducible psycho-sociological schemas, and in fact, we did reduce them when criticizing the Absolute of dialogue. Let us recall that the act-law is the true determining principle. It constitutes an order, while God is absence of order.[14] Ordinal and non-ordinal cannot

[13] "The One," writes Bréhier commenting on Plotinus, "is therefore the ever-present, infinitely fertile principle of the acts of the intellect. It is not in the One but in the intellect that the productive activity, of which the One is the principle, resides" (*La philosophie de Plotin,* [Paris, 1928], p. 143).

[14] It is well known that St. Thomas (see *ST,* Ia, q. 15, a. 1, 2) attempts despite everything to reconcile divine simplicity with the multiplicity of ideas in God. For him, the various ideas are only the divine essence insofar as it is indefinitely imitable by creatures. This theory naturally recalls the artificialist schemas (the constructor, the architect) and a finalistic exemplarism. Yet, if Sertillanges's interpretation is correct, the Thomistic position escapes anthropomorphism: "For him [St. Thomas], the world does not really preëxist under the form of ideas, even divine ideas. What preëxists is simply God, and what we call ideas are only projections into God, by our own understanding, of objects of time and of acquisitions of time" (*Le christianisme et les philosophies,* t. I, [Paris, 1941], p. 285).

be added together; they do not constitute number. They are not contradictory; they are even completely compatible, on the condition that they are not taken on the same level. Strictly speaking, we should say that the order of the act-law constitutes a level. The trans-ordinal Absolute, on the contrary, far from constituting a level in a "super-world," is *that by which* levels exist. It is superabundant spontaneity, the source of life and expansive generosity, but in a pure state, without any determination affecting its rigorously simple unity. From then on, the multiple unity that defines the act-law, can appear only as a derivation of the One. The relationship that binds them is irrecusable for whoever is not satisfied with a reduction aborted at the intelligible level. But this relationship must be interpreted in terms of a purely spiritual reciprocity: neither the God of nature (substantialist schema), nor the God of life (vitalist schema), nor the God of consciousness (psychological schema) could sustain such reciprocity as this. We must rise to the super-essential God, to the God of the mystics who are beyond dialogue, to the God of effective spirituality (religious or philosophical, on these heights the title is no longer important). This God is super-being. He refuses to enter into any correlation in which he would be compromised by the homogeneity of relationship. He gives himself only to the mind which carries the reduction to its end, to him who passes beyond the levels of reality and of truth, to him who discovers that the very notion of level is relative and uncertain. When the highest order—that of the act-law—itself appears as multiple and unstable; when everything is brought into question by consciousness, even whether there is a question; when freedom, the basis of everything, perceives that it is founded on nothing and that no object measures it, then at this moment God can be intended and attained. He is even within us, as the very nerve center of this proud and terrible need for struggle in act, for struggle without limit, the capacity to contest even the intelligible—even (and above all) to anguish freedom itself. And through this can hope come to

173

us, not that we might escape our situation entirely, but that we might go beyond all nature in order to communicate with Aseity itself.

It has therefore become impossible to imagine God as a pre-posited given weighing on consciousness, like a rival and alienating otherness. We can no longer ever be satisfied with affirming that he is not a given, but one who gives. To be precise, we must go further and recognize that the conferral of meaning belongs to the act-law and not to God. God contributes only the infinite indetermination out of which can arise, as it were by auto-spiration, the determining principle and the system of determinations. One might object that the presence of the undetermined One at the root of the auto-determining is still too much, that it suffices to posit existence as an unjustifiable gratuity. But we would have to reply that we are forced to choose between foundering on a crude facticity or discovering a supreme spontaneity. To be too easily satisfied, to be content to say merely that existence is referred to itself and that we are condemned to live and condemned to meaning and to freedom, would be to accept a fact, and to accommodate ourselves to a given, while refusing to contest it on the same grounds as all the rest. Or again, it involves an unacknowledged return to the reflective analytism of Brunschvicg, and a refusal to answer for life and matter. Finally, and above all, it involves a confusion, through inadvertence or ruse, of *auto-position* with *aseity*. But this is a gross confusion. Our prerogative is auto-determination, not to place ourselves beyond all determination. It seems to us undeniable that the finite mind remains both one and multiple. In fact, existentialism knows very well that existence imposes on itself its categories and its norms, and that it creates its own values. In the same way we would say that auto-position means that the act-law is both the positing of the self and the positing of laws. Hence there is a split within subjectivity, a division of subject and object which hardens as we descend the levels of consciousness. This is something no one would question. It is a sign that the human condition is recognized in its ambiguity; an ambiguity which arises from the threat of facticity and the precariousness of a subjectivity which cannot posit itself without creating its own existence, but which remains exposed to weariness and torpor, at times to the point of chaining itself to the past rather than constructing its future. Here consciousness encounters a difficult task: to assume itself and all its structures, without being able to escape them or to lay them down. It is creative but limited at the same time. The Absolute, on the contrary, is not subjected to any condition of this kind, nor to any condition whatever. It does not have to determine itself, or rather to create itself according to the equivocal expression *causa sui.* There is no distance or difference of level between its existence and its essence, between its *self* and its *law. Its* simplicity is beyond these correlations, and for it there is no question of doubling or of redoubling.[15] Likewise, its pure outpouring deserves the name *aseity* which, despite etymology, means not so much an auto-

[15] In examining the atheism of Sartre (see *Foi et interrogation,* p. 93 ff.), I have previously tried to show that the trinitarian God of Christianity escapes his objections. Only a monistic God (a simple axiom) or a dualistic God (relation of reflected to reflecting) is destroyed by the impossibility of reconciling the in-itself with the for-itself. I do not repeat this demonstration here because it involves a problematic which ought to be critical from the beginning. The trinitarian dogma is an extremely complex structure, and we shall return to it. Insofar as it objectifies the triple intervention of Creator, Redeemer, and Sanctifier, it seems to hypostatize certain contingent givens (which themselves were elaborated by a determined mentality). Insofar as it expresses necessary relations and attempts to reconcile the antithetical requirements of subjectivity and objectivity, it is one of the most extraordinary intuitions of the human mind. The historian will see an Alexandrian inspiration in it, and this will be no great surprise. But it is more important to grasp the meaning of an initiative of this sort, and here the critical philosopher will have his word to say. He will note, for example, that psychologism risks destroying this metaphysical construction (psychological trinities are not of the same order). He will also point out, we believe, that to give equal weight to the Trinitarian schema and the transordinal character of God is to confuse transcendence itself with its modes of apprehension. Neither St. Augustine nor Blondel entirely avoided this confusion. With Scotus Erigena and under the inspiration of the Pseudo-Dionysius, it will be necessary to repeat that God is more than Unity and more than Trinity. In no case can he be circumscribed by the intentionality which seeks to grasp him.

causation as a radical spontaneity. God does not have to posit himself (the pronominal is superfluous). Still less does he have to posit laws in order to posit himself. Auto-position and auto-regulation are terms that do not refer to him. They should be reserved for us since we alone must impose mediations upon ourselves in order to become ourselves. God, on the contrary, is perfect and supreme equation. That is why the effective passage from auto-position to Aseity can be effected only by grace, that is, by God's initiative and not by any pretension on our part.

Thus it is that Aseity dominates us and goes beyond us, and we can see in what sense. The atheist believes that he is fully justified in saying that we are not fully autonomous if, in order to be, we must derive our being from another. This is only in appearance, a difficulty inherent in language. For the relation of the mind to God is incommensurable with any other. Divine transcendence does not create the mind as a thing; it makes spiritual immanence fruitful; *it creates auto-creators.*

Because of this, we do not seek to hide this dependence but rather proclaim it. It is a fact and more than a fact; it is the mystery of our origin. As Brunschvicg said, consciousness cannot at the same time make itself both younger and older than itself. But while atheistic phenomenology revolts against an unjustifiable facticity—at the same time it dramatizes it: we observe that the mystery of the initial fact does not fail to exert some influence upon us. It does not allow itself to be revealed by analysis (every account of origins involves imaginative expression). But it enlightens us much more: it thrusts us forward and opens our eyes to human tasks. We owe it our power to exercise the totality of the functions of consciousness. At the end of its enterprises, the destiny of the spirit will be made known. The journey's beginning becomes clear only during the day's march, the end throws light on the beginning, and the arrival on the departure. The *alpha* is recovered only at the *omega*. Practically speaking, perhaps the Absolute will not be acknowledged without shame and without fear until the hypothesis will have become incarnate in an expansion of the auto-position to the measure of the Aseity. The liberation of man will then be complete. A God who is simply a benefactor will always be paternalistic. It is better than being a tyrant, but it is still a subtle form of alienation. Only a God capable of sharing his spontaneity can guarantee the salvation and dignity of the spirit. But that is a concern of living spirituality. The critic's task is limited to defining the conditions of possibility and validity for such an elevation.

3. REVELATION:
THE RELIGIOUS INTERPRETATION OF HISTORY

Does God speak? Is there an Absolute with whom we can dialogue? Can we pray to a transcendent God?

Two kinds of answers are possible. A philosopher will explain how God, in his transcendence surpasses our categories and how, nevertheless, we cannot intend him and thereby come into contact with him without passing through our categories. *Via negationis, via eminentiae,* the procedure is classical since the time of the Pseudo-Dionysius. In this context we will deliberately make use of antithetical categories and correct them, one by the other. We will accept the positive side of their signification and reject the restrictive mode of their representations. And we will not cease to relate ourselves to God according to a principle of intentionality. For no meaning could be applied to him outside a dynamic intentionality or outside a judgment in which our relation with the Absolute passes from implicit experience to explicit knowledge.

According to this method, we would have to say that God is at one and the same time silence and speech, that he does not speak and that he speaks, that he is mystery and that he is revelation. He is silence because he transcends all the determinations of language. He is speech because his presence is the source of our ability to think, to act, and to institute a system of ideas, of values,[1] and of signs. He does not speak because he is ineffable. He speaks because nothing is said except with reference to something beyond all expression. He is mystery because he is transcategorical. He is revelation because the judgment by analogy, which takes into account our relationship with him, enables us to know him. Thus in the philosopher's eyes, God initiates and justifies what we call the category of dialogue. Consequently, recourse to him is legitimate: we can affirm that God questions us, and that he awaits and arouses our answer. We can also affirm that God replies when we invoke him and that he hears our prayer, because he first arouses our recollection and supports our returning toward him.

However, this answer remains very schematic, and in many respects, even seems abstract. There is another more direct and more complete answer, which is equally precise even though it belongs to spontaneous thought. This is the answer offered by the Hebrew consciousness.[2] It will be worthwhile to consider it, for it holds the key to positive religion and to historical revelation.

No one will deny that the Bible[3] furnishes us with an extremely pure idea of transcendence. The God of Israel is the God of all nations. He is the invisible and ineffable one, whom Moses himself glimpsed only while turned away from him. For it is written: no one can see God unless he die. He escapes our gaze and is wrapped in mystery. His thoughts are not our thoughts,

[1] Especially of sacred values.

[2] I sometimes use one or other of the following terms: Hebrew, Hebraic, Jew, Israelite, Jewish, or even: Israel, Judaism, and so on. I am not, for all that, ignorant either of the characteristics of ancient Israel (previous to the conquest or even during patriarchal times) or the rupture between the two kingdoms or the ethnic or tribal denomination. Since it is not my job to retrace the history of the descendents of Jacob, but to describe a type of religious institution that concerns all the people of the Bible, I find it convenient to have at my command a rather extensive vocabulary and to use interchangeably certain names and designations.

[3] The experience of the exile definitively purified biblical theism.

178

nor his ways our ways. It would be a sacrilege to reduce him to our dimensions, to represent him (the image becomes an idol), to pray to him, or to adore him unless we keep the sense of the infinite by joining the idea of a God who is nigh with the compensating idea of a God who is hidden.

We might think that a God so transcendent, a God who continues to elude us even at the moment he announces his coming, would be averse to entering into history. Judaism draws the opposite conclusion. Because the Ineffable cannot declare himself openly, because he cannot himself speak our language, all speculative revelation becomes impossible. That is why the Bible declares fruitless all human wisdoms that claim to teach us in whole or in part what God is. The condemnation of pagan philosophies in Sacred Scripture comes from this: that it is illusory and a profanation to reflect God's wisdom in a wisdom of our fashioning, for God's wisdom belongs to a different order. It cannot allow itself to be won by even the cleverest minds, so long as these restrict themselves to building up a system of abstractions. But even if the *speculative* revelation of a living and transcendent God is not within our reach—even if it would be contradictory that the Ineffable could cease to be ineffable—a *positive* revelation remains possible, and an historical evidence of the Eternal becomes plausible. This is the central idea of Hebraic piety.

Judaism understands that God cannot speak like us, and therefore if he is to speak he must take on our way of speaking. That is why it sees in human history the supreme organ of revelation. Paganism believed that nature reveals God, that it bears his reflection or expression, and at its own level bears witness to him. Judaism concedes this to a certain point, but does not go so far. Nor does it take the same direction. Judaism's conception of the created steers it away from naturalism. According to this conception, nature's only reason for existence is in terms of man: its goal is to lead man to God, but man must know how to give it back to God through a gift-offering. This subordinate role of nature, this role as simple mediator derives from the superiority of history over things, from the primacy of human acts and of their freedom over the natural elements. Man alone is the image of God; nature is only his product. In the eyes of Judaism, nature is nothing but the theater in which man's destiny unfolds. Under these conditions it is not surprising that history should acquire a revelatory value. It is still less surprising that God can speak only through it. He cannot reveal himself except through the mediation of human witness. The Ineffable does not speak, but he communicates through the men of God, through his witnesses, and through his prophets. The category of revelation thus appears at the crossroads of two antithetical ideas, which are equally coherent and equally demanding: the divine ineffability on the one side and, on the other, the power man possesses to denote the Eternal in time, to be its witness, or rather, to bear the responsibility that is incumbent upon him to guide history in order that it may be a testimony rendered to God, that it may become his revelation, his "word."

This thesis seems to give more to man than to God—man becomes the revealer, and we are tempted to forget that it is God who takes the initiative in revealing himself. If we have this impression, it is because we have not yet grasped at what depth the movement of revelation within history originates. Judaism never exalts man at the expense of God, but the opposite is equally true. It looks upon history as revelatory, and this for two reasons. The first we already know: God reveals himself only through his witnesses. The second echoes the first: unlike nature, history is *intentional,* and this in two ways. In a banal sense, it incarnates free intentions, and receives a precise orientation from human impulse despite the resistance of natural determinisms and the weight of societies. In a religious sense (which the men of God give it), it manifests the presence of the Absolute in time. More precisely, it manifests at one and the same time both this presence and the way in which humanity reacts to its touch. However, only intentionality allows for this manifestation. Since God cannot show himself openly, he makes us seek for him, invites us to a long journey, reveals himself at the end of an indefinite quest and an unceasingly renewed effort to find him. On his side, man cannot grasp him but only intend him. God is never possessed like an object. He reveals himself as a presence—a presence that is all the more stimulating in that it remains mysterious. But history lends itself extremely well to this intending of God by man, to this motivating presence of God in man. It is both a means for God to summon man and the means for man to answer to his divine call. Seen in this perspective, it is identical with the process of revelation. And it helps us understand why all revelation of the Absolute can be only positive, that is, expressed in time, uttered in our language, and instituted according to our structures.

This interpretation has been criticized as too general, as not discriminating between sacred history and general history, as limited to contrasting cultural religion and natural religion, and as failing to establish in what way the mystical humanism of the Jewish people derives from a supernatural essence. Is this objection justified? I do not think so, for it pretends to ignore what the notion of historicity in the Judaic context implies. Everyone knows that Israel invented the category of history, but we forget that it invented this category for religious motives. History is not made in an arbitrary way. Nor is it made for any reason whatever by anyone whomsoever. According to the biblical writers, God alone makes history and causes history to be made. Likewise, only the men of God, or men united to God, make history because they make it with God and for God. In the final analysis, the only problem is the following: what is the ultimate end of man? What is the ultimate term of civilizations and of societies? The Bible answers: this end, this term, is the Eternal. Consequently, the destiny of individuals and of peoples can have only one meaning: union with God. Whatever promotes this union is good, and whatever opposes or delays it is bad. Thus the process of becoming human is made into *history;* henceforth it has an end to accomplish and stages to pass through. In turn history becomes *sacred history:* it takes form and acquires meaning and value, in a definitive way, only insofar as it is lived for God. According to the Jewish perspective, the concept of profane history does not exist, and could not exist. Historicity was discovered by Israel only as an indication of advancement toward the Absolute. Since then, we have laicized time, moral and social evolution, and history. We were justified in doing so, insofar as the ultimate end of man ought not to destroy partial or intermediary ends. But in the Hebrew context, the primacy of the supreme end is basically emphasized from the beginning. That is why history is conceived of only as an attestation, as a coming of the Eternal.

Under these conditions, the student of Judaism is never tempted to reduce sacred history to general history. Rather, he perceives how biblical religion, in its historical, prophetic, or poetical books, links all history to sacred history. And he sees that it is justified in so doing. For after all there is no history, there is no sound orientation for the becoming of man if temporality is not related to the Absolute. Modern man can speak of a meaning of history outside God because he proposes for himself short-term goals, notably in economics and politics. But this is an illusion. There are only two alternatives. Either history has no other meaning than to bring about a relative improvement in the human condition—and in this case the result attained cannot be the ultimate goal. Man will always find some flaw in any improvement whatever. History will strike out again indefinitely in an ever higher direction, continually seeking its realization beyond what has already been realized. This is proof that its end surpasses its grasp, and that its intention consists in willing ever more, in willing not the relative but the absolute. Or, as the other alternative, we may assign to history a more satisfying objective and identify as its purpose the obliteration of all division, the reconciliation of man and the world, and the establishment of a reciprocity among consciousnesses. But this universal peace, this peace of each with all and with everything and of each man with himself, this ideal peace is nothing but another name for the reintegration of all things in the Absolute.

The Marxist vision here adopts the perspective of Judaism. It adopts it without saying so, which is no crime. But it adopts it while remaining unconscious of its implications and unconscious of its applications also, and that is less pardonable. Relativist meliorisms do not hold up for long under reflection. Determined optimisms, those which militate for a unified society, obey the true logic of action. But how can we support them when they remain ignorant and scornful of their own authentic foundation?

Only Judaism succeeded in being coherent: there is no history, meaningful progress, connected stages, or hierarchical values unless the Absolute is recognized as history's driving power and goal. Otherwise we are forging false "absolutes," substitute "absolutes." We preserve the illusion of advancing and of progressing, but towards what? If everything is relative, if we are not headed for a term that permits an absolute judgment on the stages we have covered, there is neither advance nor progress: we then mark time without knowing where we are going or where we are. In fact, courage wavers and enthusiasm flags as soon as we can no longer be assured of the nature of the ultimate end or the purpose of the journey. On these two points Judaism was fully conscious of its own implications. That is why it truly founded history. It founded it on the Absolute, and more precisely on the religious relationship with the Absolute. This is not an exaggeration, if it is true that without religion, its enthusiasm and ferment, the most advanced civilization would be merely an elegant way of deferring the solution of the human problem. Having founded history, and having founded it on union with God, Israel was aware of its responsibility. In proclaiming this

183

sense of history, it understood that its vocation was to be the herald of God. This sets it aside from all other peoples. Its origins resemble those of its neighbors, and indeed it never stopped borrowing and exchanging. But in this one thing Israel was unique, for it alone uncovered the revelatory import of history. Israel alone understood that if it deliberately united itself to God and made an alliance with him, and if this alliance was not only a means of buying protection (as is the case in superstitious cults) but on its part a will to offer itself as a disinterested and loyal witness, despite the blows of fate and repeated failures, then Israel would become in the context of its history the effective revealer, the instrument and organ of divine action.

Once this is understood, it follows that Israel's becoming, its social and religious evolution, are given over entirely and in principle to inspiration. The convenant was not, as it was understood by its guides or chiefs, its prophets or writers, a ruse to win God's favors. It was an offering, an act of abandon, that established Israel as a messenger from the Most High. This is a situation which suggests to the free thinker that the Jewish people were the elect of God only because they claimed to be. More carefully considered, however, the situation imposes a paradox: when a community of men, a handful at first and then a multitude (although the multitude was always lagging behind the chosen few who led them), decide to live wholly for God, God speaks and acts through them. He speaks and acts through them because they themselves speak and act for him. Here, in its most subtle form, we encounter the mechanism of revelation and touch upon the most secret forces of history. The fact of Israel's union with God, and the fact of declaring what this union should be is the very expression of the Absolute. It is, if we dare to say it, God becoming history, God revealed in time and in the language of a people, God as the author of a religious experience, and God as the inspirer of books in which this experience is inscribed.

Why were the Jewish people the only ones to receive such a

mission—to *receive* it, since to attribute it to oneself is to prove that one carries within himself the power to which one is bearing witness? That no one can say. But it suffices to recognize that Israel would never have had the power to affirm and to live a union with God, if God himself had not enabled them to do so. Specifically religious evidence illuminates this depth: man cannot create the infinite, and if he names it, if he *speaks* it, it is because the Infinite names itself and speaks itself through him. Now, Israel has named God and spoken him, not only in a better way than other peoples, but in quite a different way.[4] Israel named him and spoke him in a covenant, in a history that does not restrict the Absolute to what we see, what we touch, and what we feel but within an intentional aim that restores his infinity and transcendence.[5] Thus it is that the Infinite and the Transcendent are revealed in and through Israel. It would be contradictory to intend the Transcendent without receiving from it the power to reach it. Under these conditions, we may conclude that Israel is really the people of God, the chosen people. It invented sacred history only because God is the Lord of history, because God has raised up a witness to his presence, because God wished to reveal that the destiny of humanity is to be a history (a progressive return towards him), and a sacred history (a return in a spirit of adoration, love, and sacrifice).

These considerations concerning the mentality of Judaism have only one purpose: to show that the problem of the word of God, the problem of a dialogue with the Absolute, the problem of the covenant and of prayer are insoluble only for a thought which rejects the category of revelation. At the heart of Judaism, as at the heart of Christianity, this category dominates

[4] A philosopher and theologian from a university outside France who had occasion to criticize my epistemology severely wrote me that if it were not for Jesus he would give no more attention to Judaism than to Buddhism. I answered him that without Judaism, Christianity would be projected outside its historical truth, and that Christian revelation began with Abraham.

[5] The Christian dogma of the incarnation respects and magnifies this rule: Christ is the Word made flesh, but we *see* man; we *believe* in the Lord.

all the others. God "reveals himself" because his word reaches us only if it flows through our words, the symbols of our language and of our attitudes. He reveals himself positively and not speculatively, historically and not ideally, because he cannot speak in the open; because he is a mystery; because he remains veiled in his unfolding; because in order to become manifest at our level he must allow himself to be seen through representations; and finally because human dynamics, history, is the sole order of reality in which we can express him in an intentional way, the only order in which he himself can incite, inspire, and attract free and responsible intentionalities. Thanks to the process of revelation, Judaism conceives an Absolute which is beyond all expression and which, therefore, borrows our ways of expression. This is an Absolute of silence and of mystery, of simplicity and of transcendence which, for this very reason, enters into our categories of dialogue, covenant, and prayer, and grounds and justifies them even in their anthropomorphic structures.[6] When we consider only his transcendent character, God

6 I hope that no doubt remains regarding my position. Through Judaism it must be said that the Ineffable speaks through his witnesses, by men of God, by the prophets. There we find the foundation for historical revelation and for inspiration. There we find the true structure of a religion based on witness. To speak, God needs men and he needs history. He even needs, as the theology of the incarnate Word has it, to enter into history, to become man. Once this is recognized, we must go still further. When the men of God, the prophets (all the more so, Christ) speak in place of God, in his name, it is really God who speaks. It is God who speaks, first, because it is the only way he can speak our language, then and above all, in this precise case the aim of the transcendent and the witness of it coincide: proof that his presence is perceived and that it is declared. The *locutio Dei* is no other than the presence of God or his action expressed in this manner, that is, positively revealed. If we understand this, we can maintain at the same time that God speaks and that he does not speak, that he is silence and that he is revelation, that he is mystery and that he is the source of understanding, and so on. Under these conditions, the dialogue with the Absolute is not a betrayal of the Absolute. It is the only revelation possible of the Absolute. This process of revelation allows the faithful to converse with God, to pray to him, while assured of being united with him. I have seemed to be negative in subordinating the dialogue with the Absolute to the Simple. I would like to be positive in showing that the transcendent exceeds our categories, but becomes involved in them to be revealed. Only revelation justifies anthropomorphism, or at least it alone justifies it fully.

does not speak our language. He does speak our language when we consider his immanence in the spirit and in history. The antinomy is only apparent; it is resolved by a distinction of perspectives. It even hides a necessity subordinate to divine freedom: if God wishes to tell us who he is and what he should mean to us, he necessarily borrows the roundabout way of our representations, and the complex apparatus of our intentionality. It is revelation that opens the way to covenant and to dialogue, that evokes and guarantees our prayers. It delivers transcendence to us without compromising it, and communicates mystery without dissipating it. That is why it can signify and make known the supernatural without alienating it, and without naturalizing it. Judaism understood all this, lived it, and gave it expression. We should recognize its originality as regards other cults, and accord it a unique destiny in the history of religions.

We can summarize this section in a few words: God does not speak, therefore he speaks. He does not appear, therefore he appears. No one sees him, therefore he shows himself. He is beyond our grasp and our categories, but he appears through them. He is the high point of our intentions, and their soul; nevertheless we must unceasingly purify our ideas and our schemas. For example, he cannot be called personal—personal in our sense—but he is more than this. It is possible and normal to address ourselves to him as to a person, provided we preserve the sense of mystery. It is also normal to make a very simple acknowledgment: he understands us, loves us, and hears our prayers. All this is true because it is viewed from the right angle. It takes into account our relationship with the Absolute, because it maintains his transcendence above and beyond this relationship. For all these predications, the process of revelation points out the path to follow. It fearlessly involves the Absolute in psychology and in history. But it never confuses them. It simply testifies that God reaches us where we are; and that what we are and what we do (if we know how to be it and to do it for him unconditionally) reaches him where he is, and as he is.

4. THE EARLY CHRISTIAN COMMUNITY:
MERGING FACT AND RELIGIOUS INTERPRETATION

When a believer reads the gospels he discovers, with all the enthusiasm of his faith, the astonishing personality of Jesus. He sees him act, hears him speak, and follows after him. The evangelical framework is so uncluttered, its psychological truth is so sober and strong, the action that it unfolds awakens in the soul such prolonged echoes, that contact with Jesus is instantly established in a direct and immediate way.

There is a great deal to say about this spontaneity that leads the believer to his master and immediately attaches him to his personality. If we are to understand it properly, we must surmount literary and human charm and consider only moral and religious value. Nevertheless, an analytical effort of this kind is still premature. There is a preliminary problem to be dealt with.

Have we not forgotten that the Gospel, which brings us into such close contact with the life of Jesus, supposes the mediation of a witness? It was not written day by day during Christ's lifetime. It is not his autobiography—Jesus wrote only on the sand. It is not the detailed account of his acts and gestures, written by a disciple at his side and reviewed and corrected by him. We have neither a private diary of the Master, nor his memoirs, nor a history composed of his day-to-day remarks. What we have is no less important—indeed, it is infinitely more valuable—but it is something quite different.

The Gospel is the expression of the initial faith of the Church, its express testimony, its manifesto signed in blood. Along with its importance as a historical proclamation, the authority of unusual witnesses, and the luster of a religious thought and experience lived in community, the sacred text thus acquires the character of a spiritual charter. It never recounts an event without relating it to the very heart of religion. In this sense, each letter of the Gospel is imbued with spirit, each fact contains its lesson and its effectiveness, each gesture of Jesus includes its significa- tion. We do not have a rough draft, a dry list of names, some annals mentioning dates, some customs, and some undertakings lacking universal import. From the beginning the evangelical narrative goes beyond the anecdotic level and establishes itself on a religious plane. It does not recall the life and death of a man. It testifies that God has manifested himself, that the Word has revealed itself and become present in humanity. Now this is the domain of faith. That is why the Gospels are the expression of the faith in the infant Church and among the early com- munities of believers, and not a profane history that preceded the faith of the Church.

If this initial mediation of the Church is not more frequently emphasized, it is because it disappears behind its result, and since we arrived after the fact, we find ourselves faced with the written account. We profit from what the Church accomplished in its early years; we admire this success of the primitive faith, this unique product, this gem of religious literature—the Gospel. We no longer realize that for human hand to preserve the lineaments of this history took an incomparably powerful inspira- tion, the impulse of a lively faith, and a whole-hearted involve- ment in an unprecedented spiritual adventure. But can we really recapture the psychology of the apostles? If the Twelve had portrayed themselves as literary authors using secular methods, we could give a nuanced, detailed, and picturesque portrait of them. In fact what we learn of them, generally from others, is less complete, but more decisive. The role they played in regard to Jesus comes to light only afterward when the fruit of their action confirmed the action itself. Certainly, their companionship with Jesus must have molded their souls. It prepared their mission and established their testimony. They participated in the public ministry, witnessed his Passion, saw him in the resurrection, and received the Holy Spirit on Pentecost. And yet they did not perceive everything with the same understanding.

189

Men of little faith, where did they finally get the grace to penetrate to the depths, and the strength to testify to the end for what at first they hardly understood? This we should never have known were it not for the doctrinal illumination of the gospels, if it were not for the New Testament as a whole. Only these documents show us how, enlightened by the Holy Spirit, they proclaimed the Galilean teacher Christ and Lord. The gospels, the Acts, and the epistles are the expression of this enlightenment, the witness to this faith which suddenly became strong enough and courageous enough to replace the synagogue by the Church in progressive stages. Instead of a fixed, though inspired text, we have a living text, inspired in its letter because it was inspired in the life and in the acts that it records.

Would we perhaps like a text as "objective," as implacable as a police report? But why should the objectivity that records the faith be as impersonal and neutral as that which the historian and the scholar affect? Are we sure, moreover, that there exists in the world even one text that is entirely dead, frozen, and which establishes a truth so inert that it does not contain the slightest hint of the writer's personal conviction? Is there any text whatever that does not reveal its author—the author and his environment, the author and his message? Above all, is there any text, even the most ancient and the most insignificant, that does not invite its reader to discover between the lines some human significance which still preserves a touch of relevance for the present? But when we are dealing with religion, when we are dealing with salvation, impersonality and neutrality becomes unthinkable. The relationship with God defined by a sacred text and the religious experience which it describes necessarily engages personal factors. This experience, this relationship with God has been lived by certain individuals, in a certain society and under certain circumstances. These conditions are not without interest for us. The problem of these individuals is also our own. It arises, for them and for us, from the same aspirations. Our expectation meets theirs. Spontaneously we undertake to verify their solution for ourselves, to see if it suits us and satisfies our need.

Now this solution cannot be like a theorem. It engages not only our understanding: it also appeals to the will. Moreover, it engages our consciousness at every level and involves the very depths of our freedom. How, then, could the great religious witnesses have depicted the object of faith without incorporating into it their own faith? Would a separation between the two make any sense? The object would disappear if the approach which was to grasp it were not of the same sort. Do we wish to consign the object of faith to general history in the same way that we attribute the phenomenon of falling bodies to physics? To do so would be to detach it from faith, for faith is not only a fact but a truth, not only history but meaning and value.

We should not be surprised that the testimony of faith envelops its object as a loving look envelops the beloved. Witness cannot isolate its object, remain aloof from it, or separate it from itself. It cannot drown it in phenomenal or even historical continuity. If by chance the object becomes accomplice to this separation and withdraws itself from the faith that supports it, it would be entirely reabsorbed in the profane and submerged. There would no longer exist an object of faith perceived as such; in fact, there would be neither object nor faith. Faith is impossible in a universe where all meaning accorded to its object must remain on the sensible or natural level.

It happens that we forget these elementary truths. Faith distrusts faith when it observes itself as a physicist studies an object. We are afraid that the Gospel would no longer be history if it became faith in act. We fear that a faith supported by the act of faith of the witnesses of Jesus may be less solid than if it were supported by facts not revealed by their testimony. That is why we would like to reduce the sacred text to profane memoirs. But this attitude, instead of adding to the text, actually detracts from it. We forget that the Church lived decades before writing its teaching down. We pretend to be

191

unaware of the fact that the Church never dreamed of relating the history of Jesus without recognizing in it its religious meaning. When the Gospel presents the good Master, it is always in the splendor of the redemption already accomplished, Pentecost already come, and the Church already established. The same holds for all apostolic writings. The entire New Testament does not give an account of Jesus' acts and attitudes without illuminating them in the light of the final events. It wishes to encompass Jesus' whole personality. It means to bring out his role in the religious history of humanity.

Does the historical cease to be historical for all that? Does history dissolve in the warmth of faith? Does the Gospel alter reality by bringing to light the spirituality it encloses? To raise such question is already to misunderstand the intention of the evangelists. They wrote what the apostles proclaimed. They recorded what the infant Church believed, thought, and lived. They gave an account of a faith they shared, under the power of an illumination that transcended them, and in reference to a collective experience that overwhelmed them. They were the editors of an oral and living testimony. Their concern was to penetrate the spiritual meaning of their sources (Lk. 1:4), even more than to control them materially (Lk. 1:3). For them it was the only way to grasp the subject at hand without ever distorting the meaning of this history with the history of facts. What purpose would the narration of vicissitudes serve if their principal author were not recognized for what he is? To name Jesus was very little; to call him Christ and Lord was everything. It meant summing up the entire Bible, affirming that the Messiah had come, that salvation had been accomplished, and that the sanctifying mediation was present here below forever. At the same time the story of Jesus, enclosed within a few dates, punctuated by meaningful events, and perceived in its religious sense, was offered to men, present and to come, as the history-type of a sinful humanity reconciled at last with God.

Thus faith did not distort this history but grasped it in its

192

deepest meaning. Its interpretation did not in any way destroy its concrete reality. Jesus was called the Christ and recognized as the Word, the mediator and redeemer, because he appeared in the flesh, was born of a woman, and became a country carpenter, preacher, and founder of a community. The apostles had seen and heard him. They had touched with their own hands him whom the first Johannine epistle calls the Word of life. This individual was neither phantom nor fiction, but a real man, a member of his race and of his time. In hailing him as God manifest and incarnate, his followers could neither have forgotten his earthly reality nor invented it. It was from the humble facts of his life, from their prolonged physical and psychological contact with him, from a fully historical context that the companions of Jesus finally grasped the full import of the message left to them by their master.

Thus at their proper level, the facts remain as an irreplaceable foundation. Yet the recognition of the Lord did not come from a purely human sympathy, from that of flesh and blood. As Jesus said to Peter, it could come only through the revelation of the Father. Nevertheless, it is indeed Jesus' humanity that hides and reveals the presence of God. And to intend God through Jesus is the initiative of faith. Fact and truth are linked together without the fact being minimized or the truth left without foundation. The incarnation is a reality and transcendence is effective. God's intervention in history is a fact. And the religious value of the experience of Jesus guarantees its meaning and fruitfulness.

All fear of the Gospel's abandoning the field of fact is thus dispelled. Its character as interpretation of faith does not prevent it from being also the testimony of a real history. The reverse is also true. Because the apostles were Jesus' associates, because the synoptics record their stand in his regard, and because the early community set a value only on that which clarified or promoted this stand, there remains no doubt that from Jesus to the Gospel there was unbroken continuity. Fundamentally, it is the same witness who observed the fact and grasped the truth, recorded the one and proclaimed the other. Consequently, the apostles were the bond that first joined the two together. History and faith are so united in their testimony as to be subsequently inseparable. The society they organized, the Church, will live from this synthesis, from this specific initiative which consisted in transforming events through a religious induction and in turning their account into sacred history. In their turn, the evangelists merely consigned to writing the brief report of this twofold teaching (fact and doctrine), in which facts serve as proof and faith serves as justification.

The mediation of the apostolic Church thus appears primary. The written Gospel corresponds to the Gospel that was spoken and lived, announced and propagated, and which defines the central conviction of the infant Church. The first teaching, the original and constitutive witness was the Gospel that existed before the gospels—the tradition established by the voice of the apostles, the Church as organized by them, around them, and after them. Everything that was handed on was then judged by reference to the apostolic lesson. Even St. Paul's message, original in so many ways, had to be linked with that of the Twelve, and in fact it was. Paul gloried in a direct and extraordinary contact with Christ, but he clearly affirmed his communion with the Twelve. He could have received only from them, first mediately and later immediately, the few events he relates from Jesus' life. If the material details of particular facts did not interest him, and if he suggested that the eternal action of Christ was of greater import than the human behavior of Jesus, it was not that he was ignorant of what was to become the theology of the Incarnation. On the contrary, from the beginning he looked on history as a witness of faith, and in this he was doing only what the Twelve had led him to do. Thus it is that faith can discern the bond that unites facts to truth, history to religion, the visible Jesus to the revelation of God. In so doing it does not take its object from fiction, but bases itself on a real personage and inserts itself into the historical, into concrete experience. It makes use of history to intend, in time, what does not belong to time.

The Church is therefore right in presenting itself simultaneously as the proof and exercise of faith, since it is established on facts that it considers revealing. The gospels derive from the Church and carry its message. This explains their complex nature. They connect us with the major events of Jesus' life, events already clarified and presented as signs. That is why it is impossible for us, after the event, to perceive these facts in their total meaning unless at the same time we acknowledge the justification that is given for them. Some unbelievers persist in reducing the facts in order to avoid taking a position on the interpretation they contain. This is a waste of effort, for the synthesis has already been made. We must accept it or reject it as a whole. The believer makes it his own because he recognizes it as correct and authentic. He understands how the apostles passed from the material vision to the vision of faith, how in turn the early Christian community was led through the psychological shock of the history of Jesus to the discovery of his spiritual message. But in retracing this journey, the believer verifies the same synthesis. The deeds are presented to him also as signs, as indices of the faith. Once he has grasped what they signify, the facts have fulfilled their function. Or rather, they constantly continue to fulfill it, since the intention of faith cannot be maintained except in and through the facts that convey it.

One difficulty remains, however. The infant Church seems to have made a selection from the mass of facts, and the result of this selection is the narrative of the gospels. Inspiration, the theologian will tell us, is the first principle of this selection. True, but its "selectivity" could not fail to respond to the psychological, moral and religious needs of the early Christians. That which fed the oral sources of the Gospel, and later took on ever more perfect form in the synoptics and the Johannine text, was that which met the most characteristic aspirations of souls, indeed that which met the practical needs of the believing community. Through the choice dictated by the religious spirit, a specific answer responded to an expectation, to an appeal, and to definite needs. Nevertheless, we are minimizing this thesis if we think that the economy of the catechesis alone explains the arrangement of the episodes, the commentary on the Lord's words, the clarification given to both of these, and the different tone in each author. This is true, but incomplete. The sacred author certainly aims at the useful, but the useful in this case is more extensive than we think. The synoptics and the Fourth Gospel distribute the events according to an obviously constructed order. But this is not merely to satisfy the daily functions of a Church in the process of formation, its preaching, eucharistic worship, and prayer. It was not enough to pick out and conventionalize the apostles' remembrances, and to insist on those points which the developing ritual could find useful, or on those, such as the Passion, that marked the culminating point in the story of Jesus. Certainly, these concerns can be detected. It is normal that the community should have made some impact on a series of facts that became the law of its life. This explains the adoption of a certain principle of selection on the basis of immediate needs. However, I do not believe that this is all that should be said. The true principle of selection is deeper. The psychological incidents, the adaptations to a given mentality, the thousand practical demands, the restricted play of possible modes of expression—all this remains on the outside. At the core of the phenomenon we are considering there lies an intentionality of far greater import. We must try to be precise about this intentionality, for with it we can perhaps disengage the true mechanism of faith.

In a general way, the intentionality comes to this, that what the texts are going to record, what is going to be perpetuated in writing from the experiences of the apostles and the infant Church is the aggregate of facts which is necessary and sufficient for every believer, present and future, to be able to pass the same judgment as the first believers on the messianic events. In view of this, an unequivocal criterion had to be established for a datum reduced to its essence. In substance, the gospels say this: here are the facts on which the faith of the great witnesses was based, and here is the judgment they made on these facts. The history they report and the interpretation they give of it are one and the same; it is a question of accepting or of rejecting them together. In fact, their religious experience is involved in both the matter and the form; both the one and the other have been condensed to the minimum that must be assumed if one is to proclaim the Church of Christ. Henceforth, religious devotion has to be sown, grow, and blossom within the limits of this matter and in dependence on this form, at least if it intends from age to age to give an account of the apostolic intuition.

At face value this seems to be an inconceivably narrow view. Was no opportunity ever opened to the Jews that the elders of Jerusalem converted or to the pagans that Paul baptized to ask for something more, either concerning Jesus' life or the meaning of his message? Does not the rather scanty text of the gospels—less than one hundred pages—reduce us to bare subsistence? Yes and no: yes, if we hunger for the pious and the picturesque; no, if we understand that a simple narrative, provided it determines an attitude of mind, can contain within its brevity the essence of religion. We shall see, moreover, that the text appeared amid a living community and comes to us accompanied by a constant oral commentary, which is one of the functions of tradition. Even considered alone in itself, however, it expresses all that need be expressed from the start. If it did not emphasize that the old covenant has been surpassed and perfected in the new, if it did not announce that God has lived among us and that our ransom for sin has been accomplished by Christ's sacrifice, it would not open the era of charity into which we are called to enter. But this it did declare; it did

197

announce the good news. That is why it is the charter of the faith in its origin and in its foundation.

The analysis could go still further. The selection of facts about which we are speaking offers us another guarantee besides the veracity of certain events and the price of certain values. We said that it reflected and circumscribed the faith of the Church of the apostles. It therefore expresses the religious attitude of mind of Jesus' companions and their immediate disciples. Now, if we exclude the privileged role of both groups, we soon discover that in them as in us the same religious aspiration nourished itself on the same essential needs. This is all the more remarkable since neither the science of their times, nor the cultural syncretism which was their source of religious categories, corresponds to our science or our culture. Almost two thousand years of civilization, of philosophical and scientific research separate us from them. Yet each of Jesus' words, each of his lessons of confidence, filial trust, and militant hope strike us to the very heart. Above all, his voluntary journey to death moves us, and his attitude of courage and renunciation wins us. That is why those who have seen in him the revealer of God, and even more those who have recognized him as Emmanuel (God with us), as God revealed in person, convince us that his conduct merits this interpretation. Certainly, their ability to convince us comes first of all from their sincerity, their proximity to the event, and their exceptional clear-sightedness. But from our point of view, our conviction is also justified within the period of our own religious experience, by the fact that the Righteous One who dies for his brethren, who proclaims the law of love, and who replaces Jewish futurism with the eternal present of union with God, also offers himself to us, and by degrees commands our respect as the supreme theophany. Jesus is the founder of the absolute religion because the Absolute could not reveal himself in a more perfect manner than in him, under the sign of total unselfishness, of love in act and thought. This is all that the gospels teach. Despite the antiquity and foreign character of their culture, they speak a language contemporary to all time. It is useless to *demythologize* their cosmological pattern, and to dissect in a scholarly way the gnostic or Judaic elements of their synthesis. They unquestionably bear the stamp of time and they reflect a certain outlook. But in this the mystery of Jesus is unique: it can be meditated during the most diverse eras, and it never ceases to awaken religious concern and to engage it on the paths of fidelity and hope.

Thus the "selector" principle of evangelical facts is stripped of the arbitrary, accidental elements that it seemed to contain. You may decant Jesus' story through the most obvious narrative techniques: telescoping episodes, pious reëditing, and chronological redistribution. You may sift it through Jewish mnemonic devices, convenient simplifications, and the community's ritual and educational activities. What remains will not be the residue of this sifting. The selection does not depend on the way it is done, but on the underlying intention. This intention can only be the one given above: to present what is decisive in the first ecclesial experience, what it contains as definitive of the first act of faith in Christ's mission. The fact is that if this experience touches us so closely it is because, from the depths of a religious psychology which has remained substantially the same throughout the ages, our forefathers in faith have strained out the "factual" element and so extricated its doctrinal import as to bring into relief values that we can still experience as our own. Even when we barely recognize ourselves in certain peripheral elements, in certain representations that did not succeed in escaping the particularism of a period, it is undeniable that the Christological vision of God remains intact for us in what is fundamental, universal, and specific within it. We spontaneously reëncounter it like an unchanging intentional vector. And we understand that if the apostolic testimony has succeeded in showing it through dated and limited cultural form, this in itself is proof that these forms deserve our attention and respect. A literal and entirely material criticism could find fault with their more or less extensive range of expression, and sometimes with their ambiguity. But when we discover the meaning that they are able to transmit, and the spiritual experience they succeed in structuring, we are obliged to recognize their effectiveness.

Thus the lesson that the Gospel text conveys to us seems to be manifold. In it the infant Church defines its attitude and proclaims its certitudes. It presents its faith and the object of faith as indissolubly united. It determines with precision the coördinates of Christian experience, and requires in advance that all subsequent experience be referred to this main axis, while showing that this requirement is legitimate since the object of faith would be destroyed if it were not intended through the perspectives that made its establishment possible. The proof that from Jesus to the Church there has been no interruption lies in the simple fact that only the Church of the Pentecost was capable of naming him Jesus Christ and Lord, that is, of recognizing him. Without the Church, the Galilean prophet would have appeared as an agitator or a pacifist, and would have died without being identified. The Christ-God is revealed to us by the Church, which understood and proclaimed his coming. It was Jesus who founded the Church, but it was the Church which, in discerning him, taught men to discern him.

Is this a vicious circle—Jesus proving the divinity of the Church and the Church proving the divinity of Christ? No, for the passage from the sign to the signified is a one way street, as it always is in the inductive method. The history of Jesus is an aggregate of signs whose enigma the apostles penetrated. The Gospel presents these signs at the same time it presents their key. It shows that for the early witnesses, just as for us, the signs become convincing the moment the illumination of faith places them in their true light. The facts *prove* the truth that *explains* them. There would be a vicious circle only if the facts and the truth were to prove each other, and on the same plane.

This observation, which applies to the faith of the apostles also, as we have suggested, applies to us. The only difficulty seems to be that the Church, once it has been instituted, becomes in turn both object and source of our belief. It is an object of faith insofar as it is a religious institution, the organ of revelation and of salvation. This presupposes that we acknowledge Jesus as Christ or Lord, and that we recognize the authenticity of the society that had its origin with him. It is a source of faith insofar as its oral and written testimony offers us the signs of redemption (it presents itself as a sign in the extension of Christological facts) and confides to us the religious meaning of these objective marks. But in both cases the initiative of faith, made in the Church and through the Church, is the same. It consists in intending a value through a sensible expression, and then having attained it, of venerating this expression as the indispensable index and the guiding mark of this value. But this is exactly what an act of faith does in regard to the person of Christ. By turns it takes the fact of Jesus as an elevation of intention towards God, and as the manifestation of God himself. Or rather, there is reason to believe that the valorization of the Church and of the fact of Jesus is simultaneous and that both are formulated as a prospective intentionality followed by a retrospective intentionality. In our case, the fact is obvious: the story of Jesus, such as the Gospel relates it, reaches us only through the Church, since the Gospel itself is derived from the Church. But this is true even in the case of the apostles. Only Pentecost enabled them to perceive the full meaning of Jesus' life. But Pentecost was the first dawn of the Church. That is why tradition seems in every way to be original and constituent. To have faith is to adopt this tradition, to consent to see through its eyes, and at the same time to make our own its premises and conclusions. If this is so, the genesis of the faith never follows an analytical outline. We do not teach first a brief concerning Jesus in order later to go back over each article. From the beginning we assimilate the whole Gospel lesson, the conviction of the Church. We accept the work of the early community as properly performed. We pose the problem of Christ and with that of the community and solve it in the same way. In the light of his teaching, this can be done without any erudition, simply by the clear-sightedness and enthusiasm of love.

The solidarity of Gospel and Church enables us to draw some conclusions, at least in a provisional way. If we understand this solidarity properly, it seems productive in a manner different from all historicism. It not only has the advantage of revealing the primacy of tradition over Scripture, it also has the advantage of recognizing the fact that religious perception belongs to a different order from that of sense perception or external experience. To each object perceived there properly corresponds an adapted subjectivity. There can be no religious object, except for the eyes of faith. We can even say that it is the function of faith to obtain for us a certain way of looking at things, without which the most striking and best organized facts would remain for us only so many uninteresting observations. It is to the glory of the Church of the apostles that it was the first to remove all ambiguity from the story of Jesus, and to bring humanity to see in a descendant of the Judaism of the first century of our era the highest manifestation of the spirit of God. That is what the New Testament means, and that is what makes it the definitive charter of religion.

5. THE EASTER MYSTERY

The primacy of tradition might lead some readers to believe that since faith is an announcement and a proclamation it is a cry. But this is only apparently so, and the play on words is misleading. If faith has had a traditional structure since its birth, then it must be something other than a subjective *élan* or a personal experience. The very fact that it is announced and that it is proclaimed proves that the neophyte's act of faith is not a cry in the sense that I understand it, a solitary, unreflective shriek without communicable significance. Since the faith is preached and communicated by testimony or by teaching, to accept it means to recognize the truth of this testimony and of this teaching. Furthermore, the preacher himself is not a visionary, a free-lancer. He is the echo, the representative and the delegate of a tradition that has vested him with a certain authority to act as its witness. To add faith to his words means to have faith in this tradition, to place oneself within it and to associate oneself to it. There can therefore be no mistake: even if we emphasize the specificity of oral transmission, the primacy of tradition has never been an argument for faith as a cry. A brief analysis will help us to understand this better.

When we are attempting to enter into an historical movement, to accept it on its own terms, to recapture the same deeds, and to accept the same representations of God, we can no longer appeal to an obscure mysticism, to a sentimental religion, to an irrationalism of heart or will. We are making a profession of *historical faith.* Jesus is the Lord, the Messiah, the Christ, the Word of God; he has appeared in the flesh, born of woman, manifested God. He is the Revealer. He is not a God to whom we attribute a legendary humanity; he is a man who has really lived, and whose life, death, and religious attitude supereminently, personally, and immediately express the presence of God.

To historical faith we add *liturgical faith.* It is in the liturgy that he becomes the Lord, for the liturgy alone (prayer, the eucharistic rite) enables us actively to recapture him as Christ, as the Word, by a joint participation that recalls him in his earthly life, but above all, invokes him as the eternal mediator at the Father's right hand.

Finally, we discover historical and liturgical faith as conditioned by the more subtle but decisive work of what we may call theophanic faith. No one, unless he die, can see God. Yet the anointed of God, the Messiah, is Emmanuel, God present in our midst, and we did not know him. He has come, but many have

203

not recognized him. Those whose eyes have been opened by the Holy Spirit have in turn been made the sons of God. They have shared in his fullness, and received grace upon grace.

By linking the Fourth Gospel with the messianism of the prophets we have restored this hidden movement of Christian faith. But in fact this way of understanding revelation runs through the whole Bible. The evangelists applied it to Jesus (who was able to apply it to himself): God manifests himself through his prophets, through his witnesses, and in a special way through his Messiah. That is why he who sees the Son sees the Father and he who acknowledges Jesus as the Messiah acknowledges that he is God speaking to us, God revealing himself to us.

Thus by degrees faith in Christ is formed and structured. Jesus, an historical personage, is truly the Lord whom we venerate in the liturgy; and he deserves this veneration because he is the Revealer, the Word of God. In other words, faith grasps the need to adapt the Jesus-event to a Christological category. It subsumes Jesus' historical intervention under the category of Messiah, then under the category of *Logos,* making this relationship between an event and a doctrine the definitive norm of its belief.

From these few characteristics we can see to what extent the early faith had an exact, positive content invested with a determined meaning. It implies the recovery of a history and the application of a meaning to this history. In all this, there is no heady illumination that would dispense with any reference to facts, and with any interpretation in terms of accepted categories, even those that Scripture itself furnishes, when reread in terms of Jesus. In this the Gospel, even when proclaimed orally before being consigned to writing, was never an indistinct cry, a gratuitous and arbitrary act of faith. We must always think of it in terms of tradition, institution, doctrinal and liturgical belief. Jesus identified as the Messiah—this initiative was established by the whole Judaic tradition. And it is the cult paid to Jesus Christ that will enable thousands, soon millions of souls, to make his attitudes their own, to participate in his sacrifice, and to adore God according to the norms and the intention of his spiritual experience. We are dealing with complex religious groupings, with a scriptural and ritual whole which will expand. We are a long way from that frustrated and indeterminate state imagined by some historians of the kerygma. Every faith has its cultural and liturgical coordinates. But the Christian faith, because it blossomed amid an already highly developed religious tradition, stands out more than any other against an important experiential and doctrinal background. It is not a cry uttered in solitude by fanatic visionaries; it is the echo both of a sublime example and an immense tradition. This is what I am going to establish in some detail, by pointing out the facts and principles which compose it.

Since, as I have said, it is impossible to dissociate the Jesus-event from the apostolic testimony within the New Testament, I shall not make the mistake of first presenting Jesus in secular history only to insert him later, suddenly and arbitrarily, into religious history. No, the person of Jesus can appear to us who came after Pentecost only within a religious aura wearing the crown of his cult. But when Jesus is thus presented to us, when he makes himself known to us as Christ and Master, we are not distorting his true history, but rather beginning to understand it. It is by restoring the full meaning that faith recognizes in his life and death, that we can best reconstruct his existence as man. Everyone must at least concede that his attitude brought about a new era in Judaism. He therefore played a decisive role. Now the result of his action belongs more closely to this action than certain manifestations of his concrete psychology. He is truly what he accomplished historically, every bit as much as he is what he said and did during his life time. If the person of Jesus could fit into the Christological perspective that the prophets had limned, and if he succeeded in becoming an object of theological speculation and the basis and center of worship, it is because he himself in his phenomenal life, in his historical passion, adopted a religious attitude capable of nourishing both faith and devotion indefinitely.

The incredulous will protest that it was his disciples who made him a God. This shows complete ignorance of the spontaneous working of the religious consciousness, which deifies only those beings whose presence clearly indicates a divine quality. Every theophany is a value judgment whose worth is proportionate to the spiritual need of the one formulating it. But in the case of Christ and his disciples, how could we refuse to concede that the theophanic judgment passed on Jesus was inspired by his own attitude which, in turn, satisfied a particularly pure conception of the nature of God, a conception so pure that it could not be excelled? What could be added to the God-Father, the God of love and the religion of love? Thus the historical Jesus established the measure of the evangelical Christ. The proof of this lies in the fact that faith concentrated on him to consider his example, to "categorize" his works, only after it had discovered in his person a form of union with God that transcended all others. He was not considered the revealer of God or recognized as the Messiah and Saviour, until after he had revealed to the world what constitutes a genuinely spiritual salvation, and what are the unimpeachable claims of the Divinity. In a word, if the Jesus-event was doctrinally and liturgically promoted, this was because he deserved it; or rather, because in the area of meanings and religious values we can go from Jesus' life to a Christological intention of God without encountering either gap or discord. Jesus *is* the Christ, because he manifests his prerogatives, performs his functions, possesses his virtues, and opens unparalleled means of access to the mystery of God. But to say this is not simply to subsume the man Jesus under the category of Christ, and then later under the category of the *Logos*. It means to hold and to declare that it is impossible to account for the religious experience of the Jesus of history unless we understand it from a Christological standpoint, in terms of messianism and revelation. Either Jesus had nothing to teach us about God, or else

his religious experience was really and historically of a Christological essence, for in fact he is the only instance of a messianism
that culminated in an unsurpassable idea of God. We were right,
therefore, in maintaining that the apostolic interpretation of the
Jesus-event is correct, and that the theology of Christ is not so
much an addition to the history of the Nazarene as it is the re-
establishment and explanation of it.

It goes without saying, however, that this explanation was not
worked out in one day. It had to be won gradually after having
been begun during Jesus' life-time. We may depict this history
from a point of view that is both religious and critical in the
following way. We shall mention only what seems to be essential, but we will see that this minimum has nothing in common
with the impoverished investigation of the rationalist historians.

Contrary to what some suppose, the Christian faith is not first
and foremost faith in Christ's birth, in his miracles, and in Good
Friday. It was an Easter faith, faith in the Resurrection. In the
account of the Acts, Pentecost itself is an announcement of the
Risen Christ. Now that is a disconcerting starting point. If we
are not to be thrown off by it, we must either become thoroughly
accustomed to the idea or make it the subject of a serious
reflection. Obviously, we prefer the second procedure, which
puts us directly under the obligation of trying to grasp the meaning of the Easter mystery.

If there were no Passion, the evangelists' account of the history
of Jesus would hardly be distinguishable from similar accounts
by many contemporary sectarians. During Jesus' life-time, messianic groups were numerous. Jesus and his apostles were one
community among others. Today we know that on the periphery
of official Judaism there existed in the desert groups of penitents
and sometimes real monks with vows and a common rule. The
Essenes were the first to be identified but there were also, it
seems, independent units such as John the Baptist and his group.
In all likelihood, Jesus gathered his followers together in much
the same way and for the same purpose, that is, to meditate on

207

the Scriptures, in particular on Deutero-Isaiah. He had been in contact with John the Baptist since he had been baptized by him. It is possible that he had learned a great deal of him, and it is certain that there was rivalry between their respective disciples. In all these groups, messianic spirituality was the dominant note, in reaction to the legalism of the Pharisees and the ritualism of the official priesthood, that is, the Sadducees. Moreover, we know that some fifty years before Christ the community called the New Covenant had lived a particularly pure messianism. Its members honored one of their leaders, called the Teacher of Righteousness, who had been persecuted by the priests of Jerusalem and put to death. However, the disciples of the Teacher believed that he had been carried up to heaven. They awaited his return, convinced that this time he would win a total triumph over evil. This conception offers more than one point in common with what was later to be the Christian faith. Some have concluded from this fact that faith in Christ was only a new edition, a revival of a similar creed. Yet this is to go too quickly, for the history of Jesus includes many different features, and no one can prove that there was any communication, direct or indirect, between the Essenian sect in question and the infant Church. It would be of interest to examine the documents to establish precise chronological details, but they do not give them. What is worth our attention is the fact that shortly before or contemporary with Jesus, Judaism could harbor, if only in peripheral groupings, messianic ideas a good deal purer than those that inspired the armed struggle against the occupying forces or promised Israel vengeance on its oppressors. The idea of a suffering Messiah was not unknown, nor was the idea of a defeat in death (an opinion that the Sadducees vigorously rejected) and a return in glory (a view widely spread by the apocolypses). Thus the structures that were to become Christian were preformed. When the primitive Church later imposed them they were less unexpected, less shocking than we may be inclined to believe. Far from seeming improper in the Judaic context of the time, they were in complete harmony with the mentality of certain groups. It is probable that Jesus himself was impressed by them, especially when he knew that his own mission was not going to succeed with the authorities. He consequently realized that as far as he was concerned suffering and death would be his lot, and that his own messianism would be more sorrowful than glorious, or rather glorious because it was sorrowful. Always his tragic end interposed itself to destroy both for him and his disciples the possibility of a triumphal messianism. The apostles might have dreamed that he would bring about the deliverance of Israel. It was not, however, the liberation of the nation but the cross that he brought them.

Many historians come to a halt before his tomb. They indicate a pause, and then they turn the page. After the chapter on Jesus' ministry, they begin a different chapter, the history of the early Church. We must protest against such a procedure. For to break so easily the bond between Jesus and the Risen Christ is to fail to respect the historical data and to make incoherence into a method. The gospels were very careful not to break this relationship, indeed they were written only on the unity which this relationship provides. They deny and make it impossible even to think that the Risen Christ is any other but Jesus. Was this only because they believed in the miracle? Because from their viewpoint it was just as easy to declare that the Son of God had escaped the consequences of death as to admit that the infant Jesus had escaped the ordinary laws of birth? Most certainly thaumaturgy was a literary style familiar to them. When God's power is in question, no believer will consent to setting limits to it. However, I do not think that we are dealing only with the category of the wondrous, of which religions make considerable use. I think that the evangelists blended together Jesus' life and his survival as a matter of spiritual fidelity that goes far beyond the plane of the miraculous. This fidelity inspired them to transfigure Christ even during his earthly existence as well as to describe this existence against the backdrop of the apparitions after his Resurrection. This means that it worked at different levels. However, in order to grasp its true meaning, we would have to know the intention it served. Now, we often fail to ask ourselves this question. What does this fidelity mean, where does it come from? This is what the critics leave out and what to me seems to be of capital importance.

It is not enough to say that the apostles believed that their Master had returned to life because he appeared to them; because, after having been crucified and buried, he suddenly manifested himself again to them, individually, or even collectively. Such manifestations of Christ are no more improbable than the apparitions in the life of Joan of Arc or in the story of Bernadette. Experts in religious psychology no longer consider such apparitions monstrous or morbid. This, however, is merely a matter of a negative, extrinsic judgment. Christ's appearances were in fact something very different from extraordinary phenomena, whether paranormal or supranormal. Some psychologists of mysticism would be inclined to compare them with those delusions of presence, visual or tactile, that compensate a sense of expectancy or dispel a state of anxiety. But this comparison is biased, crude, and inaccurate. The Easter mystery is not based on mental images that can be objectivized. It rests on a conviction whose realistic basis provides its whole strength. In keeping with the Jewish belief in the resurrection (an idea commonly subscribed to among the Essenes and Pharisees), it knows that death is not the final word, that the dead return or will return, and that more particularly the Messiah (for reasons to be explained later) cannot remain a prisoner in the tomb. In view of this—let us not hesitate to admit it—this belief has attained a level of reality, an order of life, which only an opposite belief, that is, a materialist creed, could call into question.

Consequently, this conviction is not sustained by a consoling figment of the imagination nor by a very impressive phantasmagoria. It is supported by the reality it discerns, by the continuity of its personal destiny through successive changes, and by the value of constancy which affirms itself through it amid suffering and death. If we attach importance only to sensible things, if we reduce man to a biological complex, and if we are concerned only with what he accomplishes in time and space, we obviously refuse to extend our destiny into the hereafter. But this very refusal immediately changes what happens here on earth; practically speaking, it contests the validity of every religious activity.[1] Logic here makes it necessary either to exclude or to include a perspective of transcendence both for the here and the hereafter. A choice must be made between the two directions. Religion chooses the second, or rather it constitutes itself in this choice. In accepting this initiative, it prevents itself from being defeated before it has begun. For the materialism it rejects is not simply the rejection of a salvation after death; it is also the rejection of any salvation in this life. It is the negation of all reference, present or future, to the Absolute. Mysticism, on the contrary, offers the possibility of developing an eschatology that defeats death. It discovers in the here and now of the religious act a relationship with the eternal, a level at which spiritual efficacy can be perpetuated and renewed indefinitely by contact with the divine, and a plane of values that no biological or biophysical weakness can destroy. Certainly, belief in the resurrection is filled with a mysticism of this sort. That is why it lives more in certitude than in hope. It intends and attains this level of lived eternity and perpetuity. It should even be recognized that, as outlined by faith, existence at this level

---

[1] Ancient Judaism was not familiar with the mystique of resurrection. It even advises against the cult of the dead where there appeared to be an animist danger prejudicial to monotheism. It became silent when faced with any attempt to formulate an individualist eschatology. But this deliberate reserve, this voluntary lack of imagination coincided at the same time with a total abandonment to divine providence. It can be said that the old Israel (before the exile) emphasized the service of God and took little interest in individual consequences beyond the tomb. But it cannot be said that it denied beforehand (as did the Sadducees) all eschatology of a personal nature. For the service of the Most High, fidelity to the covenant implied for each and all the values of justice and of holiness, which the Bible never at any time declared to be perishable.

211

becomes required of all those who rise above the naive or scientific worship of material elements.

Eschatology, based on this fundamental certitude, is no longer a dream. Envisioned along the same lines,[2] the Easter mystery no longer runs the risk of being the victim of an illusion. It has the assurance that there is a hereafter, that the dead rise again, and that every tomb is a temporary resting place. In regard to Christ, however, it possesses additional certitude from which we have the conclusion, not that Jesus rose from the dead (this is self-evident when we realize that all the dead will rise [1 Cor. 15:13]), but that his resurrection was the first fruits (1 Cor. 15:20), the *prototype,* which did not await the universal resurrection. The additional certitude derives from the fact that since death is the wages of sin it cannot hold the Righteous, the Holy One in its grasp (Acts 2:27; 1 Cor. 15:27, 56). This is why Jesus escaped death immediately, or at least just as soon as his death could be verified and the reality of his resurrection thus certified. To say that Christ has risen means to ratify the general belief in resurrection and to understand why Jesus had to be the first born from the dead (Col. 1:18; Rev. 1:5), the first reborn from the tomb. In both cases it is to bring to light the plane of continuity, of eternity, and of permanence of which we were speaking, that real and subsistent plane that transcends biophysical limitations. The resurrection of each and all is not therefore an imaginary entity even though imagery is used to express it, as is necessarily the case concerning an experience still in the future. Neither is the *archetypical,* the model resurrection of Christ an invention of visionaries, despite its being made known to us through Christophanic narratives, for this is only natural in an event that had witnesses to its manifestations, but not to its production.

Once established on this realistic foundation, the apparitions

2 It is not unimportant and at any rate it is in keeping with historical fact to note that belief in the resurrection of the dead preceded the event and testimony of Easter.

of the Risen Christ can no longer be equated with simple impressions of his presence. They cease to be the product of a purely subjective emotion. They have been preceded by and founded upon the objective certitude of a victory over death and of Christ's triumph over sin, and consequently over the corruption of the body (Acts 2:27; Ps. 16:10). It is only after and in reference to this objectivity that their psycho-sensorial structure can be examined without equivocation. It would be merely a question of a mirage, of a worthless and empty hallucination if the guarantee of the resurrection as an authentic fact, as an event in the life-death-glory cycle did not provide a basis for discerning the presence. But this guarantee is given; it is preliminary. Even in the episode of the doubting disciple (Jn. 20:24-29), of the disciple who had to see in order to believe, the desire for visual verification cannot be understood unless his scepticism does not go so far as to question the possibility of a resurrection. Had Thomas been convinced that God could not raise someone from the dead, he would not even have asked to see. He would have thought a request of this sort useless. No doubt he would have gone so far as to deny what he saw when he saw it, for the sight of what we know cannot be is a mystification, we are not interested in it, we are suspicious of it, and we turn our back on it. On the contrary, the apostles wholeheartedly believed in the "apparitions" of the Risen Christ. They believed in them because they confirmed a fact whose proof was not to be sought in the Christophanic sign (which is only a result), but in that history of salvation in which the destruction of death as the consequence of sin became inevitable and effective as soon as it touched him who was without sin—the Messiah, the Master. That is why the Christophanies, in turn, are convincing: because they are not satisfied with presenting the Risen Christ to those who saw him but because, on the contrary, those who saw him are also believers, and their belief leads them to a proper perspective, to an order of truth in which it would be contradictory to claim that Jesus is the Christ, the beloved of God, and that he had not broken the bonds of death (Acts 2:22–24). From this view-point the Easter mystery leaves no loophole. Either one believes that Jesus is the Messiah and because of this the first to conquer death, ahead of all his brethren; or one ought neither consider him the Messiah, nor proclaim him as the conqueror of death. The affirmation of this transcendental messiahship includes the affirmation of his resurrection and *vice versa.* The apostolic testimony, moreover, is composed of this double-yet-single affirmation. The Risen Christ of whom Peter speaks on the day of Pentecost is crowned with a messianic halo, and vested with glorified lordship.

It is evident that the rationalist critics were ill-advised to deny the Christophanic narrations all objective import. They became incapable of offering a proper analysis of the Easter mystery. More particularly, they supposed that the apostles were capable of believing in the restoration of a dead person to life without any general belief in the resurrection, and simply on the strength of the appearance of one returned from the grave. They also insinuated that this type of apparition had no more consistency than a motor hallucination, and that the resurrection was only a cry of hope in a night of illusion. In short, they implied that the perception of a phantom sufficed to launch the cult of a glorious messianism, a messianism that was victorious over death. The explanations that we have given are quite different. If they are worthwhile it is because they do not attempt to reconstruct history with disconnected strokes. After all, it is possible for the pure historian not to take sides for or against the resurrection of Jesus. It is conceivable that he be satisfied with pointing out that the apostles really believed in the Christophanies, which is an important factor since from them they gathered the courage to proclaim the Gospel. But a historian may not engage in dismantling the psycho-physiological mechanism of visions in order to deny the fact of the resurrection. Neither is it permis-sible—and at any rate it is hardly comprehensible—that he should base the complex structure of faith in the Messiah, in the

Son of God, and in Christ the Saviour on apparitions considered to be subjective and illusory.

Our own position avoids these excesses. It maintains that the resurrection is a fact, a reality, and that this fact and this reality cannot be rejected unless one rejects the system of values according to which the afterlife, the hereafter, is the only justification for death. Consequently, it holds that the Christophanies touch on something other than the imagination, that they rejoin an authentic reality and that the structure built on them is not on the point of collapse for want of empirical foundations. In return, it assumes that one is willing to grant us a certain number of things, mainly that the Easter faith was supported by Judaic belief in individual resurrection—this point should not present any difficulty—and that it was bound up with an acknowledgment of Jesus' messiahship. This last point is often badly understood, and so we must insist on it.

According to our understanding, it is inconceivable that the apostles could have believed in the immediate resurrection of someone whom they had not previously identified as the Messiah of Israel. Should someone say that during his life-time they considered him the Messiah, then when he was put to death they were distressed, disappointed, and helpless; next, that they recalled some of the Master's words on suffering, some verses from Isaiah, and also some psalms on the deliverance of the Righteous One from the bonds of death; and then that finally they "saw" him and believed or, in the words of St. John, *"If you believe, you will see"* (Jn. 11:40), they believed and they saw—all this is plausible, coherent, and in keeping with the texts. But if one asserts either that the apostles thought they saw him without believing in him, or that, though they did not believe in him or no longer believed in him, nevertheless they saw and recognized him—then such an assertion is simply inconsistent and completely arbitrary.

One position alone seems acceptable: the Easter faith is that of witnesses who are believers. They see and they believe because

215

Jesus has never ceased to be their Master, their example, and their model. The day after Calvary they fled; they did not understand why God should forsake his witness. No, they did not comprehend him, at least in time to realize, as Luke says (24:26), that it was necessary that Christ suffer these things. They did not yet understand that the suffering Messiah was still the Messiah and even that a rereading of Scripture would convince them that only a suffering Messiah is the true one. The disciples of Emmaus argued about this which, we may conclude, reflects fairly well the apostles' frame of mind after the tragic events at Jerusalem. And we know that St. Paul was obliged to go through a similar process. He had read in Deuteronomy: "There is a curse on the man who hangs on the gibbet" (Deut. 21:23; see Gal. 3:13). The crucified Jesus was therefore an object of malediction, a scandal to the Jews and a folly to the Gentiles. How could this difficulty be overcome? Paul succeeded in doing so only by discovering the redemptive power of suffering. Since he was more of a theologian than the Twelve, this conviction immediately assumed for him an extraordinary importance and distinction. He not only made the cross the central feature in a cosmo-soteriological drama, and wished to know only Jesus crucified, through a kind of compensation that consisted in changing a weak point into a strong point, but he also realized that Jesus' sacrifice forever eclipsed the Temple holocaust, with the result that the Christian faith received an entirely new ritual and sacrificial center, one freed from Jewish particularism and capable of universality in time and space. Thus, whether for the Twelve or for Paul, the decisive step of faith in the Risen Christ consisted first of all in recognizing Jesus as Christ despite his Passion, and then because of his Passion. While he was alive he was looked upon as the Messiah—this was not too difficult at a time and with a mentality which accepted messianism as a current religious principle. Once he was dead and buried, it became more difficult to continue to consider Jesus as the Messiah. After all, the idea of a Messiah who failed

216

all along the line must have seemed impossible. In order to preserve for Jesus the prerogative of the messianic attributes, it was necessary to turn the defeat into victory, cost what it might. It was necessary to give a value to suffering and even to death itself. Scripture and perhaps the atmosphere of certain contemporary groups made it possible to see how this might be done; the apostles, and later Paul, succeeded in doing it. That is why belief in the Risen Christ took on meaning for them and why, for Jesus' former companions and for Paul, the Christophanes could be quite different from an unexpected vision and unsubstantiated hallucination. The Resurrection would be only a childish myth if it did not have this spiritual content, this convincing religious value. To believe in the Risen Christ is to be convinced that Jesus is the Christ; that Christ does not die; and that death itself is an entrance into glory, a transformation, a paradoxical triumph amid an apparent defeat. This the apostles, and Paul in his turn, believed and proclaimed. Pentecost was the epiphany of the Resurrection just as the Resurrection was the Christophany of the crucifixion. We praise the courage of the apostles who, on the day of Pentecost, proclaimed the Risen Christ. But that was their cry of deliverance, the happy ending they had reached. Their real courage was in their understanding of the Passion, in the Cross, loved, surmounted and understood; in Calvary welcomed under the sign of the Resurrection; in the messianism preserved beyond the tomb, and in their belief in an immolated Christ winning for them in return the glorious vision of the Master whom they followed and served. There was in this movement of thought, and in this course of events something so brave, so courageous, so religiously stimulating that it is easy to see in it the enlivening Spirit of Pentecost. Tradition was not deceived. It spontaneously made Pentecost the founding day of the Church, the first public announcement of the Easter good news.

We have purposely laid more stress on the episode of Emmaus, on Peter's discourse at the beginning of the Acts, and on

Paul's example, than on the empty tomb. For the empty sepulchre goes back to a tradition of another vein that confirms the early tradition and provides a more convenient summary of events. No one will conclude, I hope, that my preference conceals a secret desire to deprive the Resurrection of any historical record. Not only do I not maintain that the Easter event was merely a figment of the apostles' imagination, but I believe that the Christophanies receive their objective value from a reality whose meaning they exhibit, from a resurrection without which the apparitions would be pure allegories. I further believe that the men who introduced into the Christian synthesis the concept of the resurrection, originally an Iranian notion and later a Semitic one, rendered religion an invaluable service. They did not think that Jesus had to be carried off to heaven like Elijah, or like the Master of Justice in the commentary on the book of Habakkuk. They maintained that Jesus had really risen, not merely as an immortalized soul, but as a spiritualized body, itself immortal because it had been transmuted. Now that is a schema, a suggestion of survival as strong in its way as that of any dualist immortality, which saves the soul but irremediably destroys the body. The book of Wisdom recognizes the Greek type of immortality. The apostles could have made use of it, although it is a schema that is more difficult to handle and also more vulnerable. They resorted to the only representation that respects the biospiritual unity of a human being. It is not that they intended to elaborate it metaphysically, and thus they were not worried about the danger of vitalism. They made use of their image spontaneously, directly, and functionally, so as to make clear that Jesus, the glorious Christ, had defied death by escaping from it in both body and soul, wholly and entirely.

With regard to the claim that Jesus' resurrection was wholly imaginary, outside events and outside history, I have noted that it is possible to take this position if one is a materialist. But anyone who holds that biological death is not the extinction of the person—I mean of his objective as well as his subjective aspects—but rather a transformation, an immortalization, need have no objection to resurrection. As an idea resurrection is only a schema, but a schema which intends a reality no religious mind or spiritual thinker would dream of denying. St. Paul justly links our resurrection with Christ's. If his is not real, ours is illusory; to believe in one is to believe in the other. In other words, the choice to be made lies between a spiritual personalism and a materializing biologism. From the beginning, religion leads towards the personalism, and we follow it gladly. At any rate, when we think of it, it is no more difficult to believe in the effective resurrection of Christ than in our own survival. And, as I have already said, the schema of the Risen Christ offers a more effective, more complete, and especially more concrete support to the idea of our survival than that of the immortality of the soul.

Under these conditions, it is not the "factuality" of the Easter event that becomes a problem. We can freely admit this, even with a minimum of faith in a life hereafter. The problem concerns its religious truth, its value for the spiritual life. Christianity was born on the day that Jesus' disciples understood that the crucified Messiah remained no less a Messiah, because in truth death does not weaken but rather confirms his messiahship. The entrance into glory is achieved through suffering, and not through the brilliance of an empirical triumph. One must be willing to die in order to be reborn; to be annihilated in order to rise again. Christ had to die in order to be the Christ; not a figure of armed resistance and material dominion, but rather one of obedience even unto total sacrifice and of exaltation in the hereafter. St. Paul said all this in nearly identical words. St. Peter, in the second chapter of the Acts, proclaimed it in the same way. This then is the true meaning of Easter, the foundation of Christian faith. It enabled the messianic group established by Jesus to return toward him, so that from the wounds of the Crucified the rays of the resurrection might be shed abroad. If this had not been accomplished, if the apostles had not understood that their Master had come forth alive and glorious from the tomb, history would never have known either the Church or the gospels. One Messiah among others would simply have failed, and his disciples would find no comfort in his defeat. By believing in his resurrection, Jesus' disciples brought Jewish messianism into its own, and restored its spiritual purity. They recognized that Jesus revealed the true God by his life and death and that, for this reason, there could be no other Messiah.